IGNITING THE GAMES

DAVID MILLER

IGNITING
THE GAMES

The Evolution of the Olympics
and Bach's Legacy

Foreword by
Sebastian Coe

First published by Pitch Publishing, 2022

Pitch Publishing
9 Donnington Park,
85 Birdham Road,
Chichester,
West Sussex,
PO20 7AJ
www.pitchpublishing.co.uk
info@pitchpublishing.co.uk

A CIP catalogue record is available for this book
from the British Library.

ISBN 978 180150 142 2

Typesetting and origination by Pitch Publishing
Printed and bound in Great Britain by TJ Books, Padstow

Contents

Other Books by David Miller

Our Sporting Times (anthology, 1996)

Olympic Guardians (2010)

Official History of the IOC and Olympic Games 1894-2018 (updated quadrennially from 2004)

Touching the Heart – Why Sport Matters (2019)
(Memoir in exclusive financial aid of Starlight Childrens Foundation)

Official Arsenal Opus (co-author 2011)

Earlier biographies of Matt Busby (1970),
Trevor Francis (1982), Sebastian Coe (1981, 1984,
1994), Juan Antonio Samaranch (1992), four
World Cup accounts (1970-1982)

DEDICATION

With deepest love and gratitude, this pubication is dedicated to Marita, my wife of 61 years, whose enduring devotion to her family's existence sadly closed just over four years ago. My enduring debt to her loyalty lies in common alongside that of countless wives: Marita sacrificed, in the belatedly transforming male-dichotomous Sixties, her potential professional independence so that she might support mine. A commitment many men were and still are today reluctant to acknowledge. I could never have sustained a hectic schedule as journalist and author had Marita not been the buttress of domestic solidarity with children and grandchildren.

Author and wife at 96th birthday of oldest ever IOC Member, Vladimir Stoytchev of Bulgaria, at his Sofia apartment in 1988: professional military equestrian at Paris'24, fierce opponent of fake USSR civil service 'amateurs'.

ACKNOWLEDGEMENTS

IT IS not always simple when the successful attempt to provide advantages for the less fortunate. In the early years of Pierre de Coubertin's exclusive International Olympic Committee, the majority of Olympic competitors were white, middle-class and could afford the boat fare to the Games. By the mid-20th century, many thousands of them were hard pressed either to train or pay the rail fare to regular work. While one per cent became wealthy when professionalism was accepted by the 1980s, the majority are still partially dependent on the IOC's re-investment of 90 per cent of their sponsorship and broadcast income in subsidy of athletes. While I was striving, unavailingly, for Olympic inclusion in 1956, out of pocket from training and unable to pay the electricity for a two-room apartment, I was grateful to Lord Luke, UK IOC member and director of Lloyds Bank and of Bovril, for the offer of part-time vacation work. As author and journalist, it has been rewarding to witness the countless hours of loyalty and available spare time given by a proportion of IOC members to voluntary duty: dedicated to sustaining Pierre de Coubertin's exclusive innovation which for 126 years has injected global society with a concept of honour, camaraderie and opportunity.

An easy media target by being self-elected, the IOC has had acknowledged faults, yet has survived, indeed thrived, on account of its timeless brand image: concern for the welfare of others. I first encountered this in 1972 when IOC member Willi Daume, CEO of Munich's Olympics, having seen my biography of Matt Busby with reflection on the Munich air crash, organised my tour of the city's spectacular new stadia. Daume was an organiser as profound in detail as compatriot Thomas Bach 40 years later. The longer I became concerned with Olympic administration, the more indebted to hours of time and advice from members preoccupied with delivering Games worthy of the world's best. From among the 600-plus members during my working lifetime: Michael Killanin, more clubbable than any but knotted by triangular rivalry between International Federations, National Olympic committees and IOC; Juan Antonio Samaranch, inviting me on his four exploratory tours of Africa, Central Asia, the Pacific and the Far East, from which I assembled his biography *Olympic Revolution*; details of political intrigue from, in particular, Alexandrou Siperco (Romania), Ivan Slavkov (Bulgaria), Ung Chang (North Korea); Russian empire autonomy, Vitaly Smirnov; inter-continental collaboration and media, Kevan Gosper and John Coates (Australia); essential ethics, Vladimir Stoytchev (Bulgaria), Prince de Merode (Belgium), Richard Pound (Canada); Africa's imbalances, Reggie Alexander (Kenya), Sam Ramsamy (South Africa), Henry Adefope (Nigeria); Asian emergence, Kim Un-Yong (South Korea), He Zhenliang (China), Timothy Fok and Sonny de Sales (Hong Kong), Ser Miang Ng (Singapore); Charter principles, Francisco Elizalde (Philippines), Nicos Filaritos (Greece); etiquette, Kip Keino (Kenya), Rania Elwani (Egypt), Grand Duke of Luxemborg; gender balance, Anita Defrantz (USA), Flor Fonseca (Venezuela); athlete integrity, Peter Tallberg (Finland), Anton Geesink (Netherlands); International Federations consistency, Francesco Ricci-Bitti (Italy), Philippe Chatrier (France); Gian Franco Kasper (Switzerland), Els Van Breda Vriesman (Netherlands); NOC responsibility, Walter Troeger (Germany), Raymont Gafner (Switzerland), Gunilla Lindberg (Sweden), Prince of Orange (Netherlands); India/ Pakistan relations, Ashwini Kumar (India), Wajid Ali (Pakistan); fair play, Comte Jean de Beaumont (France), Lance Cross (New Zealand), Paul Henderson (Canada); administrative discipline, Marc Hodler (Switzerland), Craig Reedie (GBR), Witold Banka

(Poland); publicity, Primo Nebiolo (Italy); broadcasting, Alex Gilady (Israel).

Initially this publication was intended to be a short extension of *Olympic Guardians*, my collective biography of the eight presidents. When the extent of Bach's reformation became apparent, an individual assessment was obvious.

My incentive was identity with Thomas's maxim: 'Change or be changed'. For inter-school matches, we used to be required to provide a linesman. For away matches, I requested as captain for permission to take a boy who 'knew the Laws'. I might as well have asked the headmaster for draught vodka in the changing room: as a Cambridge hurdler, he once arrived for training 'advice' in pinstriped trousers. A boyhood hero was double Olympic 800m champion Mal Whitfield. At White City's August British Games in 1953, preparing for the junior 100m, breathtakingly I found myself warming up centre-field beside the tracksuited icon – he telling me 'this bit is as important as the race'. The next week I bought a track-suit, and was ostracised by colleagues for 'professionalism'. In 1976, 20 years before Arsenal's revolutionary appointment of Arsene Wenger, I flew with chairman Denis Hill-Wood – under assumed names, then permissible – having persuaded him (no fee for me!) to engage Europe's foremost coach, Yugoslav/Montenegran Miljan Miljanic, the first to have defeated Liverpool at Anfield with Red Star Belgrade. We failed, Miljanic having re-signed with Santiago Bernabeu. A year later, 15 years before the Champions League was created out of the knock-out European Cup, I organised through the *Daily Express* a gathering of Glasgow Rangers, Ajax and Arsenal with UEFA secretary Hans Bangerter to discuss formation of … a league competition. Fantastic, believed the clubs! Too early, thought Europe. A year later, ten years before the IOC accepted professionalism, and convinced Daley Thompson was a decathlon champion for Moscow '80, I tried to persuade new *Express* owner Victor Matthews – Trader Vic to the tabloids – that if he would sponsor Thompson's training, I would match every £1,000 donated with a personal £100. Matthews personally preferred his own projection in golf. British sport has tended to cling to established convention. Some 40 years on, I sensed that the financial tide was turning against the future of the IOC, for all its indulgence of athletes, NOCs and IFs: that in Thomas Bach lay determination for the institution to evolve.

Alongside allegiance to the IOC, fulsome recognition is due to agencies to which I have contributed over the years; sometimes gratuitously, and with agreement to quote extracts – *Sport Intern*, with the benign collaboration of proprietor Karl Heinz Huba, Duncan Mackay's exhaustive *Insidethegames*, and Rich Perelman's expert *Sports Examiner*, together with courtesy of several extracts from the IOC's in-house *Olympic Review*. I would often have been adrift without an oar but for fellow scribes' support: Alain Lutzenfichter, Robert Pariente, Stan Greenberg, Morley Myers, Mel Watman, Philip Barker, David Owen, Franco Fava, Wolf Lyberg, Leif Josefsson, Steve Wilson and Markus Kecht. Welcome counsel from Michael Beloff QC, guidance by Jon Tibbs Associates, plus critical opinion from Antoine Duval's Asser Institute (Netherlands), and Jens Andersen's Play The Game (Denmark), sport-sensitive discerning advice from my daughter Michele (founder, Oxford University Society of Modern Dance, production manager of film features *Olympic Games LA '84*, and *Golé, World Cup '86*), latterly media/English teacher), and son Gavin (playwright/ award-winning artist, teenage member of GB Downhill Only Ski Club), and my enduring comprehensive aide Karen Game.

Enthusiastic editorial focus from Pitch Publishing's Dean Rockett, Graham Hales, Duncan Olney and Gareth Davis has been a rejuvenating filip.

FOREWORD BY SEB COE

THE GLOBAL appeal of the Olympic Games is abstract as much as physical, is mythical and ancient as well as contemporary. David Miller, an Olympic triallist for the UK's football XI for Melbourne 1956, has spent six decades as journalist and author attending 25 Games: fascinated by the complex festival of many simultaneous sports, even more by the universality of thousands of competitors sharing the Olympic Village, as Thomas Bach, Olympic fencing champion, and I both did. We began our shared but separate responsibilities in sports administration, on behalf of fellow athletes, together in 1981, elevated by emerging new IOC president Juan Antonio Samaranch, to his inaugural Athletes' Commission, at the IOC Congress at Baden-Baden. For the first time, competitive athletes were granted a demonstrative voice within the corridors of Olympic power.

Having rapidly ascended the administrative ladder within Germany's national and Olympic framework, and promoted to IOC membership in 1991, Thomas's authority expanded, becoming influential chair of the Juridical Commission. His eligibility to succeed president Rogge in 2001 was clear to all.

Over the century since Pierre de Coubertin restored Greece's classic spectacle under direction of the IOC, the appetite and appeal for both competitors and audience have modified, magnified, shifted. Change and adaptation had become essential if our unique social festival of nations' integration was to survive another 126 years. Thomas, Olympic champion of 1976, recognised the need. He envisaged detailed radical modernisation.

Having ridden and survived a succession of crises throughout his first eight years at the helm, witnessed by David Miller, Thomas carefully led the IOC into radical financial revisions, a simplified unaggressive host city election process, and the introduction of contemporary urban sports for global youth. The Olympic arena has been the fulcrum of my own existence. The world of sport has been well served by Thomas's focus on protecting and promoting the Olympic Movement for the next century and future generations. David Miller captures the perspective of sustained individual ambitions.

Sebastian Coe, President World Athletics

1

BACH'S BRINKMANSHIP, PUTIN'S ATROCITIES

THE OLYMPIC Games, renovated gift by Pierre de Coubertin, generates idealistic social and community attitudes. Can this biennial festival survive the respective barbarities of Vladimir Putin, Xi Jinping, the fortunate less extreme autocratic digressions by other despotic, ambitious politicians with their wars, totalitarianism and social contrivances? A frightening scenario.

The human race has endured, and mostly displaced, political and geographic empires throughout time, sometimes painfully. The virtue of Ancient Greece's Olympic Games has been promotion of our wiser, predominant, integrated nature: an instinctive sense of survival, of collective welfare and neighbourly association irrespective of race, creed or colour. Above all, the Olympic Games personify honour between rivals and friends, individual or nations, winner and loser, the capacity thereby to be at ease within our soul. Truly remarkable throughout history is our ability to arise with dignity out of catastrophe, as in the wake of two world wars. Even in the event of a further conflagration we can be sure – whenever the closure of the evil horror of Putin's demented empire-restoration against valiant Ukraine – of that nation's ultimate civil restoration; of Syria too, obliterated by Assad. The Olympics teach us what is good about ourselves.

Yet the risk now confronting the IOC, as its German leader Thomas Bach strives, champion of fair play, to install a transformational future, is the possible collaboration between two contemporary would-be empires, Russia and China, which could fracture the Olympic Games for decades. As observer of the last five IOC presidents, I embarked on this assessment of Games continuity, being a witness to Bach's welcome radical initiatives, with optimism. As I write, the empire lust of a Russian mass murderer, of a Chinese totalitarian dictator with designs on Taiwan and Hong Kong, portends a long-term east–west division of the globe and dissolution of Olympic ideology: universality of an attempted integrated global social equilibrium.

Do not underestimate the inflammation within what, if extended, is a war against the world: it encompasses war against truth – not the first of its kind – waged by the Kremlin's fake propaganda war. The current alarmed IOC president cannot contemplate potential Olympic termination. An apocalyptic outcome of enduring Russian annihilation could be collapse of the IOC's 'industry' in Lausanne: never mind the flamboyant, tourist Olympic Museum, but of the elaborate new headquarters, employing 600, from which 90 per cent of its multi-billion-dollar sponsorship and broadcast income subsidises many of the national Olympic committees and international federations, a majority of the latter based in Switzerland. A moral calamity in the 'minor' arena of sport hangs upon Putin's obsession and IOC victimhood. Inevitable Russian exclusion from Paris 2024 could be the trigger for their terminal banishment by an Olympic Movement equally angry and astonished on behalf of humanity.

And what if China should align with Russia? The danger is that Putin, or a successor, might attempt creation of a rival multi-Games among acolyte nations and thereby crush Bach's maxim of universality, with potential collapse of the IOC. May fortune countenance Bach's clairvoyance. Anne Hidalgo, mayor of Paris, stated on 17 March 2022, 'We will make a decision when the time comes. Vladimir Putin is breaking international law. Russia is already suspended from the Olympic Movement until December 2022, a decision on 2024 will be made by the IOC.'

How could the IOC conceivably welcome the return of a nation that thronged to fill a stadium in celebration of Putin's slaughter of women and children and historic cities of a sovereign, law-abiding nation, the perpetrators championed by the Kremlin and hundreds of fake news campaigners? Having survived World War Two, and thus far atomic capability, the world in general has become selfishly materialistic: if you desire something, therefore you deserve it – even someone else's country. The democratic world will resent competing with a nation whose military, invading unprovoked a sovereign country, assassinates mother-and-child refugees, detonates an entire rail station crowded with civilians.

In any Olympic era, the moral heart of the IOC lies with the president attempting to offer a canopy of ethics amid our multiple mundane failures. First was the partially unstructured benevolence to all (at that time amateur) by de Coubertin. Next, by Belgian banker Compte Baillet-Latour's *laissez-faire* insensitive acceptance of Hitler's intended genocide. Swedish Sigfrid Edström's diplomatically included the Soviet Union. Irish Michael Killanin's genial but inadequate grappling with professionalism, apartheid, friction between international federations and national Olympic committees, and successive boycotts of 1976–1980 left the IOC perilously weak. Spain's transformative Samaranch embraced sponsorship, professionalism, division of winter and summer Games, the return of the suspended South Africa, and established an Ethics Commission post-Salt Lake voting scandal. Gentle Belgian Olympic sailor Rogge nursed economic stability but a decade of stalled modernisation. The idealist Olympics have persistently been sabotaged by alien political thrusts.

Committed constitutional reformer Bach is harassed by Russia's endemic cheating, plagued by financially scared bidding host cities, by fractious North Korea, a global virus pandemic; perhaps terminally, the simultaneous empire ambitions of two of the three most powerful Olympic nations, each afflicted with territory kleptomania. Bach has been unwavering in upholding Olympic ethics. He would have perhaps been wiser sometimes to remain outside the political fray: his plea for peace during Beijing's ceremonies invited embarrassment in a contrived moral partnership with two conspicuously untruthful superpowers intent on world domination. This diminished rather than emphasised any degree of political power by a sporting bureau: a moral and social force entrenched in integration.

Throughout Bach's nine years at the helm thus far, while initiating his Agenda 2020 election manifesto of constitutional and financial reformations, shrewdly designed to save the IOC from its own vulnerability, he has been aware that maintaining the loyalty of the three most powerful nations, China, Russia and USA, was essential, not least financially, to the equilibrium of the Olympics. Never mind that, immediately prior to Tokyo's Games of 2020 – postponed to 2021 – the Olympic world had been largely caught off guard by the IOC Executive Board's sudden revelation of the 'advance' election of Brisbane as summer host city for 2032 – four years ahead of a normal seven-year preparation. A rainbow financial breakthrough, yet with Russia's invasion immediately following the Covid-ruptured Beijing Winter Games, the IOC now stood on a precipice.

Warring Russia and sycophantic partner Belarus then being suspended from hosting or participating in all global sport, a now retaliatory revenge withdrawal by Russia from the IOC, together with half a dozen sympathetic nations from the seven-decade former Soviet Union, would scupper Bach's triumphal objective of universality. Should China merge with such a Russian subterfuge, a whirlwind of allegiance from acolyte, beneficiary nations in Africa, Asia and the Middle East would destroy the Olympics. The mission fervently espoused by Bach could perish.

As Putin's tanks rolled into Ukraine, Bach reflected, 'A Games exclusively between nations of political alignment would sacrifice the plateau of universality. Allegations of racism are levelled against many countries, but provided the Olympic Charter is observed by all *within the Games*, the IOC must remain politically neutral. If we become politicised, we are lost. We cannot vie with one country against another, so of course we will always have our critics.' Yet observation of that principle of universality leaves the IOC in a moral cleft stick: is not protection of China's Uighur Muslims as significant as should have been that of the Jewish population at Berlin 1936, of ostracising Russia for their slaughter in Ukraine? The IOC is not the democratic world's conscience, but that is how it tends inexorably to be judged.

Moreover, the IOC is presently viewed as not being even-handed: Russia currently barred from all international involvement, yet Russia's two IOC members – Shamil Tarpishchev, president of Russian tennis, and two-time Olympic pole vault champion Yelena Isinbayeva – retaining their IOC membership. In short time, Switzerland's minister of sport, Viola Amherd, advocated their suspension. No doubt aware of the possible disintegration of the Olympic Movement on account of Putin's war, Bach was anxious to stress that sporting sanctions 'are not against Russian athletes or Russia's NOC, but for innocent competitors' "protection" in otherwise potentially hostile international competition'. Yet why would Russia not be excluded from Paris 2024, as were Germany from Antwerp 1920 and London 1948? Loyalty to some 'clean' Russian athletes – as at Rio, Pyeongchang, Tokyo and Beijing – is nothing beside loyalty to the democratic world in the face of unrestrained barbarity.

Tarpishchev and Isinbayeva extended hostility by failing to attend the concluded IOC Session post-Beijing Games. Bach acknowledged: 'Our relationship with the Russian government has dramatically deteriorated over the past years. My appeal to "give peace a chance" at the Closing Ceremony was to political leaders across the world. Our relationship with Russia's leadership has worsened following the doping scandal, the cyber attacks and even personal attacks to individuals in the IOC and Olympic Movement. The political, social and economic consequences of the Ukraine war are a turning point in world history and we cannot ignore this. The IOC is conscious, and regret, that we cannot live up to our mission – the uniting power of a peaceful sports competition, though it encourages us to work even harder.'

Bach had celebrated the relative success, under Covid duress, of both Tokyo's and Beijing's Games prior to Putin's bloodshed, 'Above all was the judgement of the athletes at both Games – so grateful that they were still achieved within the pandemic, additionally that despite negative polling beforehand, the majority of the population of both host countries proudly followed events once underway on television and were unaffected by imported Covid infection.'

True, but how could anyone rationally evaluate future Olympic Games of Paris 2024, Milan-Cortina 2026 or Los Angeles 2028 during the spring of 2022 amid bombardment of bounteous, beautiful Ukraine? Prior to the invasion, Bach was optimistic. 'I sensed the Olympic Movement had been strengthened,' he forecast, 'by two Games that had been the most widely viewed thus far, that the accusations they would be irresponsible virus-spreaders was wholly disproved by rigorous control. While contemporary youth is watching less live broadcast television, social media and TV streaming, plus different new markets, generated at both Tokyo and Beijing prominently the widest viewing ever, at Beijing higher than for Pyeongchang in 2018. Advertising ratings in France were the best ever. With our revolutionary, economising host candidate procedure that we introduced in 2021, and the election of Brisbane 2032 11 years ahead, we already have city enquiries contemplating 2036 and even 2040.'

Yet the IOC, and whoever its president, is in moral limbo regarding the Olympic Truce. Upholding that historic principle from Ancient Greece is dependent not upon the IOC – albeit permanent observer within the United Nations – but the honour of politicians. Of murderer Putin? Yet which way to turn for the IOC when harassed from every quarter, not least by Germany's *Atleten Deutsche*, demanding 'Image Sporting Rights' from sponsorship's billions, or by Rob Koehler, general secretary of agitprop Global Athlete and its commercial ambitions. The IOC is threatened not least by the avarice of competitors whom it exists to promote.

The preferred loyalty of any IOC president should be the athletes, vouched by Bach from the day of his election, but the IOC is administratively handcuffed by its own constitution: Olympic Games entry is via national Olympic committee (NOC) team selection, and thereby the aura of every Games is infused with nationalism – and many governments' perceived return on financial investment (not least in Britain) – as much or more than by individual honour. The last five IOC presidents have, to some degree, trailed unavailingly in the wake of rampant nationalism. As Malcolm Knox of the *Sydney Morning Herald* shrewdly observed during Rio 2016, 'The Games are not about you or me individually, but a special place in the world intended to celebrate sport universally … yet simultaneously they become wild in overt nationalism.' Terrifyingly, sick Putin is more overt than Stalin or Hitler. Where would lie Bach's pragmatism when Putin's butchery terminated, without inadvertently destroying universality among the innocent, which he craved? Might we hear an echo of US university professor of political science Jules Boycoff, 'Let the athletes march at the Opening Ceremony sport by sport, not by nation.' Sound sense, but who would finance the marchers?

In the maelstrom of responsibilities crowding the IOC, one single word remains too often elusive: honour. Long before Canada's Olympic swimmer and senior IOC member Dick Pound failed in his 2001 challenge to succeed president Samaranch, he proclaimed, 'If the IOC's branding of symbolism, ritualisation and honour is forfeited, de Coubertin's precious legacy will be lost.' Samaranch, a constitutional revolutionary over 20 years, by inattention all but squandered honour in the late 1990s: Bach, the first Olympic champion to be elected president, may now metaphorically need one or two moral world records in the manner of legendary pole vault champion Sergey Bubka from Ukraine (defeated for leadership of World Athletics by Seb Coe).

Despite constant criticism, much of it from the hypocritical USA, Bach could not have been more actively dedicated to IOC survival, as I sense from recording the last five IOC presidents. He reflects, 'The myths of Olympic competition reach beyond performance, go beyond values such as the Truce or governance by rules, of fairness, anti-doping. De Coubertin's objectives were not simply ethical for the sake of sport, but for social education and the concept of peace, thereby are still a major pillar of our drive for universality. The crises we have experienced in recent years have been partially on account of a triangular conflict within the idealistic concept that sport unites us: firstly, the parallel ambition of nations and potential individual medal-winners – a few hundred – to be top dog; second, the quieter motivation of the other 10,000 hoping to discover a perspective of the rest of the world; lastly, the magnet for governments and their political motivations.'

These present the IOC with what become intolerable options in this intended Garden of Eden, so often corrupted by political empires. The Olympics are a gift from history. As Barack Obama remarked prior to Rio 2016, 'The Olympics are not going to end wars, eliminate poverty, but build a sense of common humanity, of empathy. The Olympics transport us to another place … particularly for Americans, who generally feel that unless there's bad news out there, we don't need to know much about elsewhere. The Olympics offer our introduction to the world.' Chief Dan George, celebrated native American, escaping the US for Canada, author of that memorable memoir

My Spirit Soars, and campaigner to protect Indian-American reservations prior to construction for the Calgary 1988 Winter Games, proclaimed, 'To satisfy the common longing in all of us, we must respect each other.'

Having long been a commentator of the Games, tell me this: what is the historic similarity between the regal patronage of King Edward VII at London's Games of 1908, and Xi Jinping's winter festival of 2022? I will address this conundrum in a moment. Humanity's insatiable greed, whether geographic, political, financial or tribal, generated a lust for creation of empires across four millennia, many of dynastic Chinese origin: the largest, though relatively brief in the 13th century, led by Genghis Khan, stretching from Hungary to the Sea of Japan; the longest by Egypt, 1550 BC – AD 473; stridently by France, then most recently, more modest Britain, 1603–1997. Putin's newly energised but economically vulnerable Russia, and insatiable ogre China's Pacific ambitions, spark a contemporary fuse. With nursery-like posture, Western politicians pressed the IOC to confront China's alleged genocide of their Muslim minority – a cop-out by politicians shy of imposing serious retribution of financial penalties rather than evasively ride on the back of boycott by token 'rubber-duck' athletes or faceless party-pooper diplomats.

Back in 2021, Bach had stressed, 'The IOC is not a supra-world government which in the cause of upholding human rights can strip China of hosting rights – to which we elected them – because of alleged incarceration of ethnic Uighurs. Boycotts of the Olympics, on three occasions, achieved nothing. If sport can play a role in society, it lies in strengthening co-operation between neighbours, giving the young hope for a better future. The Olympics do not have responsibility, or the capacity, to solve human rights issues which generations of politicians have been unable to master.' Yet only days later, a gaggle of political poseurs from the European Parliament was calling on 'member governments and embassies to decline invitation, to attend the Games'.

As veteran IOC member Dick Pound observed, 'The only authority that can command a government is a nation's own population.' In advance of China's hosting, the IOC reached a four-Games deal with China Media Group, controller of the nation's central television, extending a long-term partnership through to Brisbane 2032, the previous contract being 2014–2022. The new deal was well in excess of the previous $550m. The cynical will say expedient: the survival of world sport is dependent on such financial advantages, obliging the IOC to covet Chinese markets. NBC's advance US advertising for Beijing 2022 had already surpassed previous levels, exceeding those advertising rates for Tokyo 2020 or Rio 2016.

So what about human rights in China? There are few empires which have gently relinquished power over their subordinate territories, though the British, in the evolving headwinds of the 20th century, attempted to do so with courtesy. Yet how would the British feel if, say, euphemistically, the Isle of Wight or the Isle of Man were 'owned' by China as financial assets, as were Hong Kong and Kowloon by the British from 1841 and 1860 respectively? The British Empire came into existence by a conspiracy of nature: an island race that developed naval power across the 16th to 18th centuries which outgunned colonies of France, Spain and Portugal: this alongside the mining of coal that propagated the steel industry revolution ahead of world rivals.

In protecting its empire, 1900–1950, Britain engaged in over 80 military skirmishes (excluding two world wars), predominantly protecting Queen Victoria's crown jewel of India and colonial Africa. It still strategically and controversially owns the Falklands and Gibraltar with uneasy tolerance from Argentina and Spain. When Britain attended Antwerp's Olympic Games of 1920, fourth in the medals table, it was in the wake of the British Army's 'Bloody Sunday' crushing of Dublin's separatist republican campaign, with the death of 300, and subsequently 4,500 interned. At Melbourne 1956, Britain could hardly protest at the Soviet Empire's suppression of Hungary's Budapest Uprising, having dejectedly failed in company with the armed forces of France and Israel, to retrieve its one-third share of the Suez Canal from rebellious President Nasser. No foreign government exerted attempt to suspend British Olympians. And avaricious France? Prior to late 18th-century domestic revolution, monarchic tentacles had occupied swathes of Caribbean, African and Asian jewels. Occupation of Algeria only ended with independence in 1962 after 130 years of conflict and some 200,000 deaths in pernicious mutual disputes.

Preceding Beijing's Winter Games, a platoon of US politicians – in concerted demand for the Games to be shunted elsewhere – displayed blindfold perspective of the USA's status as the, hitherto, most accomplished industrial and supreme military power: created by its immigrant domestic 'geographic' empire, partially dependent on an African slave population which had been denied for much of four centuries the rights of social integration, alongside subordinated indigenous Indian Americans. The USA's presence for the inaugural modern Games at Athens in 1896 came in the wake of the final 'ethnic cleansing' of 300 Indian American souls at Dakota's Wounded Knee, the final atrocity in a century's murder of folklore heroes revered to this day: witness Jim Thorpe's continuing domestic and cultural memorabilia. Travis Tygart, head of America's anti-doping agency, is reluctant to debate the imposition of President Andrew Jackson's Indian Removal Act of 1830, in which 17,000 Cherokee natives were marched, together with 2,000 slaves, on the Trail of Tears from Mississippi into Georgia, 5,000 dying of disease or starvation. Few remember that as the USA team departed for Tokyo 1964, Alabama's Robert Shelton was assembling the 50,000-strong 'United Klans of America': KKK already armed with their flaming crucifix insignia for assassination of Black Integration Freedom Fighters across Georgia and Mississippi, all, of course, in the name of honourable Christian faith. The recent Black Lives Matter campaign, extending worldwide, is a continuity of the racial inequity which disfigures the incredible achievements over the last two centuries of what has been, until now, humanity's most triumphant nation: industrial, cultural, scientific, medical.

There has seldom been an empire with a clean slate in human rights. Well-intentioned as Britain may have been in command of the Indian subcontinent, my mother-in-law, as the daughter of an army officer, had an employee sleeping on the bedroom doorstep to keep the snakes at bay. Many British military incursions involved north-west frontier protection prior to Mahatma Gandhi's independent campaign for empire release in 1947. Queensland, scheduled to host Australia's third Summer Games in 2032, will need to guard against lingering racism against Aborigines, by organisations such as the Australia Defence League, or 'Reclaim Australia', with continuing defamation of prominent sporting stars such as Adam Goodes, never mind the deification of Aborigine Cathy Freeman at Sydney 2000.

Now recall London 1908 and comparison with Beijing 2022, and the sense of entitlement as grandiose superpowers dominate the globe to a degree in which rival governments are mostly reluctant to challenge, even condemn, a host's foreign strategy or social conduct. While Edward VII eagerly graced White City Stadium, in Anglo-Egyptian Sudan in mid-1908 there was an uprising by indigenous Wad Habuba, the British Army instantly responding against religious opposition to Christian rule, and local desire to restore the Mahdist State under leadership by a veteran of the Mahdist War, Al-Qadir Muhammad Iman Wad Habuba. Britain dispatched two infantry companies to quell the uprising, led by Ernest Dickinson, governor of Blue Nile Province. Many were killed: meanwhile, packed houses in west London revelled in a glut of medals. Britain's exclusive team of judges were so prejudiced against all comers that, four years later in Stockholm, the International Athletics Federation had been created to rationalise authority in track and field.

Elements of Britain's empire linger. In 2019, Westminster found itself under obligation to end its administration of the Chagos Archipelago as rapidly as possible under order of the International Court of Justice. The Chagos Islands had been retained by the UK during negotiations for the independence of Mauritius in 1968, the islands occupied for 'defence purposes' by the UK and USA. The entire Chagos population was forcibly removed between 1967 and 1973 and prevented from returning, dispersed elsewhere. The United Nations emphasised 'protection of the human rights of those concerned' for the required reinstatement: a reversal of the Windrush scandal, many West Indies immigrants welcomed to Britain to aide post-war recovery then being declared 'illegal' seven decades later.

Across the globe, societies historically repeat their errors, seldom learn. The universality that Thomas Bach has pursued since becoming an administrator 40 years ago remains elusive. The eternal joy available in the Olympic Games was still discernible in Beijing's Winter Games: the contest against malign social nature has been recurrent: Athens initially reluctant inaugural host; Paris 1900 many months protracted; St Louis 1904 racist; London 1908 and Los Angeles 1932 nationalistic; Berlin 1936 racist; Japan 1964 threatened by Indonesia's President Sukano with prior 'separatist Games'; apartheid South Africa, suspended 1964–1992; Mexico 1968, police corrupted; Munich 1972, terrorised; three political boycotts in 1976, 1980 and 1984; political intimidation Seoul 1988, Beijing 2008, Pyeongchang 2018, Beijing 2022. Despite Bach's reformations, the IOC – benevolent in principle yet often erratic in aspects of membership enlistment – will continue to be hounded by governments, whether dictatorial or democratic: provided it survives. Contemporary life is dominated by temperamental extremists: a sense of entitlement, echoed at Boris Johnson's Bullingdon Club at Oxford University, by property billionaire Donald Trump, or empire-ambitious autocrats.

How fortunate for a century has been sport: governed – mostly – by rules which the majority respected. I was in awe of Russian sport since watching Moscow Dynamo, unknown, aged ten, on Pathe's news reel in 1946. My mother, a rebellious middle-class English teenager, joining a Belarus balalaika orchestra fleeing Lenin in the 1920s, cherished Russian culture. From numerous visits – stretching from Saint Petersburg to Siberia – I have trusted and admired Russian friends, yet can I henceforth believe a word they say? My polite message to the IOC president, for protection of the Olympic Movement as Putin's plunder of Ukraine persists, is unequivocal: remember Winston Churchill's observation of 1945, 'The Soviet Union is a riddle wrapped in a mystery inside an enigma.'

The Olympic family should exclude Russia unconditionally until Putin is either imprisoned or deceased, and thereafter subject to stringent conditional qualification at any events. Even fleeting familiarity with Russian history over centuries provides confirmation of Russia's unusual generic blend of courage and brutality: experienced by Napoleon and then by Hitler, the latter in the sieges of Leningrad (Saint Petersburg) and Stalingrad (Volgograd): philosophically, never surrender, if your colleagues do so, shoot them. Bach may not have encountered the analysis by Slava Malamud, experienced immigrant Russian-American sports columnist, source of US agency Sports Examiner: Malamud denounces Soviet/Russian sport and politics being 'inseparable and synonymous'; that for the Kremlin, since the Bolsheviks, Western sport was for the urban university elite, in Russia for the proletariat. For Stalin, international competition was acceptable only if victory was guaranteed. The first USSR football entry was for Helsinki's Olympics 1952: losing a replay against Turkey, the coach and all players were expelled permanently from the sport. Lev Yashin, heroic goalkeeper of the 1950s, symbolised national mentality: defending the border.

The appalling conflict for Bach's Olympic 'universality' maxim is that Putin's barbarism is supported by Russian

Orthodox priests and by the bulk of Russia's population, contrary to Western supposition: an echo of Christ's crucifixion approved by pontificate; disbelief that the weak shall inherit the earth. Dominic Lawson recalls in the *Sunday Times* that aristocratic French historian Astolphe de Custine, visiting Russia in 1839, recorded, 'Russia propagates tyranny as palliative to anarchy: that despotism is an endemic gene.'

Bach needs to acknowledge that Russia and Russian sport is more than just about making friends. Remember blood in the water polo pool at Melbourne's Olympics of 1956, post-Budapest anti-Soviet uprising.

Renowned historian Anthony Beevor relates in *Russia: Revolution and Civil War 1917-21* (Weidenfeld): 'Victims were bound with barbed wire and pressed into ice holes, skewered alive, roasted in train-rail furnaces, impregnated with rats then obliged to gnaw their way free. For ruthless inhumanity, the Bolsheviks were unbeatable.' This is recurring now in Ukraine, yet morally blindfold, idolised tennis millionaires lament forfeiting their ranking points at Wimbledon. How shameful.

2

WHERE STANDS
EMPIRE-INTENT XI JINPING?

THE IDEOLOGY of the Olympics lies in celebrating minorities along with the famous: the cavalcade of the unknown, strangers embracing in mutual respect. I have observed this in pursuit of what it has been a delight to call employment. The list is interminable. One of the most remarkable moments across six decades' involvement is quite recent: Yusra Mardini, survivor after swimming the Aegean for three hours when hauling a sinking raft of 14 Syrians, together with her sister Sara, to become part of Rio's emergent Refugee Team in 2016. Then there was the Kenyan adopted US refugee, Lopez Lomong, inspired as a boy watching Michael Johnson receiving adulation at Atlanta 1996 'merely for running', and rising himself to carry the US flag at Beijing 2008.

Way back, Indian American Billy Mills, close to suicide under university abuse, emerged to win the 10,000m at Tokyo 1964 with defeat of Australian record holder Ron Clarke. At Vancouver 2010, Muhammad Abbas, Himalayan villager from Pakistan, fashioned his giant-slalom skis from wood, while alongside him was Dow Travers, first ever winter entry from the Cayman Islands who found himself sharing a bus with Swiss boyhood idol Didier Cuche. The tiniest arrival at Beijing 2008 was 16-year-old Asenate Minoa from Pacific island Tuvalu, sprinting in front of a crowd larger than her national population. Marjan Kahler became at Vancouver the first Iranian woman at a Winter Games, wearing a national emblem in her head scarf when bearing Iran's Opening Ceremony flag yet forbidden to share ski-lifts with men. Rania Elwani, Egyptian obstetrician, African record-breaking semi-finalist swimmer at Sydney 2000, when questioned by an interviewer how she felt 'failing to win a medal', reflected, 'If only he understood just what it means to be part of this global celebration.' Elwani's emotion was probably exceeded by Isaquias Pueiroz of Brazil in 2016: scalded as an infant in the jungle-dominated north, losing his father aged five, sold in child trafficking before returned to a destitute mother, lost a kidney when falling from a tree on to rocks, yet government-funded in the local-transport medium of canoeing, uniquely to win three Olympic titles.

Celebration of Olympic neutrality may have to contemplate its own diminution, not on account of provocation of a fictionally declared war, but mass murder: deranged genocide, the price for which can never be recovered. The awful irony is that the guilt flows from the totemic leader of a fabulous nation which coincidentally is one cornerstone of a unique festival. As the IOC president projects, 'In achieving universality of the Olympic Games, Russia, as part of the big three together with America and China, has had an important contributory role: sporting, social and financial, alongside that of IFs. It is why when elected president, my immediate move was to establish an annual Olympic summit in December together with those three, the Executive Board and all IFs [international federations].' With cruel perversion, Russia has contrived to create, firstly in 2014, an IOC nightmare of Sochi's institutional cheating, and now a climax of a trans-continental catastrophe by devouring Ukraine, just when the reward of Bach's constitutional reforms were predicted to blossom at the Games of Paris and LA: an effective re-ignition of momentum.

For an IOC member so dedicated to the borderless interests of sport, and increasingly as president, Bach has received, mostly with forbearance, extended media criticism, not least from Germany. Eminence is often given such negativity: here, not as a Bavarian lawyer but during years of domestic sports authority, and then a deft precision within the IOC during intolerance of others' indecision, and evident in his apparent ambition. Bach's easy humour, in private, slides into objective formality behind a microphone or in front of a camera. This makes him a ready target for sports media, they seldom requited to summon testimonial evidence for their earnest, often hearsay opinions.

So Bach has focused otherwise during his often 16-hour day co-ordination of the affairs, and occasionally the lives, of 500 affiliated associations all with their own specific schedules and skin-tight finances: ignoring the rebuffs of 'suited charlatan', 'racketeer', or allegations that the IOC 'should be eradicated' – any replacement presumed by media similarly to re-invest, of course, 90 per cent of its multi-billion-dollar income in subsidies for international sport including youth scholarships and an Olympic Refugee Team. Tokyo's and Beijing's tortuously restricted routines nonetheless introduced spectacular new 'street corner' contemporary sports, a captivating blood transfusion for enlisting the energy of today's and tomorrow's youth.

There are a clutch of ardent IOC members working in league with Bach: recently deceased François Carrard, eminent Swiss lawyer, IOC director-general 1989–2003 during Samaranch's second decade and initial years of Rogge's contemplative presidency; subsequently advising discreetly in line with Bach's forward planning; Michael Payne, past marketing director who dynamically kept the hesitant but crucial TOP [The Olympic Partner Programme] sponsors onside during the Salt Lake City scandal 1998–99; and Francesco Ricci Bitti, past president of international tennis and now head of the Association of Summer Olympic International Federations (Samaranch's consultative amalgam to halt mutiny by individual IFs in search of an alternative to IOC).

During Tokyo's disruptively postponed Games of 2021, over two weeks Ricci Bitti had 31 appointments, at different event venues, to ensure efficiency of extemporised health and technical event-producers within Japan's bubble, which kept external Covid infection to a minimum. 'Ricci Bitti's limousine luxury', jibed the critics. Was he expected to travel by bicycle? 'It was a difficult adventure in Tokyo,' Ricci Bitti recalls, 'for proud organisers and athletes. ASOIF [Association of Summer Olympic International Federations] has become not just rule-maker, but value-provider sport by sport, and possibly strategist for esport introductions. Not all athletes in Tokyo were ready for the regulations under a range of authorities. In running a Games there are athletes … and admin engines. It's a two-faced operation and sometimes an admin problem: the "athletes' union" cannot be dovetailed with the "management union" responsible for smooth running.

'The IFs are on a wider expectation than ten years ago – in finance, management control, legal intelligence – and not yet fully equipped on this. International sport is under threat between performers and public investors. Business partners do not give money free to sport. The potential for athlete defection is there, unrealised as yet. While 0.01 per cent of athletes financially succeed, ASOIF's responsibility is to protect the 99.99 percentage. Besides the additional fragility of loyalty to the Olympic ethic by the 0.01 per cent, the mounting calendar of reconstructed major IF events dilute competitive appeal for Olympic honours, and achieving a peak for the Games.'

Bach concurs, 'The IFs' risks are there. Venture capital firms are interested, within sport for business. The IOC is not into business, but for sport's values and protection. IFs are autonomous, they need to study business strategy, what it means for governance, for admissions, to be on guard for maintaining proper regulations.'

IOC modernisation had begun with Samaranch's presidential election in 1980, and progress advanced with the compliant support of Richard – Dick – Pound and right-hand staffer Carrard, he latterly acutely aware of IOC's languishing amateurism. 'We had recognised with Barcelona's hosting in '92 the level of professionalism now required,' Carrard recalled. 'The huge private and public responsibilities: the so-called democratic choice which relied on many people who lacked the information and confidence for such decisions, so the need for change, for administrative evolution, was unavoidable. I used to hear Samaranch sighing, "If only the EB [Executive Board] made host city election decisions, we'd avoid many problems." Thomas was already in that advisory group recommending host city decisions should not be left to the mass [IOC] Session, evolution was fundamentally required, just as the then USOC [United States Olympic Committee] president Larry Probst had advocated. This acknowledged that the host elections and determining the sports programme were the members' only remaining prerogative and thereby posing whether the IOC democratically still needed over a hundred of them?'

When I last talked with Maître Carrard, not long prior to his passing, he had hinted at doubt whether the IOC could survive its fight for survival for another 20 years – the major vulnerability being survival of the 40-odd summer and winter IFs, 'If the IFs accept external financial subsidies, they risk losing their administrative rights and control, and thereby Olympic ethics. That is the problem, though since Thomas arrived, the IOC has strengthened their relation across the Olympic Movement – with the UN, with the international community, but we then have to explain issues like restricting suspended Russia's uniform identity regulations in Tokyo. The true test of accepting outside finance is involuntarily placing sport in the hands of business, which doesn't understand sporting ethics. And how can you suggest sport is not between nations but individuals [the universality] when the individuals are dependent on national finance? Any switch in financial power becomes administratively dominated.'

Equally informed on every IOC constitutional or financial dilemma across many years is Michael Payne, adroit negotiator behind Samaranch's sponsorship revolution of the 1980s; subsequently becoming independent guru for global contract franchises, all this divulged in his published *Olympic Turnaround*: the multitude of daring deals as broker on broadcast rights negotiated with Tokyo, Beijing and elsewhere long before Covid had intervened. He relates:

'The traditional model of prime-time rating has become no longer applicable, with so many different devices available around the clock, live, short-term clips, so the way any sport can be consumed has radically changed. As the IOC has needed to calculate: how many people, what do they want to watch, for how long, in which country? Since London 2012, the audience from India has become five times higher than ever before: the evolution of the whole industry, digitally, has exploded, so that's where the IOC has had to move.

'It has to be remembered, when considering the removal of live spectators from Tokyo, that contracts are all negotiated long before a Games occurs, so the impact of one Games reflects only on the future. I am already at work on contracts for 2032 – TOP sponsors negotiate on the long term. Thomas Bach has done a phenomenal job with increase in the value of the TOP programme, which will have moved from $1bn at the time of Rio 2016, to $3bn by the time of Paris 2024. The market is there: Tokyo's home local sponsorships negotiated pre-pandemic were the most successful ever. I was there in Tokyo for the postponed Games – it was a miracle that it happened, that the IOC gathered 206 NOCs during mid-pandemic, and a tragedy that there were no spectators allowed. Yet Thomas responded that he believed the Games could be saved, so convincingly that Tokyo's Organising Committee agreed, "We'll wait."

'Bach recognised it was impossible for 2020, and negotiated with Premier Abe for postponement, now aware that Japan still had to save face. The event's care bubble to isolate the public from the Games would work exceptionally well. The irony was that Bach had been anxious to escape from the existing risks surrounding five of his first six years of the presidency, following the opening establishment of his Agenda 2020: the Sochi 2014 hidden doping scandal, the near financial disaster of Rio 2016, the trepidation of Pyeongchang 2018 and North Korea. He had expected Tokyo to be easy, brilliant, flawless Japan. Instead, Covid!

'Yet what rescued Tokyo was digital TV innovation, that athletes unable to afford to bring their family would now instead be able to see and speak to them back in their own village, in, say, Syria, wherever, a magic technology for enlightenment, a celebration of communication. Yes, the innovative effect of new contemporary sports, skateboarding and indoor climbing, etc, was a magnet for the world, for both youth audience and competitors, a super-hit with uncomplicated venues, but it was Bach who saved the Games. Without him, they would never have happened. The Olympic Broadcast Service technology was a catalyst.'

Having achieved the remarkable feat – primarily for the athletes – of rescuing Tokyo's Games, Bach's target now was the potentially more complex challenge, within six months, of Beijing's Winter Games: threatened not so much by viral scourge as social philosophy. My father being for a while an actor, I was imbued early on with the stage, and in particular the melodies and lyrics of Noel Coward. His ironic 'Don't Let's Be Beastly to the Germans' had an articulate sophistication matched only by Victoria Wood. In World War One, did not the Brits and Germans emerge from the trenches to play football on Christmas Day? I hear an echo of Coward, sincere, in Bach's universality attitude towards the autocracies of Russia and China: innately hoping to make the world friendlier, safer. As the IOC would become inextricably committed to Beijing for 2022, 'let's democratically improve them' – while the 'free' world clamoured for China's sporting ostracism – but not against a compelling share of their commercial wealth. Bach told the IOC Session of February 2022:

'In electing Beijing, we saw the potential for China's promise of extending winter sports to 300 million enthusiasts, particularly with the arrival of different new sports, and not just for the elite. China would now become a winter sports nation, with its relevance to health and social integration. Furthermore, we worryingly detected elsewhere a growing politicisation of sport on the horizon, and the danger of memory of boycotts of the past, while we were striving for the unifying mission of the Games. In many conversations we stressed that the Games can only encourage a unification, bringing humanity together, the Games standing above all political disputes. This message was accepted, so that athletes who have overcome many preparatory uncertainties can now make their dream come true. We know that sport cannot alone create peace, nor can we take decisions on war, but symbols are important, showing how the world can look if we all respect the same rules and each other.'

Totemic Chinese leader Xi Jinping delivered his own message, Beijing becoming the first city to have hosted both summer and winter events, 'The world today, under the impact of changes unseen in a hundred years, enters a period of turbulence, facing multiple changes. The IOC has led the Olympic Movement with courage and fortitude in gathering global solidarity ... and I thank the IOC for promoting sport in China.'

Was not China's investment in winter sport an expansion of education for ordinary people? A reflection of the benevolence of sport for all? Had we not witnessed this in the character of Mikhail Bobrov, wartime mountaineer skiing hero of Saint Petersburg, perilously camouflaging the roofs of German-target churches under aircraft gunfire during the siege, and guerrilla marksman subsequently, later at the Olympics of Rome embracing a forgotten German rival whom, near fatally wounded, he had taken by sledge to hospital? Yet here now were a group of nations led by the US and including Australia, Belgium, Britain, Canada, Denmark, Estonia, Lithuania and New Zealand, opting not to send government representatives to the Games in a shallow diplomatic boycott. No bonus points: if critical of a sports rival, say so face to face. Absentees went unnoticed.

While much of Europe and Commonwealth nations nursed this smug sense of democratic superiority, this did not apply worldwide, non-autocratic nations represented among 30 dignitary enthusiasts to share China's largely artificial snow and 'friendly' trade affiliation: Argentina, Egypt, Ecuador, Luxembourg, Monaco, Mongolia, Pakistan, Poland, Serbia, Singapore, all gracing Xi's hospitality banquet following the Opening Ceremony. Downing Street's non-attendance will have had zero political impact beyond perhaps diminishing UK commercial enterprise. Despite cynical doubt expressed globally, Xi reassured his guests on China's aimed expansion into winter sports for 300 million ordinary folk. Norway, Austria, beware.

Yet the Games would not dispel international hostility to China's regimented social repressions: while Chinese media extolled domestic medal haul, an isolated publication did run the story of an indigent mother chained round the neck to the wall of a doorless shack. There is not total insensitivity to social indigence. Yet the evil deceit of the concurrent Beijing meeting of superpower presidents, Xi and Vladimir Putin, affirming 'united opposition to abuse in the affairs of international sovereign states and human rights' was exposed within three weeks in Ukraine to be valueless. A prominent UK daily begged the question of why these Games, never mind the pandemic, could not have been offered for the benefit of athletes to a country 'they deserved', free of cyber surveillance? This overlooked the reality that China had been the only realistic option following withdrawal of bids in 2015 by half a dozen democratic nations. So, abandon the Olympics of 2022? Bach campaigns for athletes, not governments.

Western media were in a lather about China's total Covid isolation bubble repression of visitors' free movement, deepening institutional prohibition of free speech: the first pragmatic under Covid, the second autocratic policy beyond any tourist option, the two facets monitored everywhere by security. Yang Yang, senior member of the organising committee and an Olympic champion, warned in *China Daily*, 'Athletes need to be responsible for what they say.' At daily official press conferences, 'irresponsible' Western questions were anaesthetised by an official 'opinion therapist'. There is no cultural key available for unlocking China's irredeemable social padlock: irate Westerners simply had to accept that the granting of the Games was a genuine long-term gift to citizens lacking short-term power over a press gang government. Domestic gold medals would bring a philosophical reward for the world's largest population. Xi, in his meeting with Bach prior to the Games, the first with a foreign dignitary in two years of Covid, expectantly proclaimed 'the importance of the Games to China's government'.

Global media's persistent but often uninformed assault on the IOC – 'dedicated to its own glorification' – hung awkwardly around two personal issues disrupting the conventional charm of an Opening Ceremony: the earlier alleged disappearance and re-emergence of prominent Chinese tennis player Peng Shuai, then the perceived 'contrived' promotion of Uighur cross-country skier Dinigeer Yilamujiang to share lighting of the Olympic Flame. In both instances, any element of political subterfuge was indeterminate. A while before the Games, Peng had publicly lodged accusation of harassment against a senior Communist party official with whom there had been an acknowledged affair – mistress-boasting being a Chinese male indulgence. Alarm was sounded by the International Tennis Federation (ITF) on Peng's whereabouts; Thomas Bach clandestinely located her and confirmed her supposed safety, met her again in Beijing upon his arrival, she then appearing at the Opening Ceremony, photographed and apparently at ease, yet declining to divulge further detail. It remained unclear whether Peng was the victim or initiator of remote social revenge in a surveillance nation where almost every private sigh is video-recorded. The complexity for Bach was whether his involvement was correct and justifiable under the IOC Charter, in response to anxiety by the ITF.

Meanwhile, an apparently joyful Yelamujiang told the Xinhua agency that such a privileged role in the Opening Ceremony was 'a huge honour': selection determined, according to the organising committee, by athletes' birth date. Led by US critics, protestors claimed the inclusion was a political diversion to counter accusations of internment and even genocide against Uighur Muslims. Aged 21, Yelamujiang had become the first Chinese cross-country skiing medallist in any international federation event in 2019. She was joined in the flame-lighting by Nordic-Combined compatriot Xhao Jiawen. Zumretay Arkino, from World Uighur Congress, alleged the inclusion was 'a propaganda event'; she was one of five athletes in China's team from the Xinjiang region. The controversy was one of many dismissed as 'Western lies' by Yan Jiarong, former delegate to the UN General Assembly and organising committee representative at daily IOC media conferences. Jiarong was also intent on assertion that Taiwan – Games participant under the title Chinese Taipei, with its own flag and anthem – is inherently part of China. Could Xi be scheduled to emulate the path of Putin in Ukraine? The US would feel obliged to respond.

From here let us consider, from the beginning of his presidency, Thomas Bach's conflicted passage towards Olympic controversies which threaten an imperishable concept. Beijing's legitimate sporting events follow in Chapter 15.

3

LONG-TERM LEGACY

THOMAS BACH was born in the southern German town of Tauberbischofsheim, and had begun fencing from the early age of six, unusually with the foil discipline, regarded almost more an artistic than sporting culture. In Bach's coaching school, fencing was more dynamic: in parallel with living alongside a prematurely ailing father, who died of heart failure when Thomas was a young teenager, the boy acquired early the instinct of self-initiative.

While he would later write glowingly of Munich's spectacular stadium and Olympic Village architecture assembled for the Games of 1972, for him aged 18 the Games were an anti-climax: excluded from the fencing team for being too young.

'The Games, at the time, were for me a de-motivation, our federation excluding two of us,' Bach smilingly recalls. 'The following year, we were part of the team that gained silver in the World Championships. During Munich's event, I'd been offered a place at a youth training camp. I'd said no thanks, went on holiday to Spain, watching the Games in a bar, and this provided a future target.' This was achieved four years later in Montreal as a member of the foil team's gold medal. Bach reflects how his performance was lifted as a team player, more than as individual, 'A different character, out of respect for the others, a sense of needing to go further … yes, I was small, but for a fencer quick on my feet.'

With the Germans poised to defend their Olympic title at Moscow in 1980, there was once again frustration, Germany taking the political decision – in contrast to Britain – to boycott the event in support of the blatantly ineffectual President Carter-led US protest against the Soviet invasion of Afghanistan. Bach was prominent among German athletes antagonised by a meaningless gesture-principle in which they played no active part. So it was logical that he was among a group of 25 Olympic medallists invited by Juan Antonio Samaranch – new IOC president from Spain elected at Moscow in succession to Michael Killanin of Ireland – to an IOC Congress of 1981 in Baden-Baden. Significant in Samaranch's extension of the hitherto male-only club was the inclusion – on the initiation of Killanin – of six female athlete 'guests', in parallel with the inaugural IOC election of two women, Flor Isava Fonseca of Venezuela and Pirjo Häggman of Finland. The women athletes were Yuko Arakida (Japan, volleyball), Irene Epple (Germany, alpine), Michelle Ford (Australia, swimming), Svetla Otsetova (Bulgaria, rowing), Vera Sosulia (USSR, luge) and Elizabeth Theurer (Austria, equestrianism). Subsequent to the Congress, Samaranch created the Athletes Commission, led by Bach and including double 1,500m champion Sebastian Coe from Britain. 'I had been so frustrated at missing Moscow,' Bach said, 'especially when knowing that the voice of athletes had not been heard, and our inclusion at Baden-Baden, taken seriously, was hugely appreciated. Coe, Kip Keino of Kenya, I and others were given real motivation for helping to steer the future development of international sport.'

By now, approaching 30, Bach was extensively into life as a lawyer, qualified at Warzburg University, and with his own practice, also invited into sport management by Willi Daume, doyen of the National Olympic Committee. Bach knew it might be a long haul, 'I didn't want what happened at Moscow to happen again; furthermore, it took a long time to promote a merger between the NOC and the governing body of German sport, the DSB. Transformation needed support of friends, including Helmut Kohl, who initially considered sport did not deserve such focus. Finally he recognised that the merger would strengthen both bodies.'

If Bach had been quick on his feet on fencing's piste, he became an adroit conference negotiator, not least in the accelerating realm of sponsorship contracts under the guidance of Adidas magnate Horst Dassler, mogul of that industry. Bach was increasingly influential, outside public gaze, by the time Samaranch was obliged, in the wake of Salt Lake City's hosting scandal of 1998–99, to create Commission 2000, an administrative ruse embracing 80 international figures – 36 from business, industry, politics and culture, including Henry Kissinger, Giuseppe Agnelli of Fiat, Peter Ueberroth from Los Angeles 1984, Boutros Boutros-Galli of the United Nations, 26 athletes and over 40 from the IOC, including international federations and NOCs – a brainbox both cosmetic and practical for introduction of constitutional reform and calm water prior to Sydney's Olympic Games of 2000. Here was Bach's presidency tutorial. A decade later came his own elevation to prominence. Through Samaranch, Bach learned to turn sports management from an amateur's hobby into a professional equation while still retaining the fundamental 'universality of the Games'.

In his three-decade ascent of IOC's administration, Bach significantly was appointed chairman of the Juridical and the Sport-and-Law Commissions: feet under the table, but without influence on the immobile debate on the Olympic Programme, for which indoor climbing, karate, roller sports and squash racquets among others repeatedly but unavailingly attempted to throw their hat in the ring. As a consequence, during Jacques Rogge's 12 years at the helm as president, the only new arrivals, accepted at Copenhagen's Session of 2009, had been golf and rugby sevens. Rogge had been reluctant, repeatedly saying, 'We cannot change the goal posts.' But whose posts?

Rogge had claimed that to rise above 28 sports would require changing the Charter. Yet the Charter was not set in stone by founder Pierre de Coubertin, it is there to be adjusted by the members as desired. There's not too much fencing or pole vaulting nowadays in Bamako, Central African Republic. Yet for over a century the IOC, loyal to its founder, had been an administrative contradiction: institutionally rigidly traditional yet upholding the right of members' individuality, i.e. believe what you like but don't rock the boat. Thus, when the Salt Lake scandal had caused Samaranch to create the Commission 2000, inviting global opinion, Rogge, presiding over his first IOC Session in 2001, encountered members opposing rule change because they considered it curtailed their independence; how to behave. Embarrassed, Rogge postponed debate to a further, Extraordinary Session in Mexico City in 2002.

Nevertheless, Bach had quietly been consolidating authority within increasingly complex financial or competition issues, legal exactitude now ever more relevant. He resolved, for instance, a skating judging corruption at Salt Lake in 2002 involving prejudice favouring Russia over Canada, asserting 'consistency is paramount'. At Turin's Winter Games of 2006, he adroitly supervised, as juridical chairman, a serious doping incident within Austria's camp, resulting in permanent Olympic suspension for six athletes and cancellation of a $1m grant to the Austrian NOC. Prior to Beijing's Summer Games of 2008, with global confusion and international street protests disrupting the torch relay, Bach had obliquely criticised Rogge when stressing, 'The mistake was to permit the relay to be identified as a Chinese event, whereas in fact it belongs not to the host country but to the IOC. We had been warned for months that there would be controversy.'

Epitomising an attitude of *laissez-faire* had been the juggling act with a wayward wrestling federation over many years. Seven months before the double election in Buenos Aires in 2013 – the city hosts for 2020 and a successor to

Rogge – the IOC belatedly awoke to the endemic dysfunction of wrestling's administration, with immediate suspension, yet simultaneously granting the possibility for re-admission when competing alongside new applicants straining at the bit. Symptomatic confusion. Two days before Bach bid for ultimate authority, wrestling was voted back into the stable. Time, millions of dollars and the ambition of other candidates had been duly squandered: hardly the way to run a sweet shop. Credibility for wrestling's federation, FILA (*Fédération Internationale des Luttes Associées*), was rescued by Nenad Lalović, an innovative Balkan whose revision had expanded women's participation and the clarification of obtuse judging. This bureaucratic jigsaw illustrated, for an incoming president, the extent to which the IOC needed to co-ordinate with international federations under the direction of the articulate Francesco Ricci Bitti, Italian president of both the Association of Summer Olympic International Federations (ASOIF) and International Tennis. As Ricci Bitti stressed, 'All federations must collaborate with the IOC to make the Games manageable for any city. The issue is not the number of sports but the number of competitors: tennis manages, in the Olympics, with half the number we have at Grand Slams, but is still a major Olympic event because players are representing their country. International federations have to adopt the same perspective. We can reduce the numbers in big sports – athletics, gymnastics, swimming, maybe boxing, rowing, wrestling. Gymnastics amounts to three sports – artistic, rhythmic, trampoline. Reducing numbers would create scope for more sports. Likewise, of course, bid cities should be restricted to a select, reduced number of presentations instead of touring the world at gross expense.'

The IOC 'club's' unpublicised cloak-and-dagger negotiations – let's not pretend they didn't exist – had swayed decisions. At the heart of the club in the early 21st century stood Sheikh Ahmad, a powerful personality from Kuwait's ruling nobility. I had been friendly with his father,

Sheikh Fahad, avid racehorse owner in the UK, president of the Olympic Council of Asia (OCA) and football fanatic, motivator of the national team which had met England in the opening round of Spain's 1982 World Cup. My wife and I had been guests of the Sheikh at a training tournament in Tunisia, while I once had the Arabian desert experience of a tented, cushion-seated lunch amid horizonless abstraction. Fahad was killed in the opening week of the Kuwait–Iraq War, Samaranch provocatively replacing him with his young son Ahmad: a smilingly discreet political figure who had quickly become manipulative across the oriental sporting landscape, and beside succeeding his father as head of OCA, rapidly rising to become president of the Association of National Olympic Committees (ANOC).

At the end of Rogge's 12-year rule, there were three immediate decisions to be made – the elections of his successor and that of the summer host city of 2020, plus the future of the troubled wrestling association. Ahmad was calculated to be a significant potential 'fixer'. Prior to the presidential election, he had stated, 'My concerns are always guided by the head rather than the heart. The Olympic Games lasts for two weeks, while my responsibilities for the interest of over 200 NOCs lasts for four years. My job is to protect and promote their welfare. It is my duty to collaborate with whoever is IOC president. Before the election, my association with any candidate is concerned with their responsibility to ensure the Olympic Movement's continuity and prosperity.' Quite a grand assumption. Through mutual Middle East business interests, Ahmad was known to be close to Bach's ambition, potentially influential, while inevitably his emotional momentum would be martialled behind Tokyo's bid for 2020.

Two years prior to this strategic crossroads in IOC history, there occurred in 2011 the seemingly straightforward election in Durban, South Africa, of Pyeongchang as winter host city for 2018. At the third attempt, bureaucratically well marshalled, enthusiastically presented even if competitively inexperienced as had been Seoul when elected in 1981, Pyeongchang only the third winter host in Asia, so why not? Except that the chief rival was the double-bid by Munich-Garmisch: thriving, financially safer European alpine hub, backed by formidable IOC members Berthold Beitz, Walter Troeger, a conspicuous Bach and prominent athlete Claudia Bokel: host to 10,000 winter events over 40 years and last Olympics 75 years ago in 1936, Munich's summer hosting in 1972 had been an architectural and administrative landmark in Olympic history. The imponderable voting 'elephant' in the Sessions' corridors at Durban was Ahmad. In two years' time Bach, with his known business allegiance in the Gulf, would expect to be sure of Asian backing for the plum post. An otherwise inexplicable 38-vote margin in favour of Pyeongchang rather than Munich, 63-25, with third candidate Annecy embarrassingly adrift on seven, will have enjoyed significant Ahmad influence. A studiously prepared address, in English, by Korea's state president could not account for that avalanche vote. 'I was indeed greatly disappointed,' Bach remembers. 'We had been informed that Pyeongchang would not come back for a third time, and though we had some issues at home, our committee had won a domestic referendum in Garmisch. Meanwhile Pyeongchang had re-entered the race. It's hard to judge the outcome, the swing in how Pyeongchang was rewarded.'

Onwards a couple of years. By 2013, Rogge's 12 years at the helm had, in his own words 'become an irrelevance': a calm, respectful orthopaedic consultant treading water in an Olympic climate oscillating in several directions. With that conservative attitude which characterises provincial medicine – dogged trust in established laboratory wisdom – Rogge had politely steadied the boat, in the wake of the Salt Lake election scandal which had threatened to sink his predecessor, if not the IOC itself. Yet the steeplechase of mounting Olympic hosting expenditure, increasingly scared cities and shifting sands between rival and newly emerging contemporary sports, had left Rogge prosaically heavy-footed.

The IOC was in urgent need of energy, ideas and constructive constitutional reform. Samaranch had partially revolutionised de Coubertin's ideological 19th-century Greek revival: among other innovations, women members, professionalism (in 1987), separation of Summer and Winter Games, some of this coalesced with Dick Pound, Montreal QC and Olympic swimmer who might have helped sustain Samaranch's advances but found himself inadvertently skewered in the presidential election of 2001 – by Samaranch.

For two decades, Pound had been Samaranch's dutiful aide, a legal mind behind strategic advance, but come the Salt Lake crisis, Samaranch appointed Pound as chair of an ad-hoc investigative commission. Pound's verdict included dismissal or embarrassed resignation of ten members. He reflected, 'To investigate conduct, I was scrutinising members who would be voting in the upcoming presidential election. In my view, it was more important to save the IOC than to curry favour with voters. I knew that a thorough investigation would compromise my prospect of becoming president.' To deepen Pound's disadvantage, the concurrent emergence of Kim Un-yong – masterful organiser of Seoul's memorable Games, by now promoted Executive Board (EB) vice-president and emergent presidential candidate – was signally one of those censured among Pound's official warnings, regarding employment of Kim's son by Salt Lake's organising committee. This steered Samaranch's subterfuge election campaigning away from Pound in favour of Rogge, ensuring the defeat of Kim, whose enthusiastic support still earned him second place behind Rogge in the voting second round, ahead of Pound – never mind Pound's deserved elevation in 1999 as inaugural chairman of the World Anti-Doping Agency (WADA).

By the time of the election in 2013 Pound's age – a member since 1978 – disqualified him as candidate, notwithstanding that he would have crucial responsibility, once again off the cuff, of internationally exposing details of Russia's endemic flagrant doping from 2011 to 2014. In one of history's perverse twists, the blocking of Pound's potential foresight as president in 2001 would leave open the door a decade later for Bach's long-conceived necessary modernisation: here were two amiably intellectually egocentric rival lawyers, one sensitively witty but his opportunity eroded, the other urbane yet adversarial Germanic reformer.

The preceding election for the summer host city of 2020 was a contest between three candidates all bearing major question marks: Istanbul wracked by Muslim insurgents backed by President Erdoğan and simultaneously on the verge of involvement with Syria's civil war; Madrid undermined by financial instability; and Tokyo riding the radiation risk from Fukushima's tsunami. It was going to be a least-risk vote. The anxieties for members were maybe less acute than for the decision of 1984, when there had been no candidate other than an independent organising committee unsupported by the city council of Los Angeles. By 2013, the enormity of a Games had become a project not for a city but a government. The IOC might now have a contingency fund to survive a cancellation, but it certainly did not need a liability from Japan, Turkey or Spain, not knowing the depth of the imponderables facing each candidate.

The obstacle for Tokyo rested on Premier Abe: could he deliver credible assurance that in seven years' time Tokyo, as opposed to Fukushima, scheduled to take a generation to recover, would be pollution-free? Tokyo had been perceived, pre-tsunami, as the safe bet. Asked what she thought of Turkey's Islamic-provoked civic riots, a young medal-winning prospect speaking for Istanbul innocently replied, 'All democracies have protests.' As sweetly naive as saying all countries experience instances of lung cancer. Ng Ser Miang, vice-president from Singapore, pondered, 'We are reduced to deciding between short-, medium- and long-term risks, and opting for what we consider the least.'

With Tokyo's trust restored, rivals were left whistling in the wind. Princess Takamodo, the first member of the

Japanese royal family to enter the debating arena, graciously upstaged Prince Felipe of Madrid with her fluency in French and English. Bid president Takeda reminded the world that Japan had never had a positive drug test, that alone worthy of the award. Francisco Elizalde of Philippines, a scrutiniser for many years and now honorary member without a vote, summed up his colleague's substantial margin, 'They wanted a city about which they could be sure, which outweighed the risks attached to the other two.'

Madrid's mayor Ana Botelo gave an irrelevant travelogue of the city's culture, state president Mariano Rajoy a political lecture, and not even Felipe could rouse the enthusiasm for Madrid. Fifty per cent unemployed among the under-25s was an economic risk too far for financial equilibrium. Turkey clearly had an exciting future, but not for this moment. Erdoğan and his bid committee had failed to confront domestic faults: when asked about 400 imprisoned dissenting journalists, there was no answer. The voting was straightforward: Tokyo 42 in the first round, Istanbul and Madrid tied on 26, Istanbul winning the play-off, but Madrid's eliminated votes failing to dent Tokyo's margin which rose to 60 against Istanbul's 36. Looking to repeat its memorable emergence in 1964 – post-atomic, morally re-invented, industrially avant-garde – Tokyo had winged it.

The IOC were happy they had cleared one hurdle and were expectant they were about to clear another with a new president. Yet subliminal questions were being asked about who really was running the IOC, global media relentlessly scrutinising the stage. The *International Herald Tribune* had just forecast, for instance, that by 2050 the combined population of Russia, Britain and France, three vote-holding members of the UN, would be exceeded by Indonesia, probably by Nigeria. While the IOC is not above but separate from politics, it would have to adjust to demographic change: Britain currently had four and Russia three voting IOC members, Indonesia none. Britain was winning the majority of its medals in expensive equipment sports: equestrian, sailing, rowing and cycling. By 2050, not many Indonesians or Brazilians, unable to afford even the bus fare to work, would be riding horses. The IOC was going to have to adjust.

Rogge's ambulatory reign had become fundamentally in need of adjustment, and now there were six candidates aligned for succession, alphabetically Thomas Bach (Germany); Sergey Bubka (Ukraine Olympic pole vault champion); Richard Carrion (Puerto Rican banker); Ng Ser Miang (Youth Games invigorator, Singapore); Denis Oswald (veteran Swiss oarsman); and Wu Ching-kuo (Taiwanese president of the International Boxing Association). In the minds of most, there was an expected outright result, as Dick Pound forecast, 'Thomas Bach, all but automatic, I would have been surprised at any other outcome.'

Respectful and gentlemanly democratic may have been this iconic self-elected club, yet those steering the wheels of fortune – Sheikh Ahmad among them – had little doubt on the betting odds: Bach possibly winning in the first round, Carrion a distant runner-up, admirable for fluent address from the podium without notes; Ng an Asian leader but subsumed beneath China's brooding power, with Oswald, Bubka and Wu elegant also-rans. This it proved to be. Bach, cosmetically astute, long ago first to announce his candidature, had relinquished his commercial liaison with the Middle East. Following comprehensive control of the German Olympic Sports Confederation over several years, he had effectively corralled his voters more by function than eloquence. I had a sense of his tactics when he invited me, as *Times* correspondent during London's Games of 2012, not for a drink but for breakfast among observant colleagues: a PR exercise. The tally in Buenos Aires in the second round was Bach 49, Carrion 29, Ng, Oswald, Bubka and Wu incidental. Bach would need to be bold, brave, even belligerent if he were to force the world's foremost cultural body to relinquish some inhibitions, conservative attitudes. Philosophies in international federations were outdated. In the glow of congratulations, Bach needed a cold shower of reality.

'Thomas was indisputably the best candidate,' recalled Carrard. 'He'd worked in depth to build his campaign, his background, Olympic title and legal experience, plus his involvement in IOC Commissions was exemplary. I witnessed this from close quarters. I liked Richard Carrion, his rival from Central America, but he was from a different world.' Dick Pound, Montreal lawyer and IOC vice-president who a decade earlier held ambition for the same transformative role as Bach now envisaged, but had been undermined by internal friction, echoed Carrard's view. 'Thomas's style was hyper-organised in his pre-planning, meticulous to a fault, carefully scripted, devoid of deviation, beyond debate by the EB. He held a deeper agenda than anyone.' Gerhard Heiberg, veteran Norwegian chief of Lillehammer 1994, was equally impressed, 'We observed Thomas's ambition, he worked so hard to make it clear, his lobbying was smart. Carrion was impressive but came from a minor background.' Craig Reedie, past chairman of the British Olympic Association and imminently new chairman of WADA, had watched Bach's cumulative authority, 'The Juridical Commission had become even more important, kept Thomas in focus, besides which he'd chaired the biggest social organisation in Germany, and crucially was multilingual.'

Equally relevant had been Bach's visible role as an ally of Rogge, who discreetly spoke in Bach's favour, never mind Ahmad's supportive flag-waving in the face of hostile German media negativity, which constantly confronted Bach's prospects, fulsomely denied. Bach's PR carried an unashamedly professional hue, 'Unity in Diversity', a central theme being protection of sport autonomy, simultaneously promoting the potential for new events. As a young fencer, he had learned the art of patience and timing. By 2010, so far had been Bach's feet already under the table that in an earlier third election for vice-president he had gained 80 out of 90 votes. In his first media foray, he emphasised his intention 'to change the host bidding procedure for future Olympics: make sustainable venue projects a priority, greater involvement of public support, not to demand extravagant city commitments', and cryptically observing that 'all bid books are written by the same people'.

Thus had ended the reign of Jacques Rogge, the second Belgian to hold the office – Compte Baillet-Latour the first when succeeding de Coubertin – Rogge having given the IOC security and dignity with a quiet face, a clarinet in comparison with Samaranch's pianoforte. Rogge had consolidated Samaranch's revolution of post-Salt Lake scandal transparency. Professor Arne Ljungqvist of Sweden, a key WADA figure, aptly observed, 'Jacques wasn't so much king as the man who held all the keys.' Iconic Olympian Sebastian Coe, mastermind of London 2012, considered Rogge's emphasis 'on athletes being the soul of the Games' and the first president to stay in the Olympic Village, his most significant message. Legendary French skier Jean-Claude Killy, co-ordination committee chairman for the upcoming Sochi 2014, defined Rogge in one word, 'integrity', adding, 'Everyone knew where they stood.' Heiberg echoed approval, 'I never heard Jacques being attacked by anybody, his door was always open.' Critics' counterpoint had been Rogge's reluctance to rethink issues already decided – furthermore to allow authority to shift towards unelected office staff in Lausanne. He had been a wise squirrel – building reserve IOC funds approaching $1bn.

LONDON 2012 MEDALS

United States of America 104 (46-29-29)
China 88 (38-27-23)
Great Britain 65 (29-17-19)
Russia 82 (24-26-32)
South Korea 28 (13-8-7)
Germany 44 (11-19-14)
France 34 (11-11-12)
Italy 28 (8-9-11)
Hungary 17 (8-4-5)

Australia 35 (7-16-12)
Japan 38 (7-14-17)
Kazakhstan 13 (7-1-5)
Netherlands 20 (6-6-8)
Ukraine 20 (6-5-9)
New Zealand 13 (6-2-5)
Cuba 14 (5-3-6)
Iran 12 (4-5-3)
Jamaica 12 (4-4-4)
Czech Republic 10 (4-3-3)
North Korea 6 (4-0-2)
Spain 17 (3-4-10)
Brazil 17 (3-5-9)
South Africa 6 (3-2-1)
Ethiopia 7 (3-1-3)
Croatia 6 (3-1-2)
Belarus 12 (2-5-5)
Romania 9 (2-5-2)
Kenya 11 (2-4-5)
Denmark 9 (2-4-3)
Azerbaijan 10 (2-2-6)
Poland 10 (2-2-6)
Turkey 5 (2-2-1)
Switzerland 4 (2-2-0)
Lithuania 5 (2-1-2)
Norway 4 (2-1-1)
Canada 18 (1-5-12)
Sweden 8 (1-4-3)
Colombia 8 (1-3-4)
Georgia 7 (1-3-3)
Mexico 7 (1-3-3)
Ireland 5 (1-1-3)
Argentina 4 (1-1-2)
Slovenia 4 (1-1-2)
Serbia 4 (1-1-2)
Tunisia 3 (1-1-1)
Dominican Republic 2 (1-1-0)
Trinidad and Tobago 4 (1-0-3)

Uzbekistan 4 (1-0-3)
Latvia 3 (1-1-1)
Algeria 1 (1-0-0)
The Bahamas 1 (1-0-0)
Grenada 1 (1-0-0)
Uganda 1 (1-0-0)
Venezuela 1 (1-0-0)
India 6 (0-2-4)
Mongolia 5 (0-2-3)
Thailand 3 (0-2-1)
Egypt 2 (0-2-0)
Slovakia 4 (0-1-3)
Armenia 3 (0-1-2)
Belgium 3 (0-1-2)
Finland 3 (0-1-2)
Bulgaria 2 (0-1-1)
Estonia 2 (0-1-1)
Indonesia 2 (0-1-1)
Malaysia 2 (0-1-1)
Puerto Rico 2 (0-1-1)
Chinese Taipei 2 (0-1-1)
Botswana 1 (0-1-0)
Cyprus (0-1-0)
Gabon (0-1-0)
Guatemala 1 (0-1-0)
Montenegro 1 (0-1-0)
Portugal 1 (0-1-0)
Greece 2 (0-0-2)
Moldova 2 (0-0-2)
Qatar 2 (0-0-2)
Singapore 2 (0-0-2)
Afghanistan 1 (0-0-1)
Bahrain 1 (0-0-1)
Hong Kong 1 (0-0-1)
Saudi Arabia 1 (0-0-1)
Kuwait 1 (0-0-1)
Morocco 1 (0-0-1)
Tajikistan 1 (0-0-1)

4

VOGT'S INAUGURAL LEAP

THE LEGACY for the new president of the IOC was a slumbering anachronistic private club needing to break free, to adapt to contemporary financial imperatives. Rogge's reign had witnessed six stable Games, though that of Athens 2004 commercially precipitous. Only a handful of 'clean' superstars such as Usain Bolt had shielded conventional Rogge from more casual criticism during the extended realm of rampant cheating which eluded WADA's as yet legal limitations.

For all the altruism – the Solidarity Fund's million-dollar scholarships being an elevating charity in over 150 countries – some International Federations remained adrift from contemporary essential adjustment; to respond to evolving events. Bach intended to do so. Directing a mammoth global organisation – a shoal of avaricious broadcasters, sponsors and athletes' agents, not to mention ten thousand competitors and a digital audience of billions – had become all but suffocating for a 'traditional' administration. Rogge had mooted a presidential shift: 'whether the Executive Board should consider my successor receiving a salary beyond regular expenses. I sense that a future President will necessarily move towards being Executive Chairman'. Aware of this possibility, the Ethics Commission had authorised the six presidential candidates to publicise their manifestos: Bach prominently the most radical. No surprise there. For some while, he had harboured the concept hinted at by Rogge, even before then by Samaranch; and earlier still. I recall an evening in the Seventies, President Killanin debating issues, as often pre-dinner at the Hotel Beau Rivage beside Lake Geneva, and musing that 'important committee decisions should always be by an uneven number – and three is probably too many!'

A missing link had been intercommunication between the three constituent bodies creating an Olympic Games, NOCs, IFs and IOC, for which Samaranch had studiously negotiated: with broadcasters, sponsors, WADA and, increasingly, governments with regard to security. Within weeks of taking office, Bach summoned a 'co-ordinating meeting' to establish a permanent dialogue among main stakeholders. Prime objectives were, first, the principle of autonomy, a prerequisite for global maintenance of sport's ethics and laws free from commercial manipulation; secondly, the sustainability of the Games through adjustment of both the host bidding procedure and the Olympic programme: Caroline Vogt of Germany the first female ski jumper accorded presence by Olympian men. Those departmental 'shakers' attending this formative gathering were Sheikh Ahmad (ANOC); Sepp Blatter (FIFA); Claudia Bokel (Athletes Commission); John Coates (IOC vice-president); Lamine Diack (IAAF); Nawal El Moutawakel (IOC vice-president); René Fasel (Association of International Winter Federations); Patrick Hickey (IOC Executive Board); Peng Liu (China NOC); Julio Maglione (FINA, swimming); Lawrence Probst (USOC); Craig Reedie (IOC vice-president); Francesco Ricci Bitti (ASOIF); Marius Vizer (SportAccord Convention); Wu Ching-kuo (IOC Executive Board); and Alex Zhukov (Russia NOC). A veritable mini-UN.

Fundamental to IOC stability has always been coherence among the international 'big guns': in de Coubertin's inauguration, France, Germany, Britain and Sweden, a century later USA, Russia and China. From the outset, Bach aimed to court the three most powerful NOCs, alongside the continuing interests of Europe, Africa, Asia and South

America. Significantly, a new revenue-sharing agreement between the IOC and the US Olympic Committee in May 2012 had been, as Rogge described, 'a crucial pillar in the Olympic Movement'. By this, USOC had retained current revenue received by its TV rights share, but this would be reduced to seven per cent in any increased broadcast deals, its sponsorship marketing share halved to ten per cent of the increased revenue. Meanwhile, China had been a recent host in 2008, and Russia was imminently inviting the world to Sochi's Winter Games of 2014: a massive virgin creation of a winter resort at the Black Sea 'secret' haven of Communist hoi polloi, for a reputed $50bn; calculated to magnify the might of both Russia's two-decade 'democracy' and its autocratic leader, Vladimir Putin. Bach well recognised where the IOC needed friends, but not soon enough a veiled evil.

An early foreign appointment for the new president – irony of ironies in the light of events – on 29 September was lighting of the Olympic Flame at Olympia prior to the usual passage, in this instance, to Sochi's Black Sea haven. In his address at Olympia's scene of ancient history, where lies de Coubertin's heart, Bach intoned, 'The Olympic flame reminds us to use the strength of our values and symbols for the positive development of global human society … our Russian partners and friends have a vital role to play in this responsibility. I am certain they will offer us and the world an excellent Games … the Torch Relay a messenger for Olympic values of excellence, friendship and respect without any form of discrimination … a reminder for all athletes and spectators of our values … a symbol of coexistence and mutual respect.' Never was a message of goodwill to be more stridently betrayed ten months later.

Worse still, in the IOC's innocent yet ineluctable descent towards humiliation, was Bach's pronouncement of judicial vigour at the Fourth World Conference on Doping in Sport at Johannesburg in November 2013. His words bristled with characteristic conviction:

- 'Sport is about athletes, more precisely about clean athletes, which is why we're here today with one goal: to produce a majority who compete in the spirit of fair play. Protecting clean athletes must be our ultimate goal, priority in all our decisions. We have to change our mentality: not extrapolate the cost of one positive test from the cost of all tests performed, not to argue that one positive test costs several hundred thousand dollars. The fight against doping is security, deterrence and prevention, to be improved still more.'

- 'Tests are indispensable in protecting clean athletes but not an end in itself. Gathered here in Johannesburg we are united in zero tolerance. The IOC will pursue this fight with determination, soon we will know the name of the new WADA president, and we look forward to strengthening co-operation, indeed with all stakeholders including governments, national, regional and international.'

- 'WADA especially should increase co-operation with governments and we need better exchange of information between state authorities with sports governing bodies and national anti-doping organisations, which means state authorities must do more to punish in doping cases: the dealers, agents, coaches, doctors and scientists.'

- 'As an athlete I argued for a lifetime ban for a first doping offence, but legal colleagues have said this is not possible. Regular sanctions from two to four years for serious violations, for which the IOC is calling, will I hope be accepted, but even this code is not enough. We need more sophisticated targeted tests, individual profiling and scientific research: whether blood and urine tests are really the most effective.'

- 'Preventive measures must be applied as early as possible in an athlete's career: not just for them, but their entourage. WADA should work more closely with NOCs and IFs.

The IOC's determination is clear from our drastically enhanced anti-doping programme for the forthcoming Games in Sochi.'

- 'When the Olympic Villages open, testing will cover the full in-competition menu of prohibited substances ... we shall be tougher than at any previous Winter Games, performing tests anywhere in the world, more flexible, more effective, the number of pre-competition tests increased from 804 at Vancouver in 2010 to 1,270 for Sochi. In all, we will perform nearly 2,500 tests compared with 2,150 in Vancouver, and will keep the samples for at least eight years, for re-analysis if new methods of identification are developed.'

- 'More than $1m will be spent on pre-competition testing outside Sochi: this expenditure is not a ploy but an investment in the future of our sport. We want to ensure fair competition and clean athletes, who deserve our commitment.'

Fate might be assigning Bach's mission to the desert, but his energy was on full drive. Now in the saddle, he was not going to dismount: an inaugural development would be a series of teleconference engagements with international media: one of the first a debate on the uncertain progress of preparations of both Rio's Summer Games of 2016 and more imminent the Sochi Winter Games, these some of the questions:

- *How advanced are safety arrangements and construction for Rio 2016?*

'Experts were there last week, progress is advanced, but on the other hand, there is no time to lose, and clearly additional government support is needed. I will be there in the next couple of months to co-ordinate operations with all stakeholders.'

- *Is the validity of Moscow's doping laboratory for Sochi established?*

'WADA's decision is that the laboratory is ready, pending certain conditions that external experts are part of the team.'

- *What are the new president's priorities for generating Olympic interest among new fans?*

'The IOC's goal is not just to generate interest, but to persuade youngsters to engage in sport. The Youth Games, the second summer event scheduled for Nanjing this year can be expanded to include more modern sports. The access of media needs to be extended.'

- *What is the function of the newly created IOC Co-ordination Commissions?*

'For the IOC, NOCs and IFs, it is necessary to protect the uniqueness of the Games as distinct from other sport, to be the guardians of this ethic; and with this ethic in mind, to formalise the calendar of all multi-sports events.'

- *What is the intention for revised bidding procedure of host cities, including members' visits?*

'There will be adjustments, as described in the election manifesto, there being insufficient scope for would-be hosts to be creative, fashioning a bid to suit their own city, country and social cultures. They should be asked how they would integrate a Games into their local environment, and the IOC's stipulated technical agenda for host application should be in place by the end of 2014, in time for prospective candidates for the Winter Games of 2022.'

- *What is the response to Russia's anti-Gay promotion law during Sochi 2014?*

'The IOC will remain intent on upholding free reporting according to fundamentals of their Charter.'

- *Is there to be creation of an in-house Olympic television network?*

'So far this is a matter of debate, recognising that between each Games there is insufficient coverage of Olympic sports, some needing more promotion to address the world's youth population. Such a network could achieve this.'

- *Is Africa ready to host a Games?*

'Any bid would find a sympathetic response, because this is a universal movement, not just for athletes but for all continents, though that does not mean a candidate would win, bidding remaining a competition.'

- *What are the benefits of the president's recent tour meeting heads of state?*

'With all of them was evident the importance of sport within modern society, within education, integration and social values, confirming that the Olympic Games are a catalyst to convey social messages, that athletes are thereby valuable role models.'

In pursuit of his multiple objectives, Bach was intent on constant communication and development of his plans with the Executive Board, and early on there had been a four-day brainstorming seminar in Montreux; centring on the key issues within his purported 'Olympic Agenda 2020'. The roadmap for the Olympic Movement, which he intended to follow, would firstly be debated within the IOC Session in Sochi: those proposals selected then forwarded to subsequent working groups, and formally presented in an Extraordinary Session in December 2014.

Discussions at the 'brainstorm' centred on five themes: the uniqueness of the Games; the central function of athletes; identification of the ethic of Olympism; the function of the IOC; and the constitution of the IOC. The prime objectives were funding of new research into anti-doping with an initial budget of $10m; the realignment of financial regulations to enhance sustainability of the Games within bidding procedure; reassessment of the Olympic programme; and protecting the legacy of any Games within each city, partially by adopting the broadest possible use of temporary and/or dismountable venues. Worldwide media was erupting over many months with vindictive criticism of Russia's alleged over-investment in construction of facilities at Sochi. Omitting intended secretive doping manipulation, what Russia had calculated to create, when schmoozing the voters at Guatemala's Session in 2007, was a modern, civic complex way beyond simply a sports hub: simultaneously establishing the permanent winter training facilities which had been lost in Armenia, Azerbaijan and Georgia with the disintegration of the Soviet Union. Amid the raucous media condemnation, and with my official IOC history of the Games contracted for a Russian translation, I took a preliminary trip to the Black Sea resort: this is what I reported for the international Sport Intern website:

'Is the world a better place on account of de Coubertin's reinvention? Is the controversy surrounding Russia's mega project culturally and practically justified? For all the extravagant criticism heaped upon the IOC by critics, the global population is marginally better off for the re-establishment of an ancient Greek tradition: as Randy Harvey, commentator of *Los Angeles Times*, had remarked during Salt Lake City's Games of 2002, "We haven't advanced that far through the Olympics in pursuit of a more perfect civilisation, but the important thing is we have the vehicle that enables us to keep trying." Interminable reference to Sochi's expenditure in excess of $50bn is predominantly fed by media ignorance, every Games having *two* parallel budgets: building facilities for 17 days of sport, the other meeting the overload of government exploitation of momentum to achieve, in seven years, civic expansion of local facilities which might otherwise take 20. Expenditure for Beijing 2008 or Moscow 1980 was immeasurable, using minimum-wage labour, possibly the same for Seoul in 1988 and now Rio for 2016; yet it can be claimed that Olympic cities are often structurally advanced by hosting, alongside the cultural and emotional welfare of the residents. Putin's mega project, creating what might be termed a Las Vegas of the Black Sea, is designed to enhance not merely his own prestige, but the domestic expansion of an almost reclusive region.

'What the Caucasus region of south-east Russia is receiving is manifold: two thermo-electric power stations, three new water purification plants, 300km of new roads, 20 tunnels and multiple bridges, an array of new schools and medical centres, 50 new hotels – all that plus the most compact state-of-the-art winter sports complex in the world. If Putin's Napoleonic ambition looks excessive, consider the past. The most glorious phase of the British Empire, the Edwardian era at the turn of the 19th century, witnessed the summit of aristocratic luxury in the wake of Queen Victoria's reign. The Albert Memorial in memory of her consort, the cost of which could have built 125,000 houses in the East End slums, was unquestioned, nor the 1908 [Franco-British] Exhibition's building of the White City Stadium for the Olympic Games. Lake Placid, the venue for the 1932 Winter Olympics at the height of the depression had been farming land initiated by abolitionists for freed slaves: the little village required massive government funding as Olympic host, and constitutional amendment for the felling of trees to conduct venue sites.

'Putin's gamble – the new rail link to Krasnaya Polyana's virgin mountain cluster costing more than Vancouver's entire investment for the Games of 2010 – can only be measured over following decades. Likewise Tokyo 1964 had been a platform for Japan's post-war electronic industry development; Munich 1972 an extravaganza of futuristic architecture and engineering to display German post-war expansion; Montreal 1976 having an operational Games profit ruined only by the mayor's grandiose stadium expenditure; Seoul 1988 transforming the political face of South Korea's military regime; Barcelona 1992 prematurely lifting Catalonia into the 21st century, redesigning and expanding the city – of their $6.7bn investment, only a third devoted to sport. The sophisticated sports venues of the Alps were developed over six decades; Sochi's in seven years.

'The Sochi security provision is as suffocating as Seoul's in 1988: Sochi's 40,000 soldiers on 24-hour alert, yet Seoul's marathon course had a soldier every three metres. Security is the burden the IOC has carried since the Israeli massacre of 1972. Thomas Bach is attempting to rationalise the IOC's multiple functions, an immense objective being to limit megalomania on three fronts: manipulative bid cities, self-important IFs, overtly demanding sponsors, alongside which must be restrained the IOC's own sometimes insular conceit. The Olympics have walked a tightrope ever since 1896 in Athens and the task of Bach was now to attempt to rationalise henceforth the entire façade.'

It could be said that Russia had achieved an ideal dual concept: a uniquely compact city cluster of specialised yet multi-purpose stadia, grouped within competitors' ten-minute walking distance to venues on the shore of the Adler suburb of Sochi, where a new international airport was now open. Simultaneously the Krasnaya Polyana mountain cluster was a minor miracle of engineering in the 45km distant mountain range. Yet it was apparent that the massive Putin-backed project could become a regional legacy of exceptional merit. The mountain range might not yet be Klosters or Whistler, but Sochi, a hideaway for Moscow's elite throughout the 20th century, could perhaps soon rival Europe's traditional destinations for cultural events and international sport.

Promised, environmentally, was the greenest Games yet: a major development in sewage treatment, ten trees planted for every tree uprooted in road-rail construction, electricity-saving technology. Coincidentally, I flew from Moscow sitting next to the director of the Voeikov geophysical observatory, a meteorologist calculating Sochi's air purity. The alpine ski centre was special: competitors would be able to view from the top the entire downhill challenge to the finishing pan, possible at no other renowned venue. The men's course was said to be ideal for television. With a spectacular altitude village for snow sports, at the residence by the sea for skating, the IOC's minimum 12 square metres living area per two athletes was trebled to 40 square metres. The Adler cluster of five stadia offered an array of functionalism, with the main stadium football-orientated for the 2018 World Cup.

As a commentator having favoured Salzburg's bid in 2007, I felt honour-bound to acknowledge the breadth of Sochi's achievement. A saunter along the harbour front, where motor yachts of minor oligarchs liltingly reflected Russia's conspicuous prosperity, all seemingly beyond protest, offered much for Bach to welcome. Speaking prior to the IOC Session, Bach fired enough arrows to convince the disillusioned of the extent of his determination on modernisation, stressing that members had to approve 'a change of attitude' regarding sustainability, credibility and the accent on youth. Following his election, he had invited rivals to discuss these views, which would be put to the test at an Extraordinary Session at Monte Carlo in December: implementation of Bach's projected Agenda 2020 crucially assessed and, optimistically, approved.

So intent was the new president on rapid advance, there were occasions when his speech-writers might have gained more impact through brevity than prolix essays – witness his address at the Opening Ceremony of the 126th IOC Session prior to Sochi's Games, a veritable 3,000-word soporific *langlauf.* The following is an edited draft of Bach's effective public expression of a private vote of thanks to Putin:

'This is a night of anticipation and dreams, athletes gathering, longing for competition, to show the world the standards they have achieved, craving for the Olympic Flame shining above the stadium. Tonight we can tell the athletes, "Your stage is ready." Remembering how things were seven years ago, after the dissolution of the USSR, Russia no longer had a winter sports centre, national championships had to be held abroad. Russia decided to resolve this using 2014 as a catalyst, with much scepticism concerning this visionary project to modernise a regional summer resort. We can see that Russia has delivered and I would like to thank President Putin for the commitment, together with the people of Sochi and the Krasnodar region for their patience, the thousands of volunteers who have welcomed us so warmly. This has demonstrated how much the Olympic Games draws the world's attention to a host city. The IOC's mission is to place sport at the service of harmonious humanity, an Olympic Games showing that competition can embrace harmony, dignity, ethics, fair play and friendship.

'These values come to life through competition and living together in an Olympic Village among athletes wanting to win but respecting each other. This can only be if we are politically neutral without being apolitical. This we can only achieve if we protect the athletes against discrimination on the grounds of race, religion, politics, gender and sexual orientation. We have been satisfied by assurance from the president and government that the Olympic Charter will be respected. The IOC is not a supra-national government, we do not have a mandate to impose measures on a sovereign state, but hope we have a positive influence on society's development through sport, remembering Nelson Mandela who so simply said, "Sport can change the world."

'The Olympic Movement stands for building bridges, not erecting walls. From 2013 to 2016 we will support athletes by providing five billion dollars directly to international federations, national Olympic committees and Olympic Games organisers to manage resources; the Olympic Movement representing the right to play sport in global solidarity; for equal rights for all athletes; for sustainable sporting development and enhancing peace through sport. This ambitious endeavour can only succeed in co-operation with political leaders: respecting the law of sport, the athletes, Olympic values and political neutrality. [Governments] must address disagreements in direct political dialogue and not on the backs of athletes ... the pinnacle of this co-operation is our relationship with the United Nations, where we enjoy the status of permanent observer, and it is my honour to welcome the secretary general to his first ever appearance at a Session, which will offer us the opportunity to study the future as we prepare our strategic roadmap, Agenda 2020.

'I began that dialogue immediately because I had promised it upon election, and it is better to make changes when an organisation is successful rather than when in crisis. We will take decisions at the Session in December, where I expect the debate to evolve around sustainability, restructuring the bidding procedure with creativity and diversity, and debating composition of the Olympic Programme. Our ultimate goal is for clean athletes, this must be our motto: therefore the IOC has already increased the number of pre-competition tests by 57 per cent compared to Vancouver 2010, also creating two funds of $10m each to advance doping research. We invite governments of the world to match this additional contribution by the IOC, which will involve about 300,000 anti-doping tests per year.

'There will be no Olympic future without youth, whom we have to convince not only to watch but to play sport, to get couch potatoes off the couch. Let us address all these topics with an open mind, let us create "University in Diversity".'

The intensity of Bach's energy could indeed be daunting. In a separate interview at the time of the Session with Sport Intern, the president confronted a stream of questions. *Would the Charter be upheld in compliance against any sexual discrimination?* 'I am confident this will be so.' *There are political gay rights protest absentees from Sochi, will this not undermine participation?* 'To political leaders we say, understand what our responsibilities are and what are yours, address your disagreements peacefully, and not on the backs of athletes. It is my conviction that this can be in the long-term political interest because people understand what it means to make ostentatious gestures that cost nothing but produce international headlines. The Olympic Games have the power to inspire and unite.' *Why did the IOC prefer Sochi to the superior bid from Salzburg recommended by the Evaluation Commission?* 'Salzburg had an excellent bid, but so did Sochi, which proposed a visionary project. We can see now that Russia has delivered on its promises. Regarding the Evaluation Commission, its report is valued, but it is not a means to an end. If it was, we wouldn't need to vote.' *Following 'expansion' Winter Games in Sochi and Pyeongchang, will a European venue with historic facilities hold advantage in 2015 bidding for 2022?* 'We have five applicant cities for 2022. To say anyone has an advantage due to location would be false, they all have an equal chance. I have encouraged them to be confident enough in their projects, not to restrict themselves solely to the blueprints of the past, but taking initiative on how they see the Olympic Games benefiting their local population.' *Snow and ice events are the definition for a century of Winter Games – with a need to introduce modern events for contemporary youth, and expand spectator interest, why not shift some summer sports, say weightlifting, to the Winter Games?* 'We have been flexible with the programme in recent years, 12 new events are added here in Sochi, most of which did not even exist 20 years ago. We aim to strike a balance between tradition and modernity.'

Wilful positivity by Bach was drawing enthusiasm way beyond Sochi, notably compliments from the *New York Times,* on his speech at the Games's Opening Ceremony. Juliet Macur declared, 'At his first Olympics as president, Bach made points that sounded like a sharp riposte at Putin and the law he signed that banned the distribution of gay propaganda to children in Russia. In the most refreshing speech by an IOC president in decades, Bach did not kowtow to the host country. He said the Olympics should set an example for "human diversity and great unity". To the athletes, he said you have come with your Olympic dream, you're welcome, no matter where you come from, or your background, it's possible as competitors to live together in harmony and tolerance and without any formal discrimination for whatever reason.'

Indeed, the plea from this past Olympic fencing champion to governments of the world, more specifically to the Kremlin, was unrelenting as his Opening Ceremony address proclaimed:

'I say to political leaders, thank you for supporting your athletes, they are the best ambassadors of your country. Please respect their message of goodwill, tolerance, excellence and peace. Have the courage to address any of your disagreements in direct political dialogue and not on the backs of these athletes. To all officials and sports fans, I say, join and support our fight for fair play, the athletes deserve it. And to you, my fellow athletes, I say respect the rules, play fair, be clean, respect your rivals in and out of competition ... Russia has set the stage for the best winter athletes on our planet, the IOC wants your dream to come true, and this is why we are investing almost all of our revenues in the worldwide development of sports. We wish you joy in your effort and a wonderful Olympic experience, and I now have the honour of inviting President Putin to declare open the 22nd Olympic Winter Games in Sochi, Russia.'

How bizarre, how criminal, that such a sumptuous welcome staged by Russia could be camouflage for the calculated corruption that was about to engulf events of the next two weeks, and remain undetected for almost two years. From a nation ever ready to be contentious, US media overflowed with unrestrained praise of Sochi's Opening Ceremony: as from Alan Abrahamson of nbcolympics.com, 'It could not have been more stunning. The crowd gasped with delight at Vladimir Putin's Olympic launch in just the perfect picture-postcard manner he doubtless always envisaged ... No wonder the organisers wanted the Games to begin before the flame was even lit on Friday night. Sport can be a wonderful distraction from regular life ... It was easy to sense that the Sochi Games may conclude looking finer and more spectacular than any of their predecessors.' In the *New York Times* David Herszenhorn declared, 'With an extravaganza that reached deep into the repertory of classical music and ballet, traversed to the sights and sounds of the world's largest geopolitical expanse, swept across millennia of history in a celebration of everything from tsarist military might to Soviet monumentalism, a swaggering, resurgent Russia turned its Winter Olympic aspirations into reality. In a big way, Russia is back – amid an economic slowdown, continuing rights abuses and suppression of political dissent that have drawn sharp criticism was a matter for another day – here was a majestic spectacle that included a glowing *troika* of horses made of

70

light streaking through a snowbound sky, the multicolour union domes of St Basil's Cathedral bobbing in the air, literary references to Gogol, Tolstoy and Nabokov, images of Stalinist skyscrapers, performances by Russia's acclaimed ballerinas, musicians and singers.' Impressed we all were.

Duly elated, the next day I made the scenic journey to the mountain cluster. The Germans know a thing or two about Winter Olympics: at their mountain HQ, their team was wide-eyed in admiration for what Russia had created on this glorious range of soaring peaks. Walter Troeger, mastermind behind Munich 1972, was euphoric, 'Our team say that this is the best they have ever seen, what Russia has done is beyond praise.' Such a view was uniform. 'Outstanding,' according to Spyros Capralos, chairman of Athens 2004. 'A legacy for decades to come,' reflected Anita DeFrantz, bronze US oarswoman from Montreal 1976 and current Executive Board member.

Every day I travelled the 16km each way on the new electric railway between central Sochi and the Adler suburb, crowded with expectant fans, my youngest fellow traveller a nine-year-old dreaming of a Russian ice hockey gold medal. Not to be. The pervasive security searches, at the rail station, media centre, every event, were unfailingly courteous, more so than at Montreal or Salt Lake. Vigilant police were infinitely polite, helping to carry one's bag. Being of an age beyond masculine eligibility, hardly a double for George Clooney, I found that to catch the eye of any Russian woman involved in this festival was to draw a smile. I say this as neither flattery nor affectation. It was to the credit of Bach that in the most exposed speech any individual has to deliver, he had been forthright in expressing indifference to absent heads of state, suggesting it was their loss. Generosity was pervasive. Dining at a hotel I was short of change for a taxi. The reception desk gave me 200 roubles ($6) saying, 'Pay us when you come back tomorrow.'

In recollection of a Games simultaneously historic for its lavish preparation and malevolence of its surreptitious, corrupted drug testing for grotesque nationalistic prestige, I have no intention to labour readers with a litany of Russian cheats, whether or not they were complicit in fraudulently concealed positive tests. There were, of course, thousands of honourable competitors, a relative handful defrauded of a legitimate medal: the rest intent on the honour of having been a competitor at such a memorably spectacular festival, however compromised it was subsequently to be revealed. There were genuine notable champions. The Ruski Gorki jumping centre, costing over $200m, was symbolic of Russia's gargantuan preparation. Carina Vogt's inaugural women's Olympic ski jump triumph for Germany was a landmark. Expectation lay between diminutive 17-year-old Sara Takanashi of Japan, dominant over the past two seasons, Austrian veteran Daniela Iraschko-Stolz, 13 years her senior, and current world champion Sarah Hendrickson, recovering from an autumn injury. Unassuming Vogt had never won a world cup event, yet here she was in the lead after her first-round jump with 103m, Takanashi lying third and meaning she would jump third to last in the final round. Iraschko-Stolz took the lead in the second round, leaving Vogt needing no more than a reliable jump to overtake her, doing so with 97.5m, which pushed Takanashi into fourth place behind Coline Mattel of France with bronze. Ingrid Vestby of Norway is thought to have been the first recorded women's ski jumper in 1862, and though men were jumping from the first Games of 1924, women had fought long to make their Olympic appearance 152 years later at Salt Lake in 2002.

The arrival of slopestyle and of ski half-pipe multiplied entertainment for packed crowds, almost as ecstatic as successful competitors. The most celebrated of all freestyle exponents, millionaire American snowboarder Shaun White, described the slopestyle course as intimidating, and withdrew to avoid injury risk that might have threatened a third half-pipe gold medal. Spared the uncertainty of slopestyle, White was ready for his triple crown. It was not to be. At 27 he was no longer young for this discipline: Iouri Podladtchikov, a Russian immigrant from Switzerland, who had crashed on his first qualifying run, now responded with a perfect execution of his trademark 'Yolo' – you only live once – a flip which White had added to his repertoire, conscious of Podladtchikov's rising threat. Now White failed even to gain bronze.

Californian Jamie Anderson had no inhibition about acknowledgement, following victory in the women's slopestyle, of her hippy lifestyle: engrossed in yoga and burning sage in her Olympic Village room, self-aware with layers of beads and necklaces around her neck upon victory. Meditation had marked the path of the 22-year-old from South Lake Tahoe, who now became queen with a style that could not be challenged.

Whoever the winner, the downhill has a particular gravitas that separates it from the newly elevated freestyle disciplines: a simplicity allied to extreme speed in which the fastest is uncomplicatedly the winner. No judges. Matthias Mayer of Austria emerged from relative obscurity on a demanding course. Aged 23, he had never won a World Cup race, fifth his highest place. Now he was six hundredths of a second quicker than Christof Innerhofer of Italy, with Kjetil Jansrud of Norway a further tenth away. Mayer entered that celebrated band of Austrian champions, Toni Sailer, Egon Zimmerman, Franz Klammer and Fritz Strobl, a relief for a fanatical alpine nation which had won no medal in the men's alpine events in Vancouver. A tie in winter sport is uncommon; rare indeed in downhill. Now it happened in the women's event: for more than half an hour Dominique Gisin of Switzerland, first down the slope, stood at the foot of the course waiting to see if anyone could surpass her time of 1:41.57. Tina Maze of Slovenia precisely equalled that, the first ever shared gold in Winter Games alpine.

There was, the knowledgeable said, something different about Ted Ligety, who became the first American to win the giant slalom. In Turin 2006, aged 21, he had been the unexpected winner of the combined: eight years later, he was now regarded as supreme at giant slalom, three times a defending world champion, regarded as unbeatable. On newly regulated skis in 2012, Ligety had fashioned a turning technique, begun early and evading deliberate impact on his legs at every gate, then immediately launching into the next turn without loss of pace. Greater pressure from the skis on less tight turns increased his speed. His winning margin was now a huge half a second.

Figure skating judges might be said to own a collective gold medal for opaque decisions, sometimes their declaration containing more drama than the preceding performances. Women's figures in Sochi were a case in point. Defending Korean champion Yuna Kim truly dazzled only to be upstaged, in the judges' opinion, by 17-year-old Moscow starlet Adelina Sotnikova. With porcelain-like elegance, Kim had led on the short programme. To the common eye, she appeared to have skated without flaw in her free programme, a picture of fluid perfection. Up stepped Sotnikova, who had finished a mere ninth in the previous World Championships, to win approval from judges – her electric technique decreed to be superior and gaining Russia's first ever title in this event. She had made seven triple jumps compared to Kim's six; fluent Caroline Kostner of Italy, with bronze, world champion in 2012, might also feel aggrieved with her seven triples. Inevitably there were protests, rising to 1.7 million electronic signatures in Korea, fuelled by comments such as that by Katarina Witt, champion of 1984 and 1988, 'I am stunned by this result.' Ottavio Cinquanta, IF chief, defended the outcome.

In speed skating, the Netherlands metaphorically left the rest of the world for dead. Their previous best medal haul had been 11 at Nagano 1998: of their 39 athletes in Sochi, 27 were speed skaters. Now the total was 23 medals out of a possible 32, surpassing the unofficial record by one country in one discipline set by Austria in alpine in 2006. Only six of the Dutch team failed to claim at least one medal: four achieved two or more, led by Ireen Wust, with 3,000m gold and silver over three other distances. The answer, to a degree, lay in one word: cycling. Endurance development of speed skaters' basic engine, thigh-power, is fashioned more comfortably on a bicycle than on ice, the Dutch being much at home on bicycles, therein their secret.

As the champagne corks continued to pop in south-east Caucasus, inspired by Sotnikova, the experience of Sochi had no previous equal: an untroubled multi-billion-dollar celebration of the ideologies and opportunities of sport, against a background of one of the world's largest, most powerful nations, busy wrestling with modernisation and searching – allegedly – for the broad democratic, egalitarian society which is the elusive desire of all countries, not least in Putin's Russia.

Sochi's Games had been brilliant beyond expectation, but the acid test was what would the Black Sea resort feel like in a decade's time. Would the magical village in the sky, Krasnoya Polyana, still throb with intent athletes and leisure-seeking holidaymakers? The future of Putin's investment would hinge on the international response to a lavish winter/summer playground which was off the hub of international air traffic. Sochi would need selling, though estate agent brochures, widely available, were offering tantalising opportunities for investment. Acknowledgement of Sochi's success was universal, Gian Franco Kasper, Swiss president of the International Ski Federation, reflecting, 'Outstanding, excellent organisation, the most modern venues, good experience with our new events, great success in the first ladies ski-jumping, what more can one ask?'

Much of the drama and global perception of any Games is conveyed by television. Israeli IOC member Alex Gilady, a television specialist, observed, 'What looked crazy seven years ago, still rocky a month ago, is maybe the best ever, close to perfection. The broadcasting has been beautiful, a perfect image of athleticism. The Russians have produced in seven years what took Europe and the Alps 150 years. The world has a great new sports destination.' In the ultimate, unintended false acclaim, IOC vice-president and head of WADA Craig Reedie reflected, 'The Games have defied almost all criticism, facilities exceptional, security efficient and unobtrusive.'

What had been the social backcloth left behind the following week? Much of Russia's overbearing domestic legislation would remain fractious: the Games had not constituted one-hundredth of the daily life of this vast nation that stretched to the Sea of Japan. Departing euphoric medal winners would be unaware that an ecologist, working on preservation of the natural wonders where new electricity pylons now stood, had just been imprisoned for three years for painting graffiti on a fence. A military general had just committed suicide, unable to collect the necessary protocol documents so as to be given morphine during terminal cancer. A foreign acquaintance of mine, resident in Russia for many years, Russian-speaking and working in public relations, observed, 'Millions have no access to proper medical care, violation of rights continues. The Games have given ordinary Russians the opportunity to feel proud, to present something worthy to the world, to show that "We are capable", but many workers are left feeling unrewarded.' Kevan Gosper of Australia, many years prominent on the Executive Board, observed, 'Sochi has raised the bar of delivery and expectation for future Winter Games to new heights.'

The Games would close with a generous, open-minded 'goodbye' from a president optimistic and as yet unaware of horrific revelations of a dishonoured Charter still two years distant, as he made his closing speech with retrospectively ironic, sincere commendation:

'Mr President of the Russian Federation, Olympic athletes, friends and fans around the world, good evening! Thank you, you have inspired us for the last magnificent 17 days, celebrated victory with dignity and accepted defeat with grace … We have enjoyed exceptional conditions, tonight we can say Russia delivered what it promised … To this success, the international federations, NOCs, sponsors and broadcasters have greatly contributed. With your warm smile, volunteers have made the sun shine for us every day, through you everybody could see the face of a new Russia, friendly, patriotic and open to the world. There is no higher compliment than to say on behalf of all participants, these were the athletes' Games. We leave as friends of the Russian people. I now declare the 22nd Olympic Winter Games closed, and in accordance with tradition, I call upon the youths of the world to assemble four years from now in Pyeongchang to celebrate with us the 23rd Olympic Winter Games.'

One further, unwittingly macabre comment hovered over the closure. Unseen alongside the spectacular sports venues was the anti-doping laboratory described by Craig Reedie, new chairman of WADA, as being 'as good as you could want'. Allegedly, the equipment was the envy of all other laboratory directors who had seen it: much of the equipment was to be transferred to Moscow, to manipulative evil beyond imagination. It was to take a while for us to learn the truth. In the broadest sense, the state-controlled propaganda – regimenting daily life existence – in sport was horrendously worse.

SOCHI 2014 MEDALS

Russia 30 (11-10-9)
Norway 26 (11-5-10)
Canada 25 (10-10-5)
United States 28 (9-9-10)
Netherlands 24 (8-7-9)
Germany 19 (8-6-5)
Switzerland 11 (7-2-2)
Belarus 6 (5-0-1)
Austria 17 (4-8-5)
France 15 (4-4-7)
Poland 6 (4-1-1)
China 9 (3-4-2)
South Korea 8 (3-3-2)
Sweden 15 (2-7-6)
Czech Republic 8 (2-4-2)
Slovenia 8 (2-2-4)
Japan 8 (1-4-3)
Finland 5 (1-3-1)
Great Britain 5 (1-1-3)
Latvia 5 (1-1-3)
Ukraine 2 (1-0-1)
Slovakia 1 (0-0-1)
Italy 8 (0-2-6)
Australia 3 (0-2-1)
Croatia 1 (0-1-0)
Kazakhstan 1 (0-0-1)

5

EVOLVING TARGETS

BARELY 12 months into office, a succession of hurdles confronted Thomas Bach in 2014. If Sochi's Winter Games had been accomplished – with a nightmare revelation to become retrospectively embarrassing – there swiftly arrived a controversial rift with Norway: an ideal but self-indulgent, politically fractious host among five candidates for 2022. Over-ambitious Summer Youth Games in Nanjing preceded an Extraordinary Session in December to analyse, and prospectively approve, the president's transformative Agenda 2020: a harvest of 40,000 proposals, such is the internet reach of the Olympic audience. If anyone doubted the validity of market research, which rated recognition of the Olympic Rings on a par with Mercedes automobiles, this proved the case. An inconspicuous French aristocrat's 19th-century educational ideology by now encircled the globe.

The new president was correct in his intuition: following 12 years of Olympic Programme stalemate, there was no time to be lost in adjusting the IOC's future course if its qualities were to be protected. It was no exaggerated fear that, amid accelerating commercialism, misjudgement by the IOC could lead to rival, athlete-enticing alternatives: the equivalent of professional boxing's multi-ring circus of rival heavyweight world titles; the abortive attempt of a handful of major European clubs in 2021 to hijack the Champions League; or the ever-expanding calendar of professional golf and tennis. Some ideas were fanciful: an annual Olympic Games. Yet the wisdom of the working groups responsible for sifting suggestions before Executive Board perusal, thence referred to the Session in December, could provoke the most productive Olympic gathering since the founding congress at the Sorbonne in 1894.

Bach's reformative luggage in 2014 would seldom leave airline conveyor belts: his most acclaimed arrival parcel was a spectacularly extended television contract with NBCUniversal in May, securing the major broadcaster's allegiance until 2032, an astonishing coup upstaging other profound constitutional changes Bach was seeking. The value of the contract approached $8bn, by which NBCU secured US broadcasting right to the Olympic Games up to the summer of 2032 – a contract of three Winter Games and three Summer Games, signed in Lausanne by Bach: a remarkable financial facelift. He reflected:

'This agreement is excellent for the entire Olympic Movement, ensuring its long-term financial security, in particular for future host cities, for the world's athletes from 204 NOCs and the international federations. The IOC has closely linked with NBC for many decades, and we are thrilled to continue with them through to 2032. NBC's expertise and commitment to Olympic values means we shall benefit from first-class coverage of the Games to the widest possible audience for many years to come.'

NBCU had acquired broadcast rights across all platforms, including free-to-air, subscription, internet and mobile. The agreement included an additional $100m signing bonus to embrace promotion of Olympism and its values between 2015 and 2020. Brian Roberts, chairman and CEO of parent company Comcast Corporation, echoed Bach's enthusiasm, 'The Olympics are the world's greatest cultural and athletic event, and presenting them to the American audience is an honour. Our long-term commitment and investment in the Olympic Movement reflects our belief in broadcasting's future as well as our confidence that our IOC partners will continue to deliver great Games. Comcast are proud to be entrusted for nine more Olympics and we look forward to using our resources to maintain our tradition of ground-breaking Olympic coverage.' NBCU CEO Steve Burke added, 'One of the most important days in our history. The Olympics are part of our company's fabric, we couldn't be more excited that today's announcement guarantees that our massively popular and profitable programming will continue to air, every two years on the broadcast, cable, digital and mobile platforms for the next two decades. No event brings families together like the Olympics, no media is better equipped to tell the athletes' stories. I thank the IOC for their faith in us.'

The funding relevance was paramount to IOC/Olympic existence. The fee for cancellation insurance of Tokyo 2020 was just over $17m, an increase of 18 per cent for similar protection of Rio '16. This was a much smaller jump for insuring the Winter Games: that for Sochi '14 was $7.6m, the rate leaping by 69 per cent to $12.8m for Pyeongchang '18.

In 2011, NBCU had acquired the rights until 2020, including Rio 2014, Pyeongchang 2018 and Tokyo 2020, and would now broadcast every Games for 18 years, with six cities yet to be elected. In addition, rights were acquired for every edition of the Youth Olympic Games. By 2032, NBCU would have covered 23 Games since its first broadcast of Tokyo 1964, unprecedented long-term commitment and expertise from both parties. Scott Blackmun, CEO of USOC, expressed delight, 'A good day for American athletes and hopefuls. NBC's ability not only to broadcast the Games, but to tell the stories of our athletes in a way that makes our nation proud, makes them an ideal partner, allows us to feel fortunate they desire such commitment.' It was a deal that would stretch way beyond US borders: an exceptional contribution to the stability of IOC revenue, more than 90 per cent redistributed among IFs, NOCs and host city organisers.

Three months earlier, five cities had announced their intention of bidding for the Winter Games of 2022, election in a year's time from the prospective talents of Almaty of Kazakhstan, Beijing, Kraków in Poland, Lviv in Ukraine, and Norwegian capital Oslo, the EB to define a shortlist in July. The IOC would be confronted with a question of principle and tradition: should the winter event be given to a city or a country? Two of the candidates, Beijing and Lviv, proposed staging events in three cities; while sailing at a Summer Games had predominantly required a venue distant from the main Games, the winter event had largely been confined to a single city. Bach, intent on host city reformation, had been openly inviting bidding cities to put their personal stamp on projected plans. Norway was about to do so, in Oslo, host city of the 1952 Winter Games; effectively jumping ahead of the president's own desires, its projected organising committee announcing, 'Preparation, planning and implementation of a Games in Norway must be conducted to ensure full respect for human and trade union rights, and sustainable development for the climate and the environment. Economic, social and ethical considerations must be addressed.'

What more could Bach ask? Oslo was meeting the March deadline for submission, confident in approval of an Evaluation Commission to be established by the IOC, experts visiting each candidate to prepare a technical report. The Oslo project was seemingly as good as it gets: an agreement between the Norwegian Confederation of Trade Unions together with Union for Professionals and the Vocational Union, alongside the NOC and Norway's Confederation of Sports, confirmation of everything Bach was seeking. Inge Andersen, NOC secretary-general, was optimistic, 'Our aim is to protect the Olympic Games, the whole Olympic ethic. There are many new people attempting to negotiate power positions, within differing subordinate associations, and it is vital that the exclusivity of the Olympic Games is shielded from possible exploitation. The project of Thomas Bach to create a platform for reformation of existing ideals needs to succeed, knowing that other organisations are contemplating other possibilities. We in Norway seek to uphold democratic principles: fair play, the rights of workers' unions, the integrity of sponsors. Without being arrogant, we would like to influence the IOC in the synchronisation of sport within society, that sponsors have a parallel objective.'

Norway's press release stressed that its objectives were companionship, tolerance, and the unique Olympic experience; that it would not incur multi-million-dollar expenditure such as projected in the campaigns by Munich and Pyeongchang when contesting the election for 2018. Oslo stressed, too, absence of social discrimination and the unity of the major work unions, 'We want Games in Norway, including our Youth Games of 2016, to be remembered for respect of human rights and labour rights, to contribute to secure employment, fair working conditions and sustainable facilities. The only way the Olympic Games can sustain exclusivity is by managing its brand in a manner true and credible, maintaining the educational value of social responsibility and ethical principle; sustainable facilities related to the number of events; upgraded existing facilities where possible; a Games connected to regional and domestic sport and the culture embracing grass roots; plus protection of climate and environment and the essential element of anti-doping control.' Could Oslo's bid fail?

Perhaps. In May, junior political coalition partners, the right-wing Progress Party – which held only 16 per cent of parliament – rejected the financial guarantees required by the IOC contract. Prime minister Erna Solberg equivocally stated, 'I believe the Olympics are a fantastic experience, but costly. It's not even the next parliament that will bear the cost, but the one after that.' Solberg claimed her majority Conservative Party had yet to make up their mind. Bach arrived to view preparations for Lillehammer's scheduled Winter Youth Games of 2016, and following lunch with King Harald, he sought to encourage positive Oslo momentum in discussion with culture minister Thorhild Widvey and Oslo's governing mayor, Stian Berger Røsland, emphasising that his Agenda 2020 project included a stipulation for a $1bn subsidy for any successful candidate. Bach's encouragement became more relevant with the expected withdrawal of Kraków through lack of support, and by Lviv through Russia's invasion. With the Progress Party in a minority, the government for the moment held firm, Gerhard Heiberg, recently retired chairman of IOC's Marketing Commission, and leader of Lillehammer's memorable Games of 1994, commenting, 'It's possible the Progressive Party's negative attitude might have the opposite effect to that intended.' Solberg continued to stall, while NOC president Børre Rognlien observed, 'We cannot be one of the world's richest countries, per capita, and only travel to other people's countries for the Games.'

Norway's planning, stemming from its Lillehammer/ Hamar youth concept, was economy-orientated, illustrative of Bach's objective, self-protective. Accompanying Bach's visit had been Angela Ruggiero, US Olympian and co-ordinating chair for Pyeongchang 2018; finance commission chair Ng Ser Miang, director-general Christophe De Kepper, and Games CEO Gilbert Felli, all acutely aware of Oslo's potential, of the gift on hand. Following their departure, Jonas Gahr Støre, foreign minister and imminent parliamentary leader of the Labour Party, announced, 'We will agree to hosting in 2022, but only if the Games can be organised and conducted in a way that brings them back towards their roots, and avoiding expensive new facilities. Should the dominant governing party of the right still approve, only fringe political resistance would remain.' Inge Andersen continued to be optimistic, 'President Bach was forthright. Equally important is that our media seem to have taken a more positive view.'

There was not, within Scandinavia, rampant sporting moral superiority, amid the wider contemporary mistrust about costly hosting: it was simply recognised as a risk. Stockholm had pulled back alongside the summer hesitancy of many cities, even several in the USA. Bach's visit had not been without camouflaged purpose: there was a need to confront media hostility that had haunted Norway ever since 1994, when members had come under continuous press abuse for shameless junketing. Excess had discoloured voting campaigns since 1986, surrounding Barcelona, through those of Atlanta, Nagano and Sydney. There was an unspoken truth that the IOC – following Sochi's extravagance and now Rio's creeping ineptitude for 2016 – needed Oslo more than Oslo needed them.

Despite the media reservation, Oslo's mayor Fabian Stang remained polite, 'If the IOC will agree to financial downsizing, then I believe a deal could be possible, jointly for Oslo-Lillehammer for 2022. But the adjustment has to be by the IOC.' Any agreement would come not from the NOC, but parliament in late autumn, with polling showing a positive swing. Prominent Labour politician Jorrod Asphjell emphasised the need for downsizing, 'If this can be realised, then all those prominent cities which have faltered can be reassured. We don't need super-stadia, never again utilised, facilities that don't reflect domestic involvement.'

Yet without Oslo's availability, the choice the following year would be limited to one of two authoritarian governments, little-experienced Kazakhstan or Beijing, the value of the Games to any city not to be lightly discarded. There are unequivocal benefits, as Spyros Capralos, executive director of the underwhelming Athens Games of 2004, remembered. 'We had the excuse to promote infrastructure that could only have been achieved over many years. The Games remodelled the city – a new airport, a new road network, three new metro lines, transforming everyday life. Our fault lay in funding two expansive stadiums for sports where we had no local tradition.' The double-city Norwegian potential of Oslo-Lillehammer was wholly acceptable within the new IOC concept, as Gilbert Felli explained, 'Increasingly the colour of bidding these days is political more than sporting, though Oslo-Lillehammer is more about sport by a famously winter sports-loving nation than other rivals. But there's a snag: the population of Norway admire the Olympics but are out of love with the IOC.' Norway's low approval poll-ranking remained adverse, though among under-30s a majority was in favour: Bach's attitude was parental, saying, 'If a city needs extra help, then we're here to provide it, though we do not do any special financial deals [beyond the Agenda 2020 promise of a $1bn subsidy].'

Come October, the right-wing element in Norway's coalition government shot their nation's Olympic prospects in the foot, disregarding the proposed IOC financial subsidy. Voluntary withdrawal, now leaving the field confined to Beijing and Almaty, was self-deluding humbug, an act of unmitigated hypocrisy. The platform on which the coalition planted its retreat was one of falsely assumed political purity. In addition to public poll antipathy – far from uniform among the multitude of sports activists in Norway's population of five million who uniquely had a skier in their national emblem – the government inaccurately identified projected costs based on inflated figures from Sochi's Games at the beginning of the year. The coalition was condemning the IOC almost entirely on account of a protocol for bid cities including 'favours' required for IOC members: a list devised not by the IOC, but maladroitly by administrative staff at Lausanne. Such favours were: a royal cocktail party prior to the Opening Ceremony; hotel welcomes for members from the manager; separate traffic lanes to Games venues, never mind the latter having contributed immensely to the success of London 2012.

The coalition's finance minister, Siv Jensen, pompously proclaimed that Norway's rejection 'is a powerful message to the IOC that it needs more modesty'. Norway's politicians conveniently overlooked their own elite conduct when entertaining, as I witnessed over many years, the world's top athletes at their Bislet Games, when professionalism was still illegal: acceptable to pour the champagne, so to speak, for Carl Lewis and Seb Coe, but not for the IOC, which for more than a century had kept afloat, with their extensive subsidies to IFs, the globe's most priceless festival. Christophe Dubi, executive director of the Games in succession to Felli, counted the withdrawal 'a missed opportunity', recalling that mayor Stang had himself staged a cocktail party for Bach and other IOC dignitaries during their earlier trip. A thwarted Bach tactically could not remonstrate.

Counter-ambition among senior operators within the maze of IOC responsibilities can generate unexpected controversy. Signs of rough water appeared for Bach in April at the opening of SportAccord's annual convention, this year taking place in Turkey. Equilibrium had been disturbed by commercial development in what had earlier been an agreeable talking shop – the annual congress of the General Assembly of International Sports Federations, a platform for exchanging information and objectives among international federations on sponsorship, coaching, television deals, equipment and other essentials. By now this event had morphed into would-be competition promoter, this objective arising through liaison between then president Rogge and his Low Countries colleague Hein Verbruggen, former leader of the International Cycling Union.

SportAccord had latterly encountered a financial hazard, finding sponsorship, notwithstanding its raised profile on account of an IOC Executive Board meeting having become an annual attachment. Conflict of interest arose with ambition by Marius Vizer, SportAccord's chair, to raise the prospect of a World Games, inevitably in conflict with the Olympics. Here was unavoidable friction for Bach, if not immediately dismissed. In his mission to uphold universality, a fortnight later he was delivering optimism at the United Nations conference in New York on 'Sport for Development and Peace': an association of increasing value in the IOC's international perspective. Bach paid due courtesy to UN president John Ashe, and to the valued continuing collaboration with general secretary Ban Ki-moon; additionally to the valuable leadership in North

Africa by Wilfried Lemke's educated interventions on sport in Tunisia, Bach reflecting, 'We know how much sport can address human and social needs in emerging countries, key topics of the current Development Goals Framework. The contribution of sport to health is relevant to both prevention of diseases and rehabilitation. We at the IOC are much concerned in partnership with NGOs to co-operate in areas of health and education.'

Onwards to a controversial Summer Youth Games in Nanjing where many considered that the IOC had lost the plot. Bach admitted, 'The Youth Games were very much part of our Agenda [2020], about its establishment, though I admit that many had different opinions beyond being simply about motivation for youth and a campaign against obesity. It should not be simply about "medals", more the experience of engaging in a multi-sports event and involving youngsters in the Olympic Movement. Many organisations had no clear sense of mission, aware the situation needed further study prior to the next occasion at Buenos Aires in 2018, identifying for youngsters how sport should take a lead within society.'

I among many had considered the IOC took a wrong turn when electing Nanjing, a 'big-time' city, rather than Poznań of Poland, more appropriate for the perceived objective. Nanjing was enlisting perceptibly the wrong youngsters: those already fully acquainted with the competitive sporting stage. The Youth Games were not intended to be another grandstanding opportunity, but to engage in the physical aspect of education: a civilising exercise deserving the backing of UNESCO. Of the 3,500 athletes attending Nanjing, all of them were already NOC-registered competitors enjoying national funding, an investment involving the IOC which could have been better utilised to gather schoolchildren at 'Olympic Camps' rather than a mini-Olympics, as vice-president Craig Reedie observed: 'These games are being held in facilities suitable for a full Olympic tournament, a legacy from the Chinese National Games back in 2003. This range of facilities is not required, and needs reviewing. A balance of these elements with its competitive atmosphere yet without spectators in large venues will need adjustment.' Willi Kaltschmitt, Executive Board member, reflected, 'The Youth Games were formalised at our Session in Guatemala, bringing children, culture and education together, so of course I'm enthusiastic,' but veteran Dick Pound remained sceptical on the value-for-money aspect, 'I too feel the IOC has missed the plot, attendance being essentially for those not already involved in Olympic sports, to find those not yet embraced by youth programmes of the various IFs. A possible formula would be to reduce entry performance levels, and to revise city-bidding credentials.' Pound imagined the same financial outlay, around $3bn gross, could be utilised on five simultaneous continental 'Olympic Camps', such a global network opening de Coubertin's intellectual originality, beneficial not just to electronic games defectors, but to those outer regions of the Olympic arena such as Aruba, Laos and Chad who urgently needed a sense of belonging.

Bach himself played down anxiety, insisting Nanjing should not become a blueprint for future Youth Games, 'Organisers should calculate their own approach, hopefully different, with a concept for youth through their own local fashions and objectives. Yet I am impressed by the facilities here in Nanjing, sustained from the Games in 2008.' In diplomatic mode, when being awarded an 'honorary professorship' at Nanjing's Sport Institute, Bach predictably praised China's comprehensive energy in the continuing expansion of sport, 'You have already hosted the Asian Youth Games last year, and prior to the Olympics of 2008 the China National Games in 2005, making use of the legacy of previous events in such a way as to establish an example for others … While many athletes have said they are happy with everything in this event, there is admittedly a wider concern over the scale of these Youth Games, and future organisers should calculate adjustment, presenting perhaps a different concept.'

The new president was well aware of concern about the rising tide of leading events in Asia: Beijing 2008, now

Nanjing, Incheon's Asian Games in Korea the following month, Pyeongchang's Winter Games of 2018, Tokyo's Summer Games of 2020. The IOC should be spreading their message geographically, there not having been a European host since Turin in 2006, and all now vainly awaiting the outcome of Oslo's bid for 2022, yet to be decided by the city's own political conference in November, which would inadvertently further extend Asia's hosting tide.

Another sports-culture question mark was being raised by preparation for an inaugural European Games in Baku, Azerbaijan, in 2015. The European Olympic Committee had voted in Rome two years earlier to launch this innovative event into an already crowded calendar, provoking widespread criticism: who would pay, who would host, were not already exhausted athletes half asleep? Yet within 30 months, a third of the time allowed to prepare for an Olympic Games, a 20-sport event was prominently forged in this financially thriving emerging city: independent from past Soviet occupation and in the wake of two millennia of Islamic history alongside culturally compatible Turkey.

Would it work? As a commentator originally harbouring doubts, I discovered evidence – as a member of a media co-ordination committee – that not merely justified any optimism, but expectation of a double impact on the sporting map. Here was a platform on which to develop the health of a population, two-thirds of them under 30, and half of those between 14 and 30: comparable to the demography which repetitively encouraged Olympic bids from Istanbul. Moreover, Azerbaijan's pro-rata sporting advance was already one of the most conspicuous anywhere for a population of ten million. Regular Olympic winners in Soviet times, since independence those figures had soared: seven medals at Beijing 2008 (1-2-4), ten at London 2012 (2-4-4). With 12 medals at the recent Nanjing Youth Games, Azerbaijan had ranked tenth in the world and fifth in Europe. Its seven non-medal athletes had all finished in the top ten: an impressive return for the government's annual grant to sport of £10m.

Bach, cautious about financial over-expansion of global sport, could not but admire the ignition demonstrated in Baku, as expressed by minister of sport Azad Rahimov, who said, 'We consider that the European Games provide inspiration for the future of our country, for the health and occupation of young people, and by these Games we can show a wide audience the competence and capability of Azerbaijan. The legacy of our new stadia will lie in their future use, they are an investment. We badly needed a real aquatic centre, not just hotel pools, and we have built a shooting venue plus a new 65,000 capacity football stadium.'

The unacknowledged political down side, headlined by humanitarian agencies but ignored by the European Olympic Committees group and its president Patrick Hickey of the Republic of Ireland, was, 'Independent Azerbaijan remained a totalitarian autocratic state in which dissenting journalists were imprisoned: to what extent would visiting sports media expose this iniquity? Does the presence of global media, as at Moscow 1980 and Beijing 2008, help initiate moves toward social integrity?' Three months after my initial visit, in December 2014, Khadija Ismayilova from Radio Free Europe was jailed for her repetitive criticism of Aliyev, the ruling president.

From western Asia to eastern, and the Asian Games of Incheon, Korea, involving 36 sports, numerically more extensive than that of the Olympics. Here should have been advance publicity for Pyeongchang's Winter Olympics four years hence. Yet over two weeks, you would never have known, so far as I detected in attendance at half a dozen events, that Pyeongchang even existed. Having stunned the world with its spectacular Summer Games in Seoul in 1988, imprinting a picture of a 'new' nation on the world stage, with its glorious cultural finesse, in a confident world power created from rubble over 35 years, now here in Incheon there was PR silence: an impending global party without a candle yet alight.

There was more news filtering out of Incheon about the Summer Games of Tokyo in 2020, two years after Pyeongchang, with not a poster or leaflet for the latter in sight. It was an absence of information urgently needing correction if Pyeongchang was to achieve anything comparable to the impact of Seoul 30 years earlier. A Bach stimulus required? He couldn't be everywhere.

6

REFORMS UP, EXPENSES DOWN

THOMAS BACH'S scheming for constitutional reformation had been long incubating in the mind of a once frustrated Olympian. Now he knew he must tread strategically when his masterplan was presented at a Session only 14 months after election. He aligned essential support: the Executive Board; key NOC figures such as John Coates and Mario Prescante of Italy; front-line IF brains, ASOIF president Ricci Bitti and Sebastian Coe from track and field; continental power-broker Sheikh Ahmad; and athletes, currently led by compatriot Claudia Bokel, chair of the Athletes Commission. Preliminary consultation was an 'Olympic Summit' of 16 world sports officials in Lausanne. Three months later at Montreux came a debate by the EB, its opinions undisclosed: in mid-November, invited athletes from across the world at the Olympic Museum in Lausanne, to arouse competitors' enthusiasm for the 40 recommendations by the EB.

Fundamental was collaboration, ever since Bach's election, with John Coates, long-time leader of Olympic affairs in Australia, not least Sydney's Games of 2000. Bach was reliant upon Coates's allegiance, 'John played his part in helping me fashion these planned reforms, a vital role. I knew him well from my work with the Juridical Commission and his function as president of Australia's NOC. We think alike, with focus on the athletes. John is pragmatic and constructive. When I was elected, he was already such a prominent figure and an obvious partner in assembling my project. This had to be formulated in Olympic Charter language, yet as organiser of a previous Games John was familiar with all the structures, not least the costing of a Games, so together we became a team. This resulted, at the Session before Sochi's Games, in many members speaking for the first time about the project: their opinions being heard, not just confronted with a decision more or less already taken. There was near unanimous reception of all 40 points, to be considered at the end of the year.'

A perceptive observer was Maître François Carrard, previously IOC director-general under Samaranch, and subsequently always available 'adviser'. He recalled, 'Yes, Agenda 2020 was a bit ambitious! It was a huge task to be accomplished, but Thomas opened the gates. Whether or not he was in control he would be governed by events around his fresh thinking, but he understood the tapestry of the IOC. One small example: the addition to the motto, "faster, higher, stronger", with the addition of "together". Some might have thought that presumptuous, yet he has the constructive urge that others lack. Jacques Rogge hadn't touched anything adventurous. Ever!

'Thomas has an aggressive German streak, he's on the move, and he was so right to activate this Agenda, the IOC needed to reassess itself, indeed the entire Olympic Movement. Maybe those 40 points might have seemed initially too much, but Thomas's merit was that he went for it, and you could sense the significant consequences.'

Of a similar perspective was Dick Pound, from whom a decade on Bach was stealing his thunder: Pound, another lawyer, once potential president, who likewise had well recognised the need for reformation in the wake of the Salt Lake scandal, and had indeed been proceeding to implement some changes under the umbrella of Rogge. He revealed, 'Not all Thomas's ideas were new, there was much on which we had already been working, but Thomas's style was impatient, he was in a hurry, whereas I had been chair of the consultative Games study group for change in 2002 and 2003.'

Ricci Bitti, intellectual head of ASOIF, would be adding parallel energy to all Bach's proposals for modernising, streamlining and economising the structure of the Olympic Programme, 'We knew we had to make the system operational, active, focus on promotion of Thomas's ideas, which were all close to my own objectives – host city procedures, the costs of that and also in the competitions; of doping procedures and, at the same time, simplification.' All members with experience were onside, including Craig Reedie, vice-president of WADA. 'When we heard the first draft at the EB meeting at Montreux, it was evident Thomas had things well planned, yet of course he needed the EB to be in line behind him. That wasn't difficult: all his ideas well drilled, it was a *tour de force*, yet cleverly compartmentalised. EB unanimity was vital for Thomas to progress, the Agenda could never have been assembled over a couple of years.' Unanimity? Some older members took a while to fall in line. 'Was Agenda 2020 necessary?' reflects Gerhard Heiberg. 'It was clearly an intelligent programme, many ideas, and if at first I was hesitant, I quickly supported it more and more.'

Through the months of 2014, the president was legalistic in assembling his base of preliminary approval among stakeholders: having begun with 14 working groups established to refine the myriad of proposals, these finalised by the EB in October, they guided by experts from civil societies such as the UN, Transparency International, the Clinton Foundation and the World Bank. At the conclusion of the EB meeting in Montreux, Bach stated, 'If there is agreement among ALL stakeholders, changes could be made to the programme. No "secrets" were revealed beyond baseball and softball possibly being returned to *after* a host has been elected, but the IOC will not impose programme changes without unanimous agreement … Hosting will become more of an invitation, a partnership, than a city's *application*, though the timespan from election to a Games will remain at seven years. This is a sound basis.'

Programme expansion would be about flexibility. A month later, in November, I debated the project with Sheikh Ahmad, to gauge the loyalty of a prime mover. How important, I asked, was a balance between the evolving appetite of athletes and the interests of the public, both as ticket holders and televised audience? Sheikh Ahmad replied, 'Balance is the key. A Games must contain great sport, and that means placing the needs of athletes first, yet great sport doesn't just mean high quality, but a universal public appeal. The Olympic Movement must stay receptive to new trends and technologies, and the key to Agenda 2020 will be to provide flexibility.' What qualifying regulation in team sports could widen the spread of medals beyond the commercially and industrially powerful top dozen nations? 'Broadening the distribution of medals is not more regulation but more participation – we need to look at additional support for NOCs in developing their level of preparation.' Would it be acceptable to make facility-expensive sports – bobsleigh, equestrianism – optional in order to widen and economise the bidding field? 'Of course we want to bring the Games to as many territories as possible, but we must not lose that distinctive identity which makes the Games unique, that identity coming from traditional sports.' To ensure continental rotation and global appeal, would a hosting cycle – Asia, Europe, Africa, Americas – be desirable, so long as there is an eligible bid city? 'Different cultures make the Games more enriching, but we must maintain flexibility to stage the Games wherever a city offers the best proposition at that moment.'

A week later, Bach was hosting, at the Olympic Museum in Lausanne, those who are the essence of Olympism: the athletes. Among them were, besides Bokel, Vincent Defrasne (France, biathlon gold); Susana Feitor (Portugal, race walking in five Games); Jessica Fox (Australia, canoe silver); Jade Jones (Great Britain, taekwondo gold); Stéphane Lambiel (Switzerland, figure skating silver); Marsha Marescia (South Africa, three Olympics hockey); Kaveh Mehrabi (Iran, badminton 2008); Koji Murofushi (Japan, hammer gold and silver); Maria Höfl-Riesch (Germany, skiing, three golds); Jean-Michel Saive (Belgium, seven-time Olympian at table tennis). Bach was asked about the desire to make changes, responding, 'We are now in the position to drive change rather than being driven. We have to take leadership, seize the moment.'

Bach is a man temperamentally never wishing himself to be driven, yet for all his infectious optimism, the IOC, and indeed many branches of world sport, were surrounded by elements of anxiety: not least by the justifiable intervention into the footlights of international sport by wealthy Middle East nations; overloaded with finance but strictly limited in experience of administration and often the ethics of sport. For instance, Doha of Qatar, mega-rich but experiencing dilemmas embracing employment, morality, geographic impartiality, administrative knowhow. Having staged an outstanding Asian Games in 2006, Qatar was now scheduled, with its tiny indigenous population, dependence on imported foreign labour and expertise to assemble the necessary facilities, to host FIFA's World Cup of 2022. Jacques Rogge had none too discreetly 'shelved' an application by Doha as Olympic host, yet World Athletics had been pitched into confusion by Doha's successful campaign to host a World Championship in preference to Eugene of Oregon, United States, historic bastion of elite track and field, disregarded notwithstanding never previously honoured.

World sports, some beyond IOC influence, were currently confronted by a massive conundrum: the diminutive yet infinitely rich Gulf states harbouring ambitions in sport as extensive as, say, China's, yet with one 3,000th of the population and a territory on a par with Mauritius. On the one hand, Qatar or UAE deserved everything they were capable of achieving by conventional means, yet demographic elements posed likely embarrassment for international federations.

World Athletics was optimistic for administrative reform in the expectation, duly fulfilled, of Coe being elected president in succession to Senegal-Frenchman Lamine Diack: upon retirement, he was abruptly charged with multiple corruption. Not a happy background in the major Olympic sport for an IOC president in search of clarity, truth and economy.

In December 2014 came presentation at an Extraordinary Session in Monaco of the 40 recommendations. Appropriately it was John Coates who opened the batting, with 'Recommendation One, Advocacy', proclaiming, 'The host bidding process has to be appealing and sustainable. Bidding cities need to be advised by the IOC that this is an invitation; that they can use temporary or dismountable venues, that entire sports or disciplines can be staged outside the host city, that there should be environmental and labour-related regulations, that the city contract should be public. The Games can become more universal if the costs are reduced.'

Here was set the tone for safeguarding and protecting the values of the Olympics, a strategic roadmap for the future with the three pillars of Credibility, Sustainability and Youth; simultaneously re-emphasising the three functional roles of the IOC in an Olympic Games as leaders, owners and, until the day the Games begin, the organisers. Beyond city bidding, these were the 39 other proposals:

2. Evaluate cities by opportunity and risks
3. Reduction of costs
4. Sustainability of venues
5. Daily sustainable operations
6. Collaboration with other domestic sports
7. Collaboration of sports with different facilities
8. Forging relationships with professional leagues
9. Creating the framework of the entire Olympic Programme
10. Adjusting programme from sport-based to event-based
11. Foster gender equality, essentially by Tokyo 2020
12. Reduce costs/increase management flexibility

13. Maximise collaboration between stakeholders
14. Strengthen sixth fundamental of Olympism (humanitarian integration)
15. Change of philosophy regarding clean athletes
16. Leverage of $20m protecting clean athletes
17. Honour clean athletes
18. Strengthen support of clean athletes
19. Launch Olympic TV channel (digital age, reaching three billion)
20. Engage strategic partnerships
21. Strengthen IOC's advocacy capability
22. Expand Olympic education
23. Engage with local communities
24. Evaluate Sport-for-Hope programme
25. Review Youth Olympic Games management
26. Further blend sport and culture
27. Enhance basic governance principles
28. Enhance autonomy
29. Enhance transparency
30. Ethics Commission independence
31. Administrative compliance
32. Strengthen ethics spectrum
33. Further involvement of sponsors
34. Expand global licensing
35. Foster allegiance with NOCs
36. Extend 'Olympic brand' non-commercially
37. Address IOC age limit
38. Targeted IOC recruitment
39. Foster society dialogue
40. Review IOC Commissions

As author legally unqualified, I am indebted for some guidance in my analysis of the recommendations, for a leavening of expertise, to Antoine Duval, senior researcher at the Netherlands' respected legal institute ASSER, and also to Jens Sejer Andersen, international director at the Play the Game research organisation: their perspectives helpful for interpretation by many Olympic stakeholders, if not a few journalists purporting to tell the IOC just what they ought to be doing. I gratefully quote Mr Duval, 'With Agenda 2020, the IOC has raised high expectations about change, and it would be suicidal for the Olympic Movement to betray its grand promises. The 40 recommendations of Agenda 2020 being released, one should not underplay them: they constitute, on paper at least, a potential leap forward.

'The media will focus on the hot stuff: the Olympic Channel, the pluri-localisation of the Games, or their dynamic format. More important, and to some extent surprising, the IOC has also fully embraced sustainability and good governance. Nonetheless, the long-term legacy of Agenda 2020 will hinge on the IOC's determination to be true to these fundamental commitments. Indeed, the devil is always in the implementation, and the laudable intents of some Recommendations will depend on future political choices by Olympic bureaucrats. For those interested in human rights and democracy, at and around the Olympics, two aspects are crucial: the IOC's confession that the autonomy of sport is intimately linked to the quality of its governance standards, and the central role the concept of sustainability is to play in the bidding process and the host city contract.'

All the recommendations carried explanatory paragraphs, detailed extensions. The devised bid process, 'Invites potential candidate cities to present an Olympic project that best matches their sports and their economic, social and environmental long-term social needs.' For reasons of sustainability, the IOC will tolerate that events do not take place in the host city but at adjacent facilities or indeed country (this would require adjustment of Charter Article 34). Duval notes that sustainability and human rights in the bidding process needed to be pivotal, the bidding process entrusting the IOC with political leverage that effectively had an impact on the life of the community. Duval reflected, 'The IOC is not shy of tackling issues and should be praised for doing so … this is a necessary move for an institution claiming to follow good governance, and will ease the work of critics scrutinising the contract, while the public will have access to the official document itself.'

As a lawyer, Bach himself was all too aware, going back to his time as competitor, and the confusion surrounding the US boycott of Moscow 1980, that the Principles of Good Governance in Recommendation 27, and transparency of accounts in Recommendation 29, with the financial statements of the IOC to be prepared and audited according to the International Financial Reporting Standards, even when not legally required, were paramount. The public are assessors more than anyone of good governance, because without that no organisation can properly profess autonomy. Agenda 2020 boasted, 'All organisations belonging to the Olympic Movement accept and comply with basic universal principles and good governance of the Olympic Movement.'

Recommendation 30 for strengthening the Ethics Commission's independence, with the chair and members to be elected by the IOC Session, was intended to establish compliance under Recommendation 31, through advice not merely to members, but IOC staff, NOCs and IFs. This stipulation would provide scrutiny of expenditure, both by the IOC and members, though there was a loophole that would not embrace declaration of members' external coincidental earnings. Here was an arena in which the Ethics Commission would need to advance its scrutiny if improved public trust was to be engendered; a branch of accountable governance.

Recommendation 4 on sustainability of facilities, proposed and utilised in a city bid, was to have its most dramatic impact seven years later in 2021. When Bach was elected, the Games of Sochi, Rio, Pyeongchang and Tokyo were all in place, and while he dramatically manoeuvred for the double election in 2017 of Paris 2024 and Los Angeles 2028 immediately prior to the postponed Tokyo Games in 2021, the 'sudden' election of Brisbane for 2032 (see Chapter 12) was the ultimate realisation of a 'sustainable' Games. Envisaged within the 2020 concept, under the original attachment in December 2014,

Brisbane fulfilled the principle 'to establish the best possible governance for the integration of sustainability throughout the organisation', while also 'introducing sustainable sourcing policies in tendering processes, sponsorship, licensing and supplier agreements for renewals or new contracts'.

That election for 2032, unimagined in 2014, directly reflected Recommendation 3, 'Reducing the number of presentations permitted, with a significant financial contribution [to the elected city] from the IOC'; alongside 'assessing key opportunities and risks' and 'the maximum use of existing facilities where no long-term venue legacy need exist or can be justified', with the Evaluation Commission 'to benefit from third-party, independent advice in such areas as social, economic and political conditions'.

In the wake of tensions surrounding Russian legislation on anti-gay rights which had provoked global condemnation surrounding Sochi, Recommendation 14, Strengthen the Sixth Fundamental Principle of Olympism, for non-discrimination on sexual orientation, was an inevitable inclusion – though needing to be adjusted to comply with the text of Article 14 of the European Convention on Human Rights, or Article 2 of the UN Universal Declaration of Human Rights. This principle already existed, of course, in the Charter and to which the IOC at all times had been stubbornly faithful, whatever the variable inclinations domestically of any host city.

However, challenging Agenda 2020's recommendation would be the International Trade Union Confederation, in alliance with Amnesty International, complaining that 'human rights did not come under the jurisdiction of the host city contract', to which Angela Ruggiero, US ice hockey champion and representative of the IOC Athletes Commission, observed, 'Olympic sport stands for fundamental values, every athlete sure of inclusion and acceptance, our message of tolerance to the rest of the world.'

Recommendation 37 on re-assessment of members' age limit was likely to be a variable debate: an accepted principle that some elderly officials, through experience, remained effectively wise and competent beyond the age of 70, and some vigorously protesting the virtue of their own continuation. One element which Bach would be instrumental in pursuing was Recommendation 38, Targeted IOC Recruitment, with implementation of gender balance: belatedly begun after more than 80 years by Samaranch in 1980 with the first two women members. By the time of Tokyo's postponed Games in 2021, Bach had advanced the presence of women across the Olympic arena exponentially: what remained was geographical imbalance, in terms of continental representation, a thorny issue in which Europe had long held imbalanced geographical sway, and there was further need for revision in Recommendation 40, Scope and Composition of IOC Commissions.

Unequivocal acceptance greeted Recommendation 19, the Olympic TV channel, providing a platform for events and athletes beyond an Olympic Games period throughout the calendar year, fully connecting within the digital arena young people and youth events across the world: a worldwide platform spreading Olympic values, sporting events, cultural and humanitarian projects, plus exposure of bidding cities to obviate expensive travel. In Duval's conclusion, he stated, 'The caveat is that law is much about interpretation of words. The IOC has a responsibility to give practicality to the intentions enshrined in Agenda 2020. The IOC cannot afford to betray the intention of trans-national concepts, there is no space for the use of newspeak or practical disregard of essential concepts. Thomas Bach has raised high expectations, a willingness to change. Such expectations cannot be disappointed: now comes the time to deliver.'

Jens Andersen was more directly critical:

'It may leave crucial questions open, but by accepting Thomas Bach's Agenda 2020 reform programme unanimously, the IOC has set the yardstick by which it will be remembered. The changes touch on other worries expressed by the public and leading politicians worldwide, at least in countries where ordinary citizens are allowed to express what they think. There is global concern over the widespread corruption in the organisations and competitions of sport, and with Agenda 2020 Thomas Bach and the IOC clearly show that they have heard the voice of the people. Moreover, Bach has entered his presidency with an energy and determination that is not only refreshing after a decade of aristocratic stagnation under his predecessor Jacques Rogge, but also inspiring optimism with regard to the outcome of reform. On the one hand the Olympic Movement propagates "the values of excellence, respect, friendship, dialogue, diversity, non-discrimination, tolerance, fair play, solidarity, development and peace", as Bach said when opening the Session in Monaco; on the other hand the Olympic Movement gladly sells its prestige to a repressive regime that contradicts each and every one of these values, if only the price is right.

'As for the autonomy of sport, the Agenda is weak when saying, "The IOC to create a template to facilitate co-operation between national authorities and sports organisations in a country.' In other words, let's not upset China, Russia, Azerbaijan, Kazakhstan, Belarus, the Arab monarchies, most of Africa and all other states where governments in reality run the Olympic committees, implying it's a contentious issue which has to be postponed. In addition to "protecting clean athletes", the IOC could have used this reform to "protect clean sports officials". Thanks to FIFA and a number of other international federations, the public perception of international sports leaders is that they are likely to be corrupt. Clear standards of good governance could have helped clean sports leaders in clearing their own federations of corruption. But although Thomas Bach has highlighted the need for better governance in his great speech at the Olympic Congress in Copenhagen in 2009, his Agenda 2020 is surprisingly tame when addressing the threat to sports' status in society.'

Predictably, John Coates was euphoric, reflecting on the immediate impact of Agenda 2020's acceptance when contributing to my official history of the IOC, republished for the fifth time in 2018, 'From a position of strength, we have been able to drive change ourselves, rather than be driven. We have been able to tackle issues head on and prepare for the future, rather than rest on our laurels and ride success of the past. There were challenges that needed to be addressed: how can we make the Games more appealing to potential cities, better engage young people with sport, better protect and support clean athletes, ensure good governance around the world?

'Unanimous approval by the IOC Session was a watershed moment for the Olympic Movement, a clear vision of where we are headed, how we can protect the uniqueness of the Olympic Games and strengthen the role of sport and Olympic values in society. A key part of this has been the launch of the Olympic Channel, a new way to communicate and showcase sports to a younger generation. By increasing the flexibility of sports on the Olympic Programme, we have been able to provide a more youthful and urban appeal. This will be seen at the Games in Tokyo: karate, skateboard, sport climbing and surfing are likely to make their debut, as will 3x3 basketball and BMX freestyle. Tokyo 2020 will be first to benefit from this new approach, the modernisation not only of the Olympic Programme, but in flexibility in how the Games are delivered with a saving of billions of dollars in revised construction budgets.'

Confident Coates might have been, but his mood was, to a degree, flying in the face of disturbingly ominous news emerging – on the same day as the Agenda's lift-off – from Germany's ARD television, echoed by the BBC and the *Sunday Times*. Investigative journalist Hajo Seppelt, in an exclusive headlined 'Doping Top Secret', revealed via a whistleblower a system of contrived positive drug test evasion by Russia during four years. Seppelt asserted, 'I believe that Putin more than anyone has recognised how to conduct politics through sport.' Prominent were accusations of concealed positive tests at London's Olympics in 2012,

IAAF's World Championships 2013, and Sochi's Winter Games. In conjunction with emerging news of charges to be brought by the US Federal Bureau of Investigation against FIFA officials for the World Cup election of 2010 – believed to embrace Sepp Blatter, also then an IOC member and extending to ultimate criminal trials beginning in May 2022 – any sense of satisfaction for Bach in Monaco was at least temporarily soured.

New WADA chief Craig Reedie was particularly alarmed by Seppelt's revelations. Although the introduction of the Athlete Biological Passport, with its blood analysis, had advanced the efficiency of urine testing, a complex of results from 2013 had exposed daunting abuse: data of positive tests from 115 countries in multiple sports exposing 225 in Russia, Turkey 188, France 108, India 95, and Belgium, Italy, Poland and Spain with tallies from 94 to 55. ARD's disclosure prompted the immediate appointment of an independent commission headed by Dick Pound – an inquiry which would last almost a year. Uneasy now beat the heart of an IOC president who might justifiably have otherwise considered he had scored a winning goal.

Bach's technical buttress, Reedie was even more on edge, 'We knew from ARD's revelations that the situation could become critical, for both IOC and for Rio's Games – "Oh my God, I need 36 hours to think what to do next." At that point WADA didn't have the legal power to handle such a development, so launched the immediate appointment of Pound's survey into the single sport of track and field, aided by his lawyer compatriot Richard McLaren. WADA's next move was to expel Rodchenkov, the whistle-blower, to suspend Russia's anti-doping agency RUSADA, and effectively persuade IAAF to suspend Russia's athletic federation, while Thomas separately set up his own inquiry through the Ethics Commission. Initially, the IOC intended to delay Russia's sanctions until *after* the Rio Games.'

7

A HUGE TASK

THE CALENDAR year of 2015 was punctuated with drama:
alien administrative deals in SportAccord; a windfall or two
from Olympic profits; an embarrassing bureaucratic divorce
and ramification from Oslo's bidding withdrawal; an apparent
bonus emerging from Agenda 2020 with five candidate cities
for 2022; confirmed corruption within two prime international
federations, FIFA and World Athletics; horrendously, the
revelation of systemic, government-manipulated doping across
five years, 2010 to 2014, by Russia; warnings of a potentially
incompetent first Games in South America in Rio. If Thomas
Bach had envied and finally acquired the top job, it had
suddenly become Himalayan: not to mention vexation for
this mundane commentator attempting to keep track news,
alternating garlands and avalanches.

To start in springtime. Riding what he no doubt liked to
feel was a friendly horse, Bach attended the UN's International
Day of Sport for Development and Peace, proudly proclaiming,
'Olympic principles are United Nations principles, we equally
need tolerance, solidarity and peace, living in a world full
of crises: political, financial, health, terrorists, war, ethnic
and religious conflict. Overcoming these obstacles requires
a concerted effort by all sectors of society. Agenda 2020 is
our particular answer to this requirement – we have to show
a sceptical world that we are living up to our responsibilities,

and Agenda 2020 addresses this need with a series of changes that increase transparency, improve governance and raise ethical standards. Many of these changes have already been implemented, while 90 per cent of IOC revenues are redistributed within sport worldwide, amounting to $3.25m a day, every day. We have strengthened our commitment to non-discrimination by amending Fundamental Principle 6 of our Charter to mirror the text of the UN's Universal Declaration of Human Rights.' Critics may mock Bach, yet virtue by association is as ancient as the prophet Moses.

At the general assembly of ASOIF in April at Sochi, during SportAccord's convention, the upgrading of grants arising from a financially outstanding Games at London 2012, found archery, for instance, see its share rise from $15m to $18m. The regrading would be in place for the respective shares for every IF arising at Rio. The approximate financial allocations were: Group A, $45m; Group B, $25m; Group C, $18m; Group D, £15m; Group E, variable. The IFs were graded as follows:

Group A unchanged – athletics, gymnastics, swimming

Group B unchanged – basketball, cycling, football, tennis, volleyball

Group C unchanged – rowing; promoted – archery, badminton, boxing, judo, table tennis, shooting, weightlifting

Group D unchanged – canoeing, fencing, sailing, taekwondo, triathlon, wrestling; demoted – equestrianism, handball, hockey

Group E demoted – modern pentathlon; new sports – golf, rugby sevens

Gross donations had risen from $296m at Beijing 2008 to $515m at London 2012. Allocations were at ASOIF's discretion rather than the IOC's.

The mood, however, within SportAccord's convention, was less comfortable with a bizarre, unpremeditated attack on the IOC and Bach by its president Marius Vizer of Romania.

Vizer accused Bach of blocking SportAccord's strategy, simultaneously condemning the new Olympic TV channel and asserting that Bach had interfered in the 'autonomy of sports organisations'. With mounting vanity, Vizer had granted his assembly the new title of 'SportAccord Convention of World Sport and Business Summit'. To Vizer's dismay, in the wake of Agenda 2020 and the economy, it was now ruled that host cities would no longer make presentations at SportAccord. The impact from his attack was instant, Bach observing, 'My impression is that your opinion is exclusively for you ... because many people have made constructive proposals which lead to closer collaboration between the IOC and IFs.'

Almost immediately, the IAAF became the first federation to resign its SportAccord membership, others swiftly following, with Vizer left in limbo despite an attempted apology. Worse for him was clandestine withdrawal of support from President Putin, a supposed friend, who had championed Vizer's election two years earlier. Now he withdrew the signing of a projected contract for consecutive SportAccord gatherings to be staged in three Russian cities, and ASOIF suspending its association with Vizer's assertive organisation. Vizer had viewed himself as an ersatz Castro, breaking free from an overlord neighbour. If Putin had a serious friend in sport, it was equivocally Bach: soon there in Moscow for the 80th birthday of Russia's IOC veteran Vitaly Smirnov, Bach being welcomed with no less than three photo ops with the state leader.

Onwards to July's Session in Kuala Lumpur, dominated by the election of a winter host for 2022 – overshadowed by the absence as a candidate of Oslo, leaving an awkward choice between two governmental autocracies, China and emerging, little-known Almaty of Kazakhstan – both of course welcomed by the IOC president in a show of optimism, but in reality a contest between an economic giant and an unknown. Here, if the IOC was prepared to recognise the opportunity, was a situation comparable to 1981, when outsider Seoul from the emerging South Korea dramatically outbid the seemingly preferred Nagoya of Japan. Hidden Kazakhstan, recently emerged from Soviet allegiance, was a crying opportunity for expansion, taking sport into a new realm of social, financial and political confidence: surely a move in line with Agenda 2020. Beijing, which would host ice events, snow sports being staged in Xhangjiakou halfway to Mongolia by train, would no doubt be viewed as the safe choice, never mind that any host city was now guaranteed the backing of a substantial IOC subsidy.

Yes, Kazakhstan was accused by some of remaining a dictatorship deficient in human rights, but in the presentation on the day, its bid vice-chairman Andrey Kryukov stubbornly asserted, 'Our country works hard to be better, our bid document guarantees observation of Article 6 of the Charter on Human Rights, and we will sign accordingly.' Almaty's message emphasised that its was a real sports venture, created ecologically by nature, uniquely compact within a 30-minute travel radius for athletes at every event. Host of a past Asian Winter Games, here was an ideal opportunity: in contrast to a prosaic presentation from the Chinese, which effectively amounted to a five-word assurance, 'Vote for us, we're big.' Almaty's mayor, Akmetzhan Yessimov, had rattled off a dozen coherent reasons why the voters should take notice of a bid that was more an investment than a gamble, 'We scrutinised 2020, our costs are low, over seven years, amounting to only 0.3 per cent of GDP. Nine of our 13 venues already exist, environmentally excluding any construction in the mountains. There will be no white elephant venues, our first metro line has already opened, hosting 2022 is part of a 15-year strategy branding Kazakhstan as an emerging nation.'

Perversely the voters opted for the safe bet, a contradiction of all that had been unanimously recommended by Agenda 2020 seven months earlier, and even with the evidence now outlined in the IOC's Evaluation Report: a potential for expanding the Winter Olympics market. With much of China's population unfamiliar with the majority of winter events, such as Nordic skiing, biathlon and ski jumping, there was the probability of seven years of limited publicity for a Winter Olympics event, as indeed would be proved. The Chinese made it by only the slimmest of margins: 44 votes to 40: three votes the other way and there would have been the first Olympic venue, summer or winter, in the vast expanse of Central Asia. But Beijing's message, 'You trusted us in 2008, trust us again,' frustratingly had proved overpowering.

A minor controversy was that one vote in Beijing's narrow majority had been illegal: that of Timothy Fok from Hong Kong, the allegiance of which to the China mainland made him ineligible to vote, but a protest from Almaty would have been vain and discourteous. The other, earlier contradiction had been a sensible but ignored recommendation by Dick Pound, past potential president, that account should have been taken of the flexibility introduced by Agenda 2020, and for the re-admission of Oslo, the withdrawal of which had been on financial grounds. Bach countered this plausible step by asserting that Almaty and Beijing had campaigned according to the rules then existing, and that the collapse of Oslo's interest had been on account of ineffectual domestic communication. By infinite good fortune, the four-vote margin would prove a saviour: in early 2022, Almaty's streets were ablaze with civic rioting against an autocratic dictatorship within the former Soviet Union.

In the wake of relative stagnation over 12 years in revision of the Olympic Programme by Rogge, expectation mounted for the potential in the Games of 2024; the first during Bach's presidency to have seven years' preparation and, in 2015, still two years away from the vote. There was at the time speculation about final sport content for Tokyo 2020: initially, the intention for two additions, a near certainty one of them being the return of baseball and softball, in Japan baseball holding equivalent prestige with football which had rapidly mushroomed with creation of the J.League in the 1990s. Such is the magnetism of Olympic inclusion that by the submission closing date of 8 June, to the Tokyo Additional Events Programme – which would reduce to a shortlist by the Executive Board by 22 June – there were 26 applications. Of these it could be said only 12 had credible status: baseball and softball, bowling, chess, indoor climbing, dance, karate, netball, orienteering, skateboarding, squash, surfing and tug of war. It was calculated Japan's preference would be baseball, softball and karate – which were indeed there on the EB's shortlist together with climbing, skateboarding and surfing. Yet amid Agenda 2020's 'flexibility', the ultimate inclusion, approved in the next year's Session at Rio, for what would become a Covid-conditioned Games of 2021, were all five – sadly, of course, with the continuing exclusion of squash (a fourth racquet sport). There would subsequently be the inclusion of breakdancing for 2024: contemporary and popular, but another judgemental sport barely distinguishable from the floor discipline of gymnastics. The most relevant of arrivals was undoubtedly skateboarding, by now universal across all age groups: at the 2013 Session in Buenos Aires, I had been all but run down twice a day on the pavement outside my hotel.

Buoyancy for the president's desired hosting enthusiasm escalated in September with announcement of five confirmed bids for 2024: Budapest, Hamburg, Los Angeles, Paris and Rome. In tune with Agenda 2020, the new host city contract was simultaneously published, together with confirmation of the IOC's subsidy of $1.7bn to the elected city. For those casual critics who imagine the IOC and Lausanne staff live a life of ease swanning around in limousines, the new contract had required 7,000 pages of technical manuals to be distilled into 350 pages: all candidates having to agree with the Agenda's 40 items, including the IOC's Code of Ethics; plus the essential non-discrimination clause. In an interview, Bach was queried by German TV ARD on the absence of a smaller city, in view of economy reform: his deflection that the five were 'diverse'. Germany's *Bild* newspaper worried about simultaneous Olympic Games and football's European Championship, which would be played across Europe. Bach responded that Germany 'was sufficiently robust'. Associated Press asked if there would be budget limits: answer, 'unenforceable', though city bidding 'launch' conferences were reduced from nine to three.

If Bach could be optimistic that future host city health might prosper, no such confidence was surrounding the following year's destination, Brazil: never mind the nation's escalating mineral wealth. Repeat alarm bells were ringing by the week, regarding finance, preparatory manpower, transport development, volunteers, plus a mounting threat from the freshwater virus Zika, a potential health hazard for water sports including long-distance swimming. With due warnings from both Bach and the Co-ordination Commission, Carlos Nuzman, chairman of the organising committee, was obliged in September to tour Europe, reassuring an anxious audience that financial and political problems were 'irrelevant'; the legacy for Brazilian sport, he insisted, was unquestionable, that water for aquatic sports would be 'as clear as freshly fallen rain'. Yet it was difficult for him to hold his nerve in face of the alarm expressed by both Bach and Co-ordination Commission chair Nawal El Moutawakel. Here was an echo of anxiety prior to Athens 2004, further emphasised a month later when Mario Andrada, Rio's director of communications, announced reductions of 30 per cent in infrastructure, in the volunteer programme, and in the extent of test sport events. The volunteer strength was to decrease by 15 per cent, with a severe reduction in the projected $3.6bn preparation budget, the national economy shrinking now by over two per cent. Bach, ever positive, refused to join the pessimists, asserting, 'Rio's situation is as always: great progress but no time to lose, credible advance with the Olympic Village and sports venues, and public transportation to be ready on time for a great legacy for the people of Rio.'

If Sochi's Winter Games were still considered, at this stage, to have been spectacular, the president was intent on an equally flamboyant inaugural South American festival in 'romantic' Rio. Nuzman had to be believed, even if there were past examples of dodgy conditions preceding several earlier Games such as those of Mexico 1968, Montreal 1976, Seoul 1988 and Athens 2004. Nonetheless, Nuzman's re-assurance remained equivocal. The potential glamour for Rio surrounded not merely social and some structural advance, but its raised sporting and cultural reputation across the world.

One of the most populous and industrious of nations, Brazil thus far in sport trailed far behind most major countries: spontaneously and exhilaratingly athletic by nature, yet predominantly obsessed only with a single sport in football. Annihilation at the previous year's World Cup at home to Germany had felt like national amputation. Now Brazil was heading towards an inaugural continental Games, with only distant familiarity with most of the sports, Nuzman admitting, 'We are a relatively young country – remember, we won the right to be hosts without even having an established stadium for Olympic sports. I believe we can generate wider social appetite in the future for all sports.' Prior to World War Two, Brazil had boasted only a single gold medal in 40 years: rapid-fire pistol by Guilherme Paraense at Antwerp 1920. In the first eight post-war Games, there were two golds, one silver and 12 bronze, though form advanced at Moscow 1980 and accelerated at Atlanta 1996, with 17th place in the medal tally; finally beginning to blossom at Athens, Beijing and London with a medal total of 42 including 11 golds. Prestige would be on the line in 2016, both sporting and social.

Anxious concerning the imminent findings by Dick Pound's investigation, Bach staged a 'summit' meeting in Lausanne in October 2015, together with Reedie, from which emerged a radical proposal: drug testing removed from national anti-doping bodies to independent laboratories, thereby separating the procedure from individual officials who might have vested interest or corrupt motives. As Pound observed, 'They've recognised the conflict between promoting sport and enforcing its rules.' The looming thunder cloud from December 2014 further exploded in early November: Pound presenting an early release – demonstrating that neither WADA nor IOC were withholding the truth – containing devastating details of Russia's internal conspiracy of technological camouflage. Besides formal laboratory chemical tampering to reverse positive tests, a shoal of cheating competitors from many sports, most conspicuously from track and field – long suspected in a broken sport which now faced disintegration of major competitions: worse, the upcoming Rio Games. The damage extended way beyond track and field IFs and competitors: a potential mortal blow upon sponsors who sustained many leading sports. If the revelations were a detonation landing on Bach's canvas of benevolent social integration through the medium of sport, the pain was more instant for the recently elected president of IAAF, Sebastian Coe. The IOC had immediately announced the suspension of past IAAF president Lamine Diack, pending criminal charges brought by French prosecution – through facts from Pound's commission passed to Interpol. WADA's leader Craig Reedie vainly tried to apply a silver brush to a portrait from Hades when suggesting, 'The investigation is hugely positive for clean athletes, as it contains significant recommendations on how WADA and its partners in the anti-doping community can take swift corrective action to ensure anti-doping programmes of the highest order are in place across the board.' This was less than reassuring; Reedie, ever well-intentioned, adding, 'Pound's commission contains findings that will shock athletes and fans worldwide, and many issues which highlight current deficiencies in Russia's anti-doping system.' No surprise there, in the wake of decades of suspicion surrounding the former USSR and like-minded autocracies such as GDR, Cuba, Bulgaria and elsewhere. Pound's personal announcement, from Geneva, had been characteristically frank:

'The present crisis in sport does not just stop with FIFA and IAAF. If the public view is that you cannot believe in results, this should cause all sports to face self-examination. A lot of people are going to have to walk the plank. The charges laid bare are indeed appalling, and clearly Russia should be suspended. The director of Moscow's testing laboratory destroyed 1,417 samples. London 2012 results were sabotaged. Five Russian athletes should have lifetime bans. Corruption amounted to State-supported doping, comparable to former GDR. Corruption was so prevalent that the Sports Minister was not possibly unaware. The Moscow laboratory should be disbanded and the director fired. RUSADA [the country's doping body] knew that coaches were out of control.'

Pound was not categoric that Russia could be unable to repair its disease in time to send a team to Rio, suggesting, 'If Russia do the surgery, they can still be there. If not, then that's the price of their neglect. They have the better part of a year, could do it, and I hope they can.' In response to doubts expressed by media about Coe's capability to lead IAAF's fight for survival, Pound stressed he was confident that Coe 'is the right man'. He stressed that his commission's findings had been accelerated to be in time for the following week's meeting of WADA in the USA; hoping that Russia would volunteer their own suspension prior to essential radical reform. 'If not, time will play itself out. If you want to participate, you accept the regulations.' Pound emphasised that the Commission had not been dealing with verbal evidence but documentary fact; that corruption could not have happened without national federation consent. 'It was worse than we expected.' His commission had invited Russia's minister of sport to meet them in Switzerland, stressing he would be unhappy with what they had to tell him, but hoping Russia would seize the opportunity 'to attack the problem which can destroy sport'.

The IAAF election back in August, between Coe and Ukraine rival Sergey Bubka – as successor to soon-to-be defamed Diack – had centred on future public credibility, even prior to Russia's drug exposure. The reputation of track and field was already rock bottom, riddled by predominantly cheating sprinters and throwers, but short on scientific evidence. Election manifestos of the pair pandered around 'development of grassroot coaches, sponsorship expansion, grants to minor countries', yet the fundamental context had to be about character: which of two candidates could rescue a sport by now sustained mainly through the imperishable brilliance of a single, avowedly clean athlete? Usain Bolt? Without diminishing the credibility of Bubka, a multiple pole vault record holder of agreeable disposition, the choice surely had to be Coe: equally exceptional athlete as middle distance icon, subsequently the mastermind of London 2012 (if I may here disregard a personal association over 40 years in collaboration with Coe on three books). As a *Sunday Times* editorial declared, 'Coe has it in him to be a great reforming president – to clean out the cheats and those who protect them in national federations.'

The outcome, a narrow margin by 12 votes for Coe: never mind having to ride widespread media allegations that he had been aware during the campaign of Diack's earlier corruption yet had given feigned retirement his approval. Hostility would have scuppered his own chance, would it not? Come December's revelation, Coe was confronted with a global rehabilitation project for his sport that arguably surpassed the extreme demands of both his own track career and direction of London 2012. A curt acknowledgement by Moscow's Ministry of Sport, in response to Pound's Commission, that 'appropriate measures will be adopted' was no more than a charade mask on the face of evil. Coe's immediate response to his sport's confirmed iniquity was typically simple, 'Whatever the frailties that may be revealed within the IAAF, we will fix it. If this means suspension of the Russian federation, yes we will.' Would Bach concur? An earth-shifting confrontation was at hand. Putin's press secretary Dmitry Peskov added fuel to furnace with a statement through the TASS agency that Pound's allegations 'were groundless, lacking evidence, without proof'.

Ten days after lightning's strike, Bach was addressing in Prague the general assembly of European Olympic Committees, and attempted to allay fears of collapsed civilisation: that WADA was resolved to make anti-doping procedures independent of sports organisations, and that therefore the EOC should consider three intended proposals:

Firstly, with an independent test and results management, sports federations should transfer their anti-doping systems to this new body.

Secondly, the independent body would establish an intelligence gathering unit, which would monitor compliance by associated agency laboratories.

Thirdly, sanctions to be pronounced exclusively by CAS, the right to appeal upheld.

Aware that the Olympic oyster pearl was flawed, Bach pronounced to the assembly, 'WADA will lead intelligence gathering funded by the IOC to make testing in the lead-up to Rio's Games as efficient and independent as possible. Out-of-competition testing during the Games will be guided by this intelligence group to make it more targeted, more effective. As in previous Olympic Games, WADA observers will supervise all aspects of the doping control programme during Rio's Games.' The sporting world held its breath, waiting to discover if promises rested on reliable foundations. Once again, it would not be a relaxed Christmas and new year for the IOC president.

Perversely, there was a ray of sunshine in Norway, where Lillehammer was about to host the Winter Youth Games. In common with every 'senior' Games, the former host city of 1994 would be dependent upon the assistant workforce of volunteers, currently some 3,000. Of that number, mostly students, 500 places had been allocated to young foreigners. And the number of applications for that opportunity to share the unique Norwegian bonhomie we all experienced in 1994, was beyond the gross total required. Heading foreign applicants were the former Soviet Union states: Russia 841, Azerbaijan

356, Ukraine 122, Belarus 110, plus Germany with 159. Also seeking to enjoy these low-budget Games were students from Britain, China, Georgia and Kazakhstan, more than 50 apiece, plus a host of others from Canada, Egypt, France, Kyrgyzstan, Poland, Switzerland and Tajikistan, plus a handful from India, Bosnia, Nigeria and Zimbabwe. As Inge Andersen, general secretary of Norway's NOC, reflected on this extension of the Olympic envelope, 'The numbers wanting to come to Norway reveals a splendid opportunity to get to know another part of the world, a knowledge of a nation for many beyond those attending as athletes.'

8

EVIL EXPOSED

IT WAS a tremulous new year: the prospect of Rio's Olympic Games ruptured by the scandal of Russia's malignant doping 'industry', and an unseemly likely squabble, legal or otherwise, over eligibility of 'Putin's puppets': whether collectively or individually guilty, or those technically innocent. The simmering malcontent which would be generated by the presence of past Russian drug cheat swimmer Yuliya Yefimova nullified the joy that would greet Fiji's rugby sevens champions, Usain Bolt, South Africa's Wayde van Niekerk and Mo Farah on track, all-time phenomena Simone Biles and Kōhei Uchimura in gymnastics. The figure at the heart of the IOC's perplexity, other than the president, was the convener of the charge sheet: Dick Pound, once again a reluctant yet emphatic adjudicator of sporting malevolence, this time on a scale beyond comprehension. And he was not mincing his words:

'Everyone in sport knew unofficially what had been going on. From USSR days, Putin was aware [of corrupt testing], and little had changed. But how bad was it? Uncertain, yet evidence from the gold-medal era of GDR had form: when the daily events programme of the Sydney Olympics had published the all-time track performances, they tended to be East German from the 1970s! Was I now surprised at what our investigation discovered? Well, not really, thanks to whistle-blowers, and now being able technically to have access to laboratory information, learning that there had been no such thing as a "surprise" test in Russia!'

The Pound commission found that Grigory Rodchenkov, head of the Moscow lab – and Seppelt's whistleblower – had destroyed 1,417 test samples prior to a WADA visit, Rodchenkov subsequently telling the *New York Times* that he had doped 15 medal winners in Sochi, giving details of swapped samples. Contrasting, divisive opinion would begin to take root within IOC ranks, that of WADA and of individual IFs: expel Russia outright, or be conciliatory towards athletes demonstrably not implicated in cheating? Bach himself would be walking an unenviable tightrope: alert, from his time as performer, to protection of honourable athletes, yet conscious of poisoned IOC credibility, further insinuated by media allegations of his known bonhomie with Putin as being a major Olympic 'player'. There were those who considered Bach's rhetoric in favour of resolute discipline against Russia was not ultimately matched by action: he retained the principle of justice for the innocent athlete.

Although as yet unaware of the full horror of institutional perversion, Bach was appreciative of Russia's creation of a sparkling new winter sports arena, 'That legacy was valuable, what Russia had achieved. Don't forget, they were not the first candidate originally for 2014, I'd been chair of the evaluation committee for the presentation in Guatemala. So Pound's investigation had indeed been a shock, and the first [Richard] McLaren investigation would alarmingly expand this. The IOC reaction all along was get the cheats, protect the clean, I didn't want any athlete simply punished by passport, but to maintain justice. Soon we realised there was no choice but to delegate eligibility through each IF, they would know who was clean, though in swimming they would go against our will and accept individuals who had previously been positive. The IOC never wanted to hide, and banked on IFs being compliant. It all became a very heated debate across two fronts, with so much under suspicion.'

The situation in early 2016 was, to an extent, that Bach unavoidably was being driven for the moment by responses from Putin: the Russian leader publicly admitting that their doping administration had to be overhauled, and Bach's response being optimistic that RUSADA was capable of achieving this under a necessarily re-established laboratory. For the moment, there was a wish not to antagonise Russia – never mind that WADA's Anti-Doping Rule Violation Report for 2014 revealed Russia as the leading doping offender with 148 failed tests. Seemingly immune to global offence, Russia was squeezing credibility, a ministerial announcement of a projected team of 400 athletes for Rio on a $7.6m training programme, with Coe already committed to suspending the track team.

Having advocated expulsion of IOC members 17 years earlier in the Salt Lake imbroglio, Pound was now unequivocal on Russia's collective guilt, as would be WADA, after a hesitant first reaction, and an adamant IAAF led by Coe. Pound stated, 'Everyone in Russian sport, from the top down, was part of the equation, all of them benefitted. WADA had all the information they needed, before Rio's Games, not to consider these were just "allegations", and it didn't make sense for a new damning exposé by Richard McLaren not to be released just before the Games.' Of which more later.

For the moment, Bach was metaphorically playing it cool, with a new year beam of goodwill, embracing the prospects for Rio, 'The message of Agenda 2020 was change or be changed. Events of the last 12 months indicate this is ever more urgent, to safeguard the credibility of sports organisations, and to protect clean athletes. Recent events in some sports cast a shadow across the world's expectations. It is a shared response to provide answers. Most of the Agenda reforms have already been implemented, the principle of good governance applied, our code published for the prevention of competition manipulation, the protection of clean athletes and sanctioning of doped athletes independent from sports organisations, our focus in the road ahead.' This included a January visit to the Refugee Reception Centre in Athens, partially aided by a $2m IOC emergency fund, and refugees to be included in the Torch Relay circuit. Bach had initiated the prospect of a Refugee Team, funded by scholarships, participating in Rio's Opening Ceremony, 'We want to give refugees the opportunity of coming together and creating their own small Olympic community in the competition.'

A bigger Olympic community was gathering meanwhile in Lillehammer for the Youth Winter Games, coincidentally under assessment by Turkish IOC member Uğur Erdener, chairman of a working group to evaluate the event's relevance. Angela Ruggiero, US hockey Olympic champion, considered these Games 'not so much a mini Olympics as a lesson in life, exposing 15- to 18-year-olds to lifetime ideals – and for the IOC twofold, cultural education alongside brand experimentation with programme events, in a Games conducted strictly according to budget'. Norway's organising committee had exemplified Scandinavia's style of tidy socialist modesty. King Harald unostentatiously fronted a full-house Opening Ceremony crowd of 14,000: an illustration of the orderly opportunity squandered by Oslo's imprudent, avoidable political withdrawal as candidate for the major event of 2022. Some 11,000 competitors paraded, vying for 15 events, traditionally led by Greece and the cauldron lit by Princess Ingrid Alexandra, daughter of Crown Prince Haakon, who had done so in 1994. The Russian flag-bearer was composed: no wish to exclude a disgraced NOC from this benevolent youth integration.

The media precursors of agitprop were busier, attempting to lasso IAAF president Seb Coe for being disqualified to haul the federation out of its perceived pit of iniquity with their litany of false smear accusations against him: these even including allegations by the House of Commons Select Committee for Culture, Media and Sport on issues legally beyond their remit. This committee absurdly compared Coe's 'lack of curiosity', regarding retired president Lamine Diack's corruption, with the BBC's infamous failure to expose the wanton paedophilia of a famous TV presenter. Notwithstanding media malevolence, Coe had published in January a 20,000-word manifesto for rehabilitation of his beleaguered sport, promising, 'Changes will ensure the recent past can never happen again. Be under no illusion about how seriously I take these issues ... the federation is under serious scrutiny. My vision is to create a sport that attracts more young people, who once more can trust competing on a level playing field, with the proposal for a new constitution scheduled for the campaign of 2017 brought forward to this year ... there not being a single person named in Pound's investigation who has not already been sanctioned. Whatever President Putin may predict, or Thomas Bach, there is no certainty that the Russian federation will be compliant in time for Rio. It's a matter of only if and when. People forget I was driving for creation of our Ethics Commission way before WADA's appointment of Pound's investigation. Remember, in 2007 the IAAF adopted the Athlete Blood Passport 11 months before WADA guidelines.' Coe was leading virtue's pace-setters.

Meanwhile, meeting Russia's NOC president Alex Zhukov in Lausanne, Bach was guardedly optimistic that WADA and IAAF in conjunction might ensure compliance within Russia in time for Rio's Games. Bach's view was prompted by a deceptive early demand from Putin, subsequently hollow, 'For immediate attention, the most open and proficient collaboration with anti-doping agencies. We in Russia must do everything to eliminate this problem ... The Sports Ministry must give this matter immediate attention within the framework of our Federal Targeted Programme for 2016–2020.' Nice idea, if true.

Concurrent with the urgent appointment in mid-May of additional investigation by Professor Richard McLaren, the IOC were intent on raising the fight against cheats with a re-testing of 454 selected doping samples way back from Beijing

2008, and simultaneously 250 samples from London 2012, particular emphasis being on medal winners from both Games. Whatever critics might allege, Bach was on the warpath as he said, 'All these measures are a powerful strike against cheats, who shall have no place to hide. The re-tests from 2008 and 2012 follow the worrying allegations from Sochi. By confronting many doped athletes planning participation in Rio, we will demonstrate our will to protect the integrity of the Olympics, especially the anti-doping laboratory in Rio.'

The IOC was further supporting the Global Declaration Against Corruption, adopted at an international summit recently organised by then-British prime minister David Cameron, where the IOC was represented by Sir Philip Craven, president of the Paralympics, and IOC Ethics Commission leader Pâquerette Girard Zappelli. Aware of global anxiety, Bach released an extended statement in May stressing the IOC's anxiety to obliterate abuse, saying that if allegations were true, it revealed shocking new dimensions in doping, and indeed criminality: that the IOC and IFs would have to make the difficult decision between collective responsibility and individual justice, and reminding the public that already the previous year there had been a move to make the anti-doping system independent from sports organisations, 'With all these measures within our zero-tolerance policy, we would prove that protection of clean athletes, from corruption, manipulation and suspicion, is the focus of our effort. Because of my athlete's background, I understand emotional requests from many athletes who stand for fair play. We must give fair procedure to everybody.'

In a teleconference of the Executive Board, Bach related that in mid-May immediate action had been requested from WADA in what had become the IOC's most vital activity since the Extraordinary Session of 2000 with revision of the Charter in the wake of the Salt Lake scandal.

Unknowingly in line with Putin's false prospect of internal discipline would be later sane advice from an international lawyer familiar with Moscow's ministry of sport: François Carrard. This was that Russia's response to malignant detail – yet to come in July in a further bombshell exposure by Pound's Canadian colleague McLaren – should be to accept the truth of the accusations, incalculably damaging; make a dignified exit and not provocatively challenge the findings, simultaneously suggesting to the IOC that Russia's NOC be immediately suspended but given, say, six months to reconstitute their administration: for the IOC not to be dependent on arbitrary decisions by CAS of Russia's eligibility for Rio. Such cold reasoning would have been legally adroit and wise on both sides, yet emotions were far too intense under the focus of global scrutiny. Russia's wilful political deceit, and Bach's inherently protective instinct on behalf of the genuinely innocent, provoked a drama that would screechingly evolve over the next six months to the satisfaction of neither camp; not that the guilty were ever of a mind to relent.

Craig Reedie, head of WADA, recalls, 'By May our situation had become acute, and it wasn't just in athletics but the whole of Russian sport. Initially there was a mood within the IOC to delay release of McLaren's investigation until after the Rio Games, but in WADA we said no, we recommend a deadline on the question of Russia's entry, and it was then that Thomas decided to pass judgement on individuals to respective IFs. When Russia was not unilaterally banned, we could hear the thunder of media protest. When WADA held a teleconference, it was apparent that five IOC members present remained strangely silent. We knew that Thomas considered Russia such a significant country in the framework of the Olympic Movement, but within WADA we were not in the mood to compromise.'

Francesco Ricci Bitti, head of ASOIF, and present in the teleconference, was conscious it was too early for WADA to take a unilateral drastic step on the issue of discipline, on authority or athlete, collective or individual. 'We were in such a new situation, there needed to be sympathy for all sports. It was difficult for an IF to ban entire teams, to "suspend Russia", and in many instances we would have lost an appeal lodged with CAS, and the escalation of legal costs could have been prohibitive.'

When Russia's athletic federation had been suspended by IAAF in November 2015, sports minister Vitaly Mutko had predicted it would take only a couple of months to become again compliant with WADA's code. Vain ambition. Further revelations by Seppelt showed that Anna Anzelovich, the new head of RUSADA, was recorded as informing athletes in advance of dope testing dates. Pound's report exposed Mutko himself directing manipulation of test samples, and intimidation of laboratory operators. Of equal alarm for Coe would have been a comment from the IAAF anti-doping department, 'Nobody should be surprised by the culture, it works for Russia, for Ukraine, Belarus and Kazakhstan, for all the former Soviet nations.' It was from publication in May 2016 in the USA of allegations by Rodchenkov, that WADA had evidence of Russian state involvement which could be investigated by McLaren, and that this was immediately initiated.

Amid the global gloom in early June came Bach's announcement of a formal Refugee Team to participate in Rio, gathered in collaboration with the UN High Commission for Refugees. Announcing this unique formation, Bach proclaimed, 'The team can send a symbol of hope around the world. Our ambition is that such a team should become established, that they and other refugees can become absorbed by host countries.' The *chef de mission* was to be Olympian and former marathon world record holder Tegla Loroupe of Kenya; Geraldo de Moraes Bernardes of Brazil the head coach. The team would be Rami Anis (male), origin Syria, host NOC of Belgium, swimming; Yiech Pur Biel (m), Sudan, host Kenya, track 800m; James Chiengjiek (m), Sudan, host Kenya, track 400m; Yonas Kinde (m), Ethiopia, host Luxembourg, marathon; Anjelina Lohalith (f), Sudan, host Kenya, track

1,500m; Rose Lokonyen (f), Sudan, host Kenya, track 800m; Paulo Amotun Lokoro (m), Sudan, host Kenya, track 1,500m; Yolande Mabika (f), Congo, host Brazil, judo 70kg; Yusra Mardini (f), Syria, host Germany, swimming; Popole Misenga (m), Congo, host Brazil, judo 90kg. The team would be accommodated in the Village, with a welcome ceremony, IOC uniforms, competing under the Olympic flag. All costs met by Olympic Solidarity.

On 17 June, IAAF reconfirmed their November suspension of Russia's track federation, following news of continuing failure of doping tests in Russia and lack of laboratory compliance. Rune Andersen, head of IAAF's doping task force and a former WADA director, said that on legal advice 'a crack in the door' was being left for Russian athletes who could prove they had been training outside the country, and would compete under a neutral banner, these including another whistle-blower in Yuliya Stepanova. Andersen added, 'Because the system in Russia has been tainted from the top down, we can't trust that what we might call clean athletes are clean.' A new WADA report had disclosed that, even since Russia had been suspended, 736 tests under supervisory conditions had nonetheless been cancelled.

The next day, in the wake of IAAF retention of Russia's suspension, Bach summoned his four IOC vice-presidents, two IF leaders – Coe and Julio Maglione of Uruguay, president of FINA – Patrick Hickey of European NOCs, Erdener of Turkey from the medical commission and Russian IOC member Zhukov, to assess whether IAAF's ban of Russia's athletic federation was acceptable. What about rowers, swimmers, weightlifters and the rest in a 28-sport spectrum? The summit was consultative, not rule-making, having to bear in mind that under Charter regulations eligibility for any Games is determined by each IF, a principle widely understood and respected. Indeed, recognised in commentary by *The Times*, 'A legal manoeuvre to protect those genuinely innocent from the manipulative guilty.' The summit would advocate the principle of individual eligibility, case by case, by respective IFs; ignoring such random comments as that by IOC vice-president John Coates that 'Russia is rotten to the core', and habitual prejudice from US sources long inhabiting a proverbial glass house.

If it seemed Russia's position could not become even more bleak, it did so a month later on 18 July: the publication of McLaren's WADA-requested investigation of Rodchenkov's allegations: a 97-page report following a 57-day legal sprint, itself reviewing thousands of documents, forensic analysis of urine sample bottles, and other items. The report concluded 'beyond reasonable doubt' that the Ministry of Sport and the WADA-accredited Moscow laboratory 'had operated for the protection of doped Russian athletes within a state-directed failsafe system using the "Disappearing Positive-test Methodology"'. The report calculated that DPM had operated from late 2011 to August 2015, used on 643 positive samples: a number calculated to be only a minimum, due to limited access. WADA president Craig Reedie admitted the timing of the release was destabilising so close to Rio's Games, but recognised the need for action without delay, 'Given the seriousness of the revelations, WADA has facilitated the transfer of relevant information, concerning individual athletes from the McLaren investigation, to international federations. It should be noted that Professor McLaren's focus was intent on establishing State involvement more than individual athletes' benefit.' A tetchy reaction from the IOC president was that the WADA's release inflamed controversy around the IOC, Bach saying, 'We cannot be made responsible either for the timing or the reasons of these revelations, which we are now having to address so close to the opening of the Games.' The details of McLaren's investigation, which would have stretched the imagination of crime novelist Agatha Christie, were stark:

'Individuals who were identified to give interview were fearful of speaking. The commission uncovered a system for doping athletes by senior coaching officials ... by corruption of officials under direction of RUSADA ... assisted by informed medical personnel. Coaches were using familiar systems with anabolic steroid without understanding the outcome; this became evident in the Athlete Blood Passport, but was not initially understood in Russia. The WADA accreditation laboratory was controlled by the state ... if manipulative doping control failed, the lab's role was to make the positive result "disappear". The Soviet laboratory urine-swapping scheme was unique ... a greater systematic scheme operated by Moscow Laboratory for false reporting of positive samples was supported by Disappearing Positive Methodology ... efficiently directed under Deputy Minister of Sport to force the laboratory to report any positive test as negative.

'The DPM followed abysmal medal count at Vancouver Games. A new deputy minister of sport, Yuri Nagornykh, member of NOC, was appointed in 2010 by order of President Putin to report to Mutko. Nagornykh determined who would benefit from cover-up and who would not be protected; all positives were reported to Nagornykh and labelled "save" or "quarantine" ... the former to be reported "negative", the laboratory then falsifying the screen result to show negative. Surreptitious removal of urine sample bottle caps developed at Sochi to replace positive samples. The DPM in operation at IAAF Championships 2013; investigation confirmed bottle-tops could be removed without evidence visible to the naked eye, allowing athletes to compete while "dirty", through sample swapping. Co-ordination of the system by Irina Rodionova, deputy director of the Centre for Sports Preparation of National Teams, subordinate of the minister of sport, Rodionova also on NOC staff for London 2012. Rodionova would co-ordinate freezing of clean urine samples for subsequent swapping with dirty samples. Whistle-blower Rodchenkov provided credible evidence that exchanging "clean" and "dirty" bottles would pass through a secure zone, where clean urine from the freezer would be exchanged, and the process reversed ... Rodchenkov's role to ensure the matching of specific gravity of exchanged urine on the Department Control Form.'

On 21 July, the Court of Arbitration for Sport rejected the appeal by Russia's NOC and 68 track and field athletes to compete at Rio, this ban originally implemented in November 2015. The same day, WADA, now increasingly under fire for its 'zero-tolerance' attitude, received a much-needed message of confidence from 19 European sports ministers. In an informal statement initiated by Denmark, they underlined support for WADA and invited comparable support elsewhere, in contrast to Bach, who in a media conference had partially blamed WADA for escalation of the crisis. The European message stated, 'While respecting autonomy of the sports movement, we consider in relation to recent events that it is important to emphasise our support for the work of WADA, and the rights of clean athletes to perform in a doping-free environment. We call upon all states that have signed the UNESCO International Convention against doping to fully comply, through evidence, with the Convention's principles, and upon all sports organisations to fully comply with WADA in promotion of initiatives to protect integrity and clean athletes.'

On 24 July, however, the IOC rejected WADA's recommendation to ban Russia from the Games, announcing the decision would be made by each IF, that decision then to be approved by CAS as arbitrator. Reedie expressed disappointment in the light of McLaren's profound evidence. The Executive Board's decision stated, 'The IOC will not accept entry of any Russian athlete without the following provisions: acceptance from his or her IF in relation to WADA code, and provision of an anti-doping test with analysis of each athlete's anti-doping record, the Russian NOC prohibited from entering any athlete who has ever been sanctioned, and any Russian athlete ultimately accepted subject to additional out-of-competition testing.'

In this most profound IOC crisis since the Arab–Israeli massacre during the Munich Games of 1972, existential opinion was distinctly divided, respectively led by two articulate lawyers: by Bach, from his own experience as frustrated Olympian intent that justice for any innocent Russian competitor was as imperative as damnation for institutional cheating, and by Pound, former would-be president, adamant in harmony with his compatriot McLaren and WADA, that Putin's governmental mafia had so comprehensively shamed both domestic and world sport that the nation deserved total exclusion. Just as, say, two red cards in football effectively destroy nine innocent colleagues. Nonetheless, Bach remained resolute, announcing, 'This blanket ban of Russia has been called by some the "nuclear option", and innocent athletes would have to be considered as collateral damage. Leaving aside that such a comparison is completely out of proportion within the rules of sport, let us consider the consequence of a nuclear option. The cynical collateral damage is not what the Olympic Movement represents. If CAS upholds the IAAF ban, most observers expect it will increase the pressure on the IOC to consider a broader ban on all Russians. But Pound, who is also a former president of WADA, believes the IOC will not budge [this was true, although Pound in fact believed in such a ban]. I have the impression that the IOC is reluctant to think about total exclusion, even though there exists institutionalised cheating on a wide scale across a whole range of sport in that country.'

Though aware of the IOC's inclination, Pound warned of the dangers of inaction, 'I think the Olympics have to be careful, having said for so long, "We have zero tolerance," and should avoid turning that into "zero tolerance except for Russia". If you do take the tough line and walk the walk, I think a significant portion of the world would be pleased.'

Bach exercised his authority on 30 July in partnership with the Executive Board, installing a three-man emergency panel to determine Russian athlete approval in compliance with CAS adjudication, following individual IF recommendation. The three were Claudia Bokel, Germany's IOC Athletes Commission chair; Turkey's IOC Medical Commission chair

Erdener; and Juan Antonio Samaranch (Junior) of Spain. They would be dependent on mutual agreement from CAS, Bach believing this was the only way to demonstrate that the IOC were still in charge.

Two days later, in his address at the opening of the 129th IOC Session, Bach would re-emphasise his egalitarian judicial principle. The assembled audience of the Olympic Movement – IOC members, NOCs, IFs, WADA – accepted in near silence his long-standing conviction, 'Justice has to be independent from politics. Whoever responds to a violation of the law with another violation is destroying justice.' He was testing members' credulity when claiming that 'the Russian side has not yet been heard'. His address concluded on an upbeat, welcoming the launch of the new Olympic TV channel at the conclusion of the Games, 'Young people are going to be living in a new digital reality, and this is the way we need to go. Here in Rio, together with the people, the IOC has faced enormous challenges, but we never gave up. Rio is ready to deliver history.'

Inevitably showing signs of stress – who would not have? – Bach sought once more to unload some of the blame for administrative chaos upon luckless, enduring WADA at a fraught media interview – never mind WADA being 50 per cent funded by IOC, and a third of its executive being IOC members. With only five days to go to the opening of the Games at the Maracanã Stadium, Bach was on edge with the media, they eager as ever in crocodile mode to seize upon morsels. Asked if the Russian crisis amounted to 'a Games failure for the IOC', Bach responded, 'The IOC is not responsible for the timing of the McLaren report, nor for the fact that different information which was offered to WADA a couple of years ago was not utilised. The IOC is not responsible for the accreditation or supervision of anti-doping laboratories, so therefore the IOC cannot be made responsible either for the timing or the reasons for these incidents which we have now had to face prior to the Games.'

There was no chance for a Reedie riposte. Asked if this was the outbreak of a new Cold War in sports, the WADA president deferred the moment for analysis, 'Not now, after the Games there will be more time to address these affairs of emotional and passionate debate.' Yet in no way could WADA be held responsible for unprecedented Russian evil, the extent of this having been surgically laid bare only a couple of weeks earlier. Now under the exhaustive scrutiny of WADA, IFs and CAS, together with the Executive Board club-of-three, the ultimate Russian contingent acceptable for competition was going to be a slim 282 athletes in 26 sports. Bach was caught between the proverbial rock and a hard place.

From amid the stress of the past six months, Bach's relatively brief address at the Opening Ceremony brought two moments of particular relief: recognition of the Refugee Team, and presentation of an inaugural Olympic Laurel to legendary Kip Keino, once a contemporary athlete with Bach four decades earlier, and dedicated philanthropist for children back home in Kenya. Perhaps through fatigue, it was for Bach a comparatively brief address, reminding everyone, 'In this Olympic world we are all equal. We see that the values of our shared humanity are stronger than the forces which want to divide us. So I call upon you, Olympic athletes, respect each other and the values which make the Olympic Games unique for the whole world. We are living in a time when selfishness is gaining ground, where some claim to be superior to others, and here is our answer: in the spirit of Olympic solidarity, we welcome the Refugee Olympic Team. Dear refugee athletes, you are sending a message of hope to the many millions of refugees around the globe. You had to flee from your homes because of violence, hunger, or just because you are different. Now with your talent and spirit you are making a great contribution to society.

'There are millions around the world who contribute to make it a better place. To honour such outstanding personalities, the IOC has created a new distinction which we award for the first time. In recognition of his outstanding achievements in the field of education, culture, development and peace through sport, in the true Olympic spirit this Olympic Laurel is awarded to that great champion and philanthropist, Mr Kipchoge Keino. And now let us all celebrate together the Olympic Games *a la* Brazil.'

Rio's administration lived hand-to-mouth throughout their Games, Bach and colleagues not knowing where mayhem might next strike, the favela slums barely conscious of the world's favourite festival. Bach today admits, 'Administratively, every day was a crisis, on the edge – financial issues, mostly minor rather than major, one night having to change the field of play rather than otherwise halt the next day's event. The ticket situation was uncomfortable, sometimes holders not getting access, security not efficient. Yet the wider public should not really be worried too much by such problems. Our job in the IOC is not to complain, we're here to help both athletes and public. It's a kind of mirage, admin crises are not the same as athletes' trophies: the athletes are OK so long as we deliver a successful Games.'

There were as ever many memorable performances, not least by diminutive Fiji, as recollected by rugby sevens captain Osea Kolinisau in the wake of a gold medal gallop against Great Britain in the innovative tournament:

'Rio will never be forgotten, I will cherish the memory for the rest of my life – my first Olympics, the time rugby was re-introduced, the first time we Fijians had won a medal, and that it was gold. I am thankful to God, who has been our source of strength and victory … I never dreamt of becoming an Olympian, let alone a medallist, supposing that the closest I would ever get was in front of a television set just trying to imitate the athletes. We would race on the road with friends, or jump in the water and imagine we were champions. Entering the Olympic Village was an eye-opener, getting to mix with different athletes, professionals whom you normally watch on television, having Rafa Nadal walk past you in the dining hall, meeting NBA stars at the Opening Ceremony, discovering why it's the mecca of sports. Being Fiji's flag-bearer was a humbling honour, having Serena Williams take a selfie of us together sealed a rare moment. When we kicked off in earnest, we knew we needed to have fire in our heart but ice in our mind.'

Twenty minutes before Usain Bolt was to win his third straight 100m title, Wayde van Niekerk of South Africa projected himself as a target for the future with his spectacular 400m world record, lowering Michael Johnson's 17-year-old peak with 43.03s, the only man outside the US ever to have come within half a second of Johnson's 43.18s. What made his achievement the more remarkable was that, drawn in lane eight, he did not see another runner during the entire race. While events confirmed Bolt was no longer the Achilles of 2008 and 2009, he remained unequivocally the master – sometimes even with a smile. Now came a unique third 100m title, for him a modest 9.81s, leaving in his wake controversial, previously suspended American Justin Gatlin. If there were other reputations to sustain, none was pitched higher than Mo Farah's, the Somali-born distance runner who had become as engagingly British as a London bus. What he now created was a distinguished club of two: alongside legendary Finn Lasse Virén, achiever of the double-double of 10,000m and 5,000, in 1972 and 1976. Farah's summit now shared with Virén's survival of a fall in the 10,000m, climbing off the floor to retain his title. Being an Olympian is an honour, becoming a champion a triumph, defending a title supreme: David Rudisha of Kenya with modesty did the latter in the 800m, his 1:42.15 the fastest in four years but just short of his world record in London.

Of all Olympic sports, gymnastics offers the ultimate voyeuristic fishbowl in which every performer is subjected to prolonged scrutiny, the tiniest error apparent and influential. Now there was conflicting focus between two exceptional gymnasts, man and woman: diminutive American Simone

Biles, so athletically engaging that she overshadowed near-perfect all-round defending champion Kōhei Uchimura of Japan. Uchimura, less demonstrative than exuberant Biles, nonetheless gave evidence that he was maybe the best his sport had ever known, though there was parallel acclaim for the esoteric American girl, with her muscular capacity to project her short frame nine feet into the air, creating an aura on a par with past legends Korbut and Comăneci. Michael Phelps, swimming's foremost celebrity, was moved to say – on account of equivocal jurisdiction for Rio by the IF – that he doubted whether he had ever competed in a totally clean event. Mack Horton, Australian rival in their 400m freestyle final, denounced Chinese counterpart Sun Yang as a cheat, refusing to withdraw condemnation after protest from China's NOC. Sun had served a three-month ban in 2014. The British head coach was dismayed by several UK swimmers missing a medal behind known offenders accredited by FINA. Targeted by rival women was Russian Yulia Yefimova, banned for 16 months in 2013 for anabolic steroids. Fiona Doyle of Ireland, failing to qualify in a heat behind Yefimova, protested, 'She has tested positive five times and got away with it … there are signs all over the village saying this is a clean sport, and it's not.'

A *Sydney Morning Herald* commentator had nicely observed that, in Brazil, 'There are games and there's *the* game.' He might have said the only game. In Rio's varying emotional involvement in a multiple sports festival with much of which they were unfamiliar, football, both men's and women's, were the high moments. For the men's final, as the fortnight moved towards its close, the country metaphorically stood still – and not just because it was a repeat of the semi-final encounter in the World Cup two years earlier, in which Germany had lashed seven goals against a nation whose heart beats with the referee's whistle. If these Olympics mattered to Rio, then football mattered more than anything. Even before kick-off there existed in the stadium that fabulous mood that graces

Brazilians: expectation provoking a sense of ennoblement. They are living just for this: not least because four years previously in London they had surrendered to Mexico at Wembley. For 120 minutes the tension was electric. Neymar, a legend with Barcelona but burdened with criticism for earlier unadventurous displays, now gave hint of becoming his nation's idol, and did so with a genius of a free kick to give Brazil the lead. Germany soon levelled: national pulse rate soared as a penalty shoot-out became necessary. In a perfect script, Neymar scored the decisive kick; the nation could breathe again.

It had been a fraught, occasionally fractured festival, sometimes in the arena, regularly behind the scenes in administration: no one could have been more relieved than the IOC president when closure arrived for this historic inaugural South American pinnacle. In his closing speech, Bach was, inevitably and doggedly, upbeat, 'These were marvellous Games in *the* marvellous city. They are leaving a unique legacy: history will talk about a Rio de Janeiro beforehand, and a much better Rio after the Games. The IOC would like to honour those who made this happen. One hundred and ten years ago, the founder of the modern Games, Pierre de Coubertin, created a unique award – the Olympic Cup. Tonight, this cup goes to the cariocas! The IOC has invited six of you to accept this Olympic Cup … I now call upon the youth of the world to assemble four years hence in Tokyo, Japan.' For a reformist president, those years, like the immediate past, were going to be no siesta.

RIO 2016 MEDALS
United States 121 (46-37-38)
Great Britain 67 (27-23-17)
China 70 (26-18-26)
Russia 56 (19-17-20)
Germany 42 (17-10-15)
Japan 41 (12-8-21)
France 42 (10-18-14)

South Korea 21 (9-3-9)
Italy 28 (8-12-8)
Australia 29 (8-11-10)
Netherlands 19 (8-7-4)
Hungary 15 (8-3-4)
Brazil 19 (7-6-6)
Spain 17 (7-4-6)
Kenya 13 (6-6-1)
Jamaica 11 (6-3-2)
Croatia 10 (5-3-2)
Cuba 11 (5-2-4)
New Zealand 18 (4-9-5)
Canada 22 (4-3-15)
Uzbekistan 13 (4-2-7)
Kazakhstan 18 (3-5-10)
Colombia 8 (3-2-3)
Switzerland 7 (3-2-2)
Iran 8 (3-1-4)
Greece 6 (3-1-2)
Argentina 4 (3-1-0)
Denmark 15 (2-6-7)
Sweden 11 (2-6-3)
South Africa 10 (2-6-2)
Ukraine 11 (2-5-4)
Serbia 8 (2-4-2)
Poland 11 (2-3-6)
North Korea 7 (2-3-2)
Belgium 6 (2-2-2)
Thailand 6 (2-2-2)
Slovakia 4 (2-2-0)
Georgia 7 (2-1-4)
Azerbaijan 18 (1-7-10)
Belarus 9 (1-4-4)
Turkey 8 (1-3-4)
Armenia 4 (1-3-0)
Czech Republic 10 (1-2-7)
Ethiopia 8 (1-2-5)
Slovenia 4 (1-2-1)
Indonesia 3 (1-2-0)
Romania 4 (1-1-2)

Bahrain 2 (1-1-0)
Vietnam 2 (1-1-0)
Chinese Taipei 3 (1-0-2)
Bahamas 2 (1-0-1)
Independent Olympic Athletes 2 (1-0-1)
Ivory Coast 2 (1-0-1)
Fiji 1 (1-0-0)
Jordan 1 (1-0-0)
Kosovo 1 (1-0-0)
Puerto Rico 1 (1-0-0)
Singapore 1 (1-0-0)
Tajikistan 1 (1-0-0)
Malaysia 5 (0-4-1)
Mexico 5 (0-3-2)
Venezuela 3 (0-2-1)
Algeria 2 (0-2-0)
Ireland 2 (0-2-0)
Lithuania 4 (0-1-3)
Bulgaria 3 (0-1-2)
India 2 (0-1-1)
Mongolia 2 (0-1-1)
Burundi 1 (0-1-0)
Grenada 1 (0-1-0)
Niger 1 (0-1-0)
Philippines 1 (0-1-0)
Qatar 1 (0-1-0)
Norway 4 (0-0-4)
Finland 1 (0-0-1)
Morocco 1 (0-0-1)
Nigeria 1 (0-0-1)
Portugal 1 (0-0-1)
Trinidad and Tobago 1 (0-0-1)
United Arab Emirates 1 (0-0-1)
Egypt 3 (0-0-3)
Tunisia 3 (0-0-3)
Israel 2 (0-0-2)
Austria 1 (0-0-1)
Dominican Republic 1 (0-0-1)
Estonia 1 (0-0-1)

9

DOUBLE-CITY CELEBRATION

A ROUGH ride has been unsurprising for any IOC president, not excluding de Coubertin himself. Following the inaugural Games of 1896, querulously accepted by a Greek government influenced by internationalist moderator Vikelas, the founder was at the helm for five Games: two uncertain celebrations, at his home in Paris and absent from St Louis, prior to London and Stockholm creating a durable framework and acclaimed reputation (if ignoring London's prejudiced exclusive judging) followed by Antwerp and again Paris.

De Coubertin's successor, Belgian banker Baillet-Latour, uncomfortably straddled a threatened boycott of Hitler's rampant fascism at Berlin 1936. Masterful Swedish industrialist Edström adroitly steered post-World War One inclusion of the revolutionary Soviet Union at London 1948. Dogmatic, amateur-idealist, Chicago property magnate Avery Brundage financially subsidised IOC's mini-office continuity; jockeyed conflicting goodwill and lamentable public relations when confronted by warring IFs and NOCs, through Rome, Tokyo and Mexico, prior to two social time bombs from South Africa's apartheid and Munich's Arab terrorism.

Clubbable, genial, under-funded Irishman Michael Killanin stumbled on apartheid protest at Montreal, and then on Moscow's Cold War relations. A visionary Samaranch, intuitive Franco-apologist integrator, stabilised a near-bankrupt club thanks to transformative economics at Los

Angeles 1984; he recognised, too, the existence both of women members and then professionalism by 1988, but not some of the strands of geographic prejudice and financial greed disfiguring Barcelona 1992 and the centenary Games of Atlanta 1996, which preceded the worse Salt Lake scandal of 1999. Bland, provincial Belgian medic Rogge protected the IOC's piggybank and its entrenched conservatism through Salt Lake, Athens, Beijing and London: seemingly unaware during 12 mostly storm-free years that a dignified 19th-century old boys' club urgently required 21st-century management revision.

Thomas Bach had long perceived he was the man needed for the emerging digital and litigious age, with a sedate takeover, legally sound. Four years into office and the hazards had reached parallel levels of readjustment and potentially crippling setbacks: realisation of Agenda 2020 objectives, alongside government-ordained cheating. The emotional demand, extending across the remainder of 2016 and the whole of the following year, would require all of his calm but resolute drive. Concealed state immorality confronting the IOC was not swiftly to be erased, either before or following Rio's Games and the Paralympics event, from which – in contrast to Bach's legally guided, individual IF eligibility scrutiny for the prime event – Russia had been summarily expelled by leader Philip Craven, describing Russia's conduct as 'disgusting'. In response to this acclaimed decision, Valentina Matviyenko, speaker of the Kremlin's upper parliamentary chamber, dismissed the penalty as 'cruel and inhumane, jeopardising not only Russia but the whole world's sports community, holding hostage the Paralympic Movement through immoral and destructive political games'.

Such is the power of political indoctrination: when I had travelled by Trans-Siberian rail to Japan for Tokyo's Games in 1964, a charming schoolteacher guide in her 20s, during a stopover in the capital Khabarovsk, had assured me categorically, 'USSR and Britain certainly were not allies in World War Two.' Really? The teacher's duty was the perfunctory but obligatory removal of me from my hotel for KGB inspection of my luggage (my notes on prospective Olympic high jump winner Valery Brumel?). However, the outburst of Mme Matviyenko in 2017 was in conflict with Putin's deputed 'salvation commission' led by Vitaly Smirnov: an attempt to collaborate with intense WADA activity to 'sanitise' a newly appointed RUSADA and the Moscow laboratory.

In December 2016 came publication of McLaren's extended analysis – worse than the first – and a further report by former Swiss president Samuel Schmid. Russia's participation in Pyeongchang's Winter Games of 2018 would be shrouded in doubt throughout the coming year. The double charge sheet was blistering, the worldwide clamour for expulsion unceasing. McLaren's evidence was explicit: conspiracy of cover-up by Ministry of Sport, RUSADA officials and Moscow laboratory, the athletes not acting individually; the system refined for London 2012, Universiade 2013, IAAF World Championships in 2013, Sochi 2014; swapping of urine samples primarily at Moscow laboratory; his first report now confirmed by forensic testing 2011–2015; 1,000 athletes benefited in manipulated reports to WADA; 15 'false' medals identified at London 2012; four samples swapped at 2013 World Championships; at Sochi, two test swaps male with female, four involving gold medals with impossible salt content physiology, contaminated samples with 12 medals, and in six out of 21 medals in the Paralympics.

The report by Schmid, an Ethics Commission member – in partnership with Robin Mitchell of Fiji, Athletes Commission member Yang Yang, ASOIF executive director Andrew Ryan and Wolfgang Schobersberger from the Association of International Olympic Winter Sports Federations – was more exact on proposed penalties, carefully measured against potential legal appeal. The report damningly confirmed, 'Within evolution of the system, evidence shows that Dr

Rodchenkov played a key role, his scientific abilities enabling detection methods to improve the fight against doping, and winning international credibility ... but simultaneously to design better doping products and protocols ensuring they were less detectable and to establish the methodology of cover-up tests. Email exchanges confirm participation of individuals within the Ministry of Sport, and its subordinate bodies including RUSADA and the laboratories of Sochi and Moscow, by forensic and biological analysis. On many occasions reference was made on Ministry of Sport involvement, but no indication, *independent* or *impartial*, to corroborate involvement or knowledge at a higher level of the state.' This re-emphasised the legal impossibility of blanket Russian expulsion.

With appraisal of both McLaren's and Schmid's evidence, the EB, aware of such conspicuous failure to respect sporting obligations, immediately ruled as follows: suspension of Russian Olympic Committee; invitation to individual Russian athletes, under strict conditions, to the Pyeongchang Games, theirs the title 'Olympic Athlete from Russia (OAR)'; the Olympic anthem played in any medal ceremony; all Russian MOS officials banned from Pyeongchang; Vitaly Mutko, MOS chair, and deputy Yuri Nagornykh barred from all future Games; Sochi 2014 CEO Dmitry Chernyshenko deleted from Beijing 2022 Co-ordination Commission; IOC member and ROC president Alex Zhukov suspended; ROC to reimburse IOC and Independent Testing Authority (ITA) expenditure on investigations of $15m; ROC suspension potentially to be lifted for closing ceremony at Pyeongchang provided all conditions upheld. Russian athletes' inclusion determined by ITA if considered demonstrably clean, never previously ineligible under any anti-doping rule; clean in pre-Games targeted testing; receiving identical technical and logistical support as other Olympic athletes.

The IOC might have considered the nettle finally grasped, yet disenchantment remained widespread: even in China. *China Sports Daily* reported, 'Money now rules sport, even here in China sport to be run by government, dominated by investors, concerned only with money.' World opinion remained soured, primarily if not exclusively by Russia's infamy: in three Games, Beijing, London and Sochi, out of 230 positive tests – and excluding those deceitfully camouflaged – Russia had garnered 77. Bach, asked whether he regretted Russia not having been wholly suspended from Rio, emphasised, 'There was no time enough to follow a legal process, the IAAF suspension of Russia's track team was the consequence of internal presidential IF manipulation.' If the Executive Board's ruling regarding Pyeongchang fell short of media and public demand for Russia's crucifixion, yet were in line with Bach's socially principled legal guidance to protect the innocent, still incendiary for Bach was the incessant negativity from US anti-doping leader Travis Tygart: seemingly oblivious to the abysmal litany of cheating within America's own ranks. Yet was not Russia entitled to question the extent of Therapeutic Use Exemption (TUEs) randomly exploited in Europe, Africa and the US? The crisis for the IOC – and equally for Craig Reedie scrambling to expand WADA's surveillance and, essentially, its budget – was to rein in not just Russia but a myriad of other offenders in China, Kazakhstan, Kenya, Turkey, Ukraine and elsewhere. Legal restraints could not be ignored: Schmid had re-emphasised that 'only evidence forensically and biologically corroborated' could be incorporated in legal penalties.

Not that the IOC was immune to the inflation of favourable news – during a period of acute criticism where their perceived privileged existence was vulnerable. A masterpiece in PR greeted the Christmas shopping season with a publication designed to charm the doubtful. Every Olympic Games, by its experience, participation, performance and broadcast is exceptional; 28 concurrent world championships. So, how special, really, was Rio? Desperate for restored equilibrium and the appeal of future hosting, the IOC needed to celebrate retrospectively the 'glory' of Rio: this exercise was achieved with a nine-point pamphlet following an Executive Board meeting, by which the world was asked to believe that Rio surpassed the excellence of both Beijing and London. The basic motive, seemingly, was more a matter of future finance than simple self-promotion. The IOC craved the continuation of willing cities, these having become increasingly shy: an instinct furthered by Rio having hovered close to bankruptcy. However, close examination of the EB document revealed that barely a fifth of the conclusions derived direct credit from expertise, innovation or legacy offered by Rio, but on external, essentially communication/media facilities and the contributory supremacy of foreign teams. Of 12 examples under the heading 'Excellence', only two related to Rio, the rest to global media coverage. Rio's public transport improvement had been a single metro line, while the value of new venues would bear the question mark of those at Athens 2004: time would tell. Under 'Legacy', all would depend on maintenance, an innovative golf course already in decline, while within the claim of 'Stunning Achievements', out of 13 only one was Brazilian, judoka's heroine Rafael Silva. Twelve elements of 'Universality' exclusively attributable to foreign eminence. The most fulsome impression by Brazil on the visiting world, then and as always infectious, had been the nation's uniquely joyous spirit.

Early in 2017, Usain Bolt found himself deprived of one of his nine Olympic gold medals by the retrospective disqualification of Jamaican colleague Nesta Carter in Rio's 4x100m relay; likewise Tatyana Lebedeva of Russia, double silver winner in Beijing's triple and long jump events, this followed by Mariya Savinova surrendering her London 2012 800m title when ruled by CAS to have been 'positive' for three seasons: Caster Semenya of South Africa, champion subsequently in Rio, gaining a retrospective double. Vitaly Mutko, now promoted to deputy prime minister, meanwhile announced that under Russia's involuntary 'rehabilitated' doping control – supervised with some disruption by the

UK's affiliated body UKAD – there were to be 6,000 tests in the current year in an anxious attempt to be 'compliant' in time for Pyeongchang 2018. Bad news, certainly for the IOC, was withdrawal of Budapest as bid candidate for 2024 – leaving only Paris and Los Angeles in view – plus an admission by director-general Christophe De Kepper of insufficient evidence for CAS ever to have contemplated blanket Russian expulsion from 2018.

In March, Mark Adams, Bach's aide-de-camp, attending a Congressional sub-committee hearing at Washington, sought political backing for the IOC's initiative to establish total independence of both CAS and WADA from the IOC; while at Krasnoyarsk, Siberia's capital – where I once visited with Ted Turner and his wife Jane Fonda when lobbying as a potential Goodwill Games venue – President Putin was openly asserting, 'We must heed the facts of the McLaren reports – the Russian anti-doping system failed, it was our fault, and we must establish a new system, the Ministry of Sport transferring an independent organisation to Moscow State University.'

At the same time I was in Moscow hoping better to understand the profundity of Russia's sporting disaster: firstly meeting Professor Vladimir Lukin, benign academic of historical sciences, former ambassador to the UN, professed anglophile and president of Russia's Paralympics Committee. His crucial summary of Russia's scandal was eloquently brief, 'This was not a state conspiracy, but a conspiracy within a state.' Acceptable if true, but where then came the initiative? The distinction was important: was Professor Lukin philosophically innocent of the generic politics-sport syndrome? Putin had claimed manipulative testing was not a ministry-directed project: whether sports minister Mutko was *aware* will never be known, but by now Putin was on the front foot, having appointed veteran IOC member Smirnov as mastermind of an 'independent commission' tasked with establishing, in collaboration with WADA, a new compliant anti-doping agency. Professor Lukin and Smirnov both confirmed Putin's decree that the new RUSADA and a re-orientated NOC 'must be independent of the ministry'.

Lukin guardedly admitted Russia's delinquency, 'But not all details, especially concerning our Paralympic team, because international political issues cloud the arena of sports criticism, provoking an assumption of uniform guilt. Our president is confident that a new independent RUSADA will be established in co-operation with WADA and the IOC.' The steps taken by Smirnov's commission were extensive: the Russian Federal Crime Code adapted to convict induced doping in sport as an offence; RUSADA to be financed by the federal budget, not the ministry, and increased threefold; education seminars extended to 75 national sports federations; 3,000 doping tests over 18 months initially under jurisdiction of the UK agency, leading to a compulsory 20,000 Russian doping tests annually. Could and would these edicts be upheld?

Smirnov had long been *eminence grise* not merely within Russia but the Olympic Movement: his involvement beginning with Rome 1960, and becoming head of the NOC upon USSR's disintegration in 1991, when he had warned national coaches to be wary of doping development as Russian competitors increasingly began to train abroad with foreign coaches. 'I left in 2001, a Ministry of Sport having been created in '99, and I felt I had become irrelevant, better to be working within the IOC. Here at home, the ministry became more powerful, the NOC less dominant. Before the collapse of USSR, our whole sporting administration was under the state roof, but afterwards, all national federations became self-administered. The NOC was advised by Rogge in 2009 about an alarming increase in positives. When our medal haul evaporated at Vancouver in 2010, Rodchenkov, director of the RUSADA laboratory, sensed an opportunity, with massive doping from 2011 onwards to Sochi, athletes simultaneously being given manipulated clean samples.'

Alexander Zhukov, president of Russia's NOC, was frank and forthright in our meeting; friendly, but propaganda?

He acknowledged that a substantial IOC fine would be a demonstrative signal for concluding their extreme reprimand, accepting the guilt which had been inescapable. Zhukov made no attempt to hide this monumental scandal. We were talking at their Olympic office alongside the Moskva river in Moscow, the corridors festooned with celebratory pictures of momentous Olympic champions from a distinguished past, never mind Zhukov's acceptance of imminent penalties in the present circumstance: a substantial fine would help restore global public trust in the IOC's handling of such a destructive affair. Zhukov stated that all administrative officials directly implicated had already been dismissed. While he placed much of the blame on Rodchenkov, both for initiating and subsequently revealing Russia's cheating, he conceded, 'Rodchenkov failed us, yes, but there were other coaches and doctors involved, he wasn't acting on his own.'

It was understandable that whistleblowers domestically provoked negative sentiments. Back in the days of Stalin's farming collectivism and infamous widespread death by starvation, peasants could be executed for hiding grain for their families' survival. One such peasant was historically revealed when Red Army officialdom had questioned his innocent 12-year-old informant son: the farmer furiously killed the boy. Communist propaganda hailed the son as a hero for 'civic honour', peasant folk deplored his disloyalty: what you knew remained silent. In Russia, brutality rules. Zhukov reflected, 'We should not allow another Rodchenkov, but in future we have new anti-doping laws, a new RUSADA. With current testing by UK Anti-Doping, our results reveal performances which show no decline on previous years, indicating that McLaren's deduction – that our success reflected the doping – was inaccurate. We understand the need for preservation and protection of the Olympic Movement, yet I believe that our continued exclusion would be not only a disaster for Russia, but for the credibility of international sport.'

Zhukov hoped for IOC moderation in line with Bach's implemented policy in Rio: clean athletes to be accepted. 'We are ready for as many pre-Pyeongchang tests as possible.' WADA's interim UK testing had been allegedly obstructed by lack of random access within certain cities, but Zhukov was confident that special appointees would counteract this problem. Yet WADA was concerned about the neutrality of RUSADA's soon-to-be-elected new director-general: disapproval already recorded for the appointment of double Olympic pole vault champion Yelena Isinbayeva as chair of a new supervisory board, though her democratic election by the Athletes Commission to the IOC made her position unassailable. Speaking to news agency TASS, Isinbayeva had said, 'The number one task is to establish a wholly efficient anti-doping system that will be globally respected.' Smirnov, on the defensive, admitted, 'We are a big country, we haven't had the capacity to monitor all regions all the way to the Pacific. With an increased budget that would become possible, yet there has to be harmony and collaboration with WADA and the IOC. It does not help for the UK to proclaim that Russia should be suspended "to save the IOC"!'

My visit to Moscow opened an opportunity for an email Q&A interview with President Putin, published by US agency Associated Press. The autocratic superpower leader was positive, though a shade modest regarding his country's irregularities, 'might have experienced certain ups and downs with regard to results'. Yes indeed! This was our conversational exchange: I leave readers to draw their own conclusion in the light of Putin's military assignment in Ukraine.

DM, 'Might Moscow subsequently contemplate a host city bid for 2028?'

Putin, 'I would rather speak of Russia generally, not necessarily about Moscow. Apart from the capital, we have a number of cities which could potentially host Summer Olympics. There is Sochi, of course, but also Saint Petersburg and possibly Kazan. We are not going to make any specific statements, yet. In 2014, our country successfully hosted the Winter Games in Sochi. However, I do not rule out the possibility that Russia will decide to enter the bidding process for the right to host another Games. Regarding Los Angeles for 2028, it is not for us to estimate the city's chances. This must be done by the IOC. USA is one of the leading sports countries, and I believe has a good chance of getting the honour. It is well known that LA hosted in 1984 and the USSR team unfortunately did not participate – just like the US team which did not come to Moscow in 1980. Neither country benefited from this.'

DM, 'In Russia's cultural, social and political global relationships, how important is it to return to the front line of Olympic competition and international prominence?'

P, 'Russia always has been, and I hope always will be, one of the leading international sports countries. What kind of return to the front line are we talking about? Our athletes still produce great results in international competition, set new records and win gold medals. Yes, like any country, we might have experienced certain ups and downs with regard to results, but in no way does this cast any doubt on Russia's status as one of the leading countries in sport.

'You know, I always had a problem when someone was trying to place sport in social and political context. Sport is a separate and unique kind of human activity, which functions under its own rules and principles. It has nothing to do with the political agenda, and neither should it. When politics interferes with sport, unjust things happen, like the story of Russia's Paralympic athletes who were banned from international competition where they had a right to participate like everyone else. Once it became clear that our Paralympians would miss the Rio Games through no fault of their own, I decided to meet the athletes. My goal was to support them, to have a simple talk with them. I was particularly proud of these people, because it was evident that they would not give up – they will continue to stand up to the challenge.'

DM, 'How confident are you that Russian athletes and Russian society will acknowledge and support the necessity for strict anti-doping compliance – provided WADA is equally effective worldwide?'

P, 'We are currently developing a completely new system in the fight against doping in Russia. We have established an Independent Public Anti-Doping Commission. The Russian Anti-Doping agency RUSADA and our testing laboratory are no longer controlled by the state and the Ministry of Sport, but gaining full autonomy – just as in many other countries. I believe that positive processes which we have started, to reform anti-doping structures, are irreversible. We must listen to what WADA has to say, because we have to admit that we have several cases of proven doping violation. This is unacceptable. We will do everything to organise efficient and fruitful work with all our partners, including WADA and the IOC. I hope they have the same intentions.

'At the same time, it is important to understand that the international anti-doping system is not perfect. This fact is admitted by the leaders of the Olympic Movement. One of the most serious issues is Therapeutic Use Exemption. We do not want sport to become competition between different kinds of stimulators, most of which are highly dangerous for athletes' health, do we? Russia is ready for an open and consistent participation in work to establish an accomplished global anti-doping system. Once again, I would like to reiterate something that we have always stated: Russia never had, and I hope will never have, a state-backed system of doping support. On the contrary – we will fight doping.'

DM, 'In recognition of the threat to global public affection for Olympic sport caused by doping offences in many countries, might Russia consider offering a donation to WADA to extend scrutiny facilities to ensure fair competition?'

P, 'As I said, we are open for co-operation with the IOC, WADA and other international organisations who can assist us in developing our own new anti-doping system. In fact, we believe that we can launch the system *only* with successful collaboration with WADA and IOC. In our relations with WADA, we adhere, and will continue doing so, to the principles and rules of this organisation, including financial obligations towards the Olympic Movement.'

* * *

Learning of Putin's determination for Russia's NOC to overhaul and legitimise domestic doping control, Craig Reedie responded, 'WADA has been working with Russia's independent commission, under Smirnov's leadership, and I am much encouraged by these assurances.' Putin's denial of state-organised doping had been accepted in the McLaren Report with alteration to 'institutionalised'. It would be essential for a penitent Russia to be back on track for Pyeongchang. Doubt remained incurable, substantiated by events in Beijing's Winter Games.

By summer 2017, conditions were beginning to open towards Russia's conditional re-admission as participants at Pyeongchang during the coming winter. In parallel was the need for clarity by the sub-commission headed by Swiss IOC member Denis Oswald on identifiable previous-offending Russian individual performers, alongside Reedie's stipulation that Russia 'must fulfil 12 criteria before it can be ruled compliant' – primarily, acceptance of McLaren's conclusions. Zhukov promised this would be so, implicating 'all criteria in place by this fall'. Reedie was predicting pre-competition Russian testing for Pyeongchang to the point of mutual exhaustion. The temperature was not eased by North Korea's launch of a ballistic missile over Japan, a weapon capable of pan-Pacific US destination: described by Japan's Premier Abe as 'a grave threat', President Trump promising retaliation with 'fire and fury' if the US was threatened. South Korea's President Moon merely again broached the peninsular political bonus of the North's participation in the Games.

One fading embarrassment welcomed another emerging in October. Brazilian court judges conditionally released from jail the former head of Rio's Olympic Committee, now charged with corruption in an alleged vote-buying scandal during the bidding for 2016. Carlos Nuzman, 75, had been arrested at his home, charged for his role in a $2m fraud to secure votes for Rio's election in 2009. 'Preventive detention' was replaced by conditional release, stated the Superior Court of Justice. Under terms of release, Nuzman was prevented from leaving Rio and forbidden from visiting the NOC. Prosecutors stated that Lamine Diack, former IAAF chief, and his son Papa Massata Diack, were also accused; that Nuzman and former Rio governor Sergio Cabral solicited payment of $2m to Papa Massata to secure votes, Rio defeating Chicago, Madrid and Tokyo. The IOC instantly responded by suspending Brazil's NOC, stripping Nuzman of his now honorary IOC membership, though emphasising the principle of innocence without proof of guilt. A police raid of his home had discovered more cash than he possessed in the bank. An IOC statement declared, 'Our Ethics and Compliance office has requested Brazilian authorities for full information immediately after the allegations were made. Given the facts, the Ethics Commission may consider provisional measures while respecting Mr Nuzman's right to be heard, reiterating that the presumption of innocence prevails.'

In November, conditions surrounding Russia's reinstatement faltered over the extent of ongoing compliance. Belatedly, the Compliance Review Committee conditionally reinstated RUSADA, collaborative in 29 out of 31 WADA-imposed conditions, provided it fulfilled two paramount demands by 31 December: fulsome acknowledgement of the systemic government-orientated manipulated testing from 2011 to 2014, and the granting of access to laboratory data, thereby opening the door to imposition of penalties for those infringements identified by McLaren (to enable medal re-assessments). Olympic sport had held its breath for three years. Clarity that RUSADA now faced a definitive deadline came from Sergey Khrychkov, head of Europe's Sports Convention Division and member of RUSADA's new supervisory board, when admitting, 'Russia has the possibility to overcome its crisis if it meets all the conditions specified by WADA. If not, Russia's position will significantly deteriorate.' If justice had finally overtaken Russia, WADA had by no means ended a continuing universal threat, but at least a discredited, provisionally readmitted Russia now become eligible to send a rigidly tested squad to Pyeongchang 2018. A conclusion that would enable Bach, if not worldwide critics, to breathe more easily in the coming new year while also knowing that his transformative pursuit for host city election realities was in train, in the wake of peaceful constitutional negotiations achieved in September's Session at Lima, Peru.

The gratifying aspect in early 2017 had been the enthusiasm expressed by two remaining eager bid city candidates, admittedly the most conspicuous of hosts; both previously persistent applicants and now equal contenders for 2024, though each aware of the IOC's already expressed sentiment for possibility of a double election, simultaneously embracing 2028. Casey Wasserman, chair of LA's committee, had already expressed theoretical acceptance of such a double decision, believing that for all parties it made sense. On the other hand, rival Tony Estanguet, heading the Paris bid, had clearly stated that the French capital would not be prepared, if defeated, to renew their attempt for 2028. For the IOC, the prospect was wholly logical, not least on the financial front, if acceptable to one or other of the two. Wasserman had already said, 'It's exactly the kind of idea and strategic initiative the IOC should be contemplating.' Wasserman emphasised the stability of both bids, free of political opposition, uniform encouragement from local citizens, manageable budgets, 'All that, it calms and creates stability.' Yet he, like Estanguet, maintained that LA's focus remained on winning for 2024, 'There's been no discussion with the IOC as yet about the possibility of a joint double award, other than some public statements we've heard.' The main reflection would be that the IOC was gratified simply to have two such powerful contenders for 2024, though Wasserman, business-astute, conceded that the Olympic Movement at this stage 'is at a turning point, the next host needs to get it right'.

Several IOC members had already voiced concern about a potential double election: rumours escalating in recent months, on the knowledge that this was a proposal for which Bach was known to favour, to avoid a situation where 'there are too many losers'. Bach had resisted enquiries inviting denial of the potential, but general opinion remained equivocal, even John Coates having acknowledged there was no plan as yet on how such a prospect, outside the Charter, might be devised; vice-president Erdener observing that it was irregular, moreover that other potential applicant cities would forfeit their opportunity. Coates admitted that it could not be claimed whoever came second would receive an alternative, until the first event had been concluded, 'The proposal would have to be accepted at an Olympic Session.' Gerhard Heiberg from Norway was more emphatic, 'If we awarded the Games for two different years, we should have advised that was the plan from the outset, not towards the end of the race.' Charter Rule 33.2. states, 'Save in exceptional circumstances, such election takes place seven years before the celebration of the Games.' At that moment, Paris and LA were jointly focused on 2024, though Dick Pound, as astute as Bach, reflected, 'In the present climate, I would have no objection to a joint decision for 2024 and 2028, particularly if the cities might agree who should be elected the first.'

By early June and a report from the Evaluation Commission on submissions by the two cities, chaired by Swiss Patrick Baumann, official emphasis was still on a singular contest for 2024, their enthusiasm for either bid optimistic: Los Angeles 'forward-looking, innovative, vibrant' and Paris 'historical, cultural, iconic, amazing backdrops'. Baumann acclaimed these two great cities, their projects contrasted but authentic, each planning to use a record number of existing or temporary venues. Here, for a Summer Games, was the IOC in gratifyingly commanding poise for its intended recycling of

Games management under five categories: concept, experience, sustainability, legacy and delivery. However, in the present game of 'blind man's buff', consideration was deferred to a joint candidate briefing in Lausanne plus an Extraordinary Session, prior to dénouement in September. At last, with the Executive Board having stepped out of the shadows, to call for an Extraordinary Session, the IOC came clean publicly on its ambition: that there should be evolution of the candidature process, Bach emphasising at interview that awarding the projected festivals was all about seizing a unique opportunity in a candidature process that has become too expensive and too onerous. Grandly, Bach had predicted, 'We'll have some interesting days in Lausanne, some very important decisions will be taken.' They were indeed.

On 11 July 2017, the Extraordinary Session authorised the EB to contrive a tripartite agreement with Paris and LA, and their respective NOCs, for simultaneous election, as mooted clandestinely for many months, for 2024 and 2028: confirmation then scheduled for the 131st Session at Lima. Should the EB's tripartite agreement be frictionless, the Lima Session's rubber stamp would elect one city for each of the two dates: whereby the seven-year deadline within the Charter would be waived. In a metaphorical brush of the hand, the constitution had somersaulted. Bach, delighted as he had every reason to be that the proposal had been unanimously endorsed, stated the IOC had grasped a golden opportunity with two great cities, particularly at a time when hosting interest had faded. Was he revolutionary? Hardly. De Coubertin had sought a joint hosting when the IOC had struggled to recover stability following World War One devastation. Now, in the tripartite agreement (IOC/Paris/LA) embracing negotiations, the prime IOC objective was to find which of the two cities might volunteer to host the later date. A separate candidature process would then be launched for 2028, during which a further Evaluation Commission's visit would be made, again chaired by Patrick Baumann of Switzerland.

Prevalent indication was that Paris would stick with 2024: the dual response between the respective city mayors, Anne Hidalgo and Eric Garcetti, indicating this to be the likely outcome, linking arms together in a joint celebration, never mind that rubber-stamp approval in September was still an awaited formality. Legal consultation, perhaps surprisingly, had indicated that in fact no change of the Charter was required: opinion of both Coates and former director-general François Carrard, never mind an ad-hoc challenge by several members. IOC Athletes Commission reps Adam Pengilly of Britain and Yelena Isinbayeva of Russia each raised concerns about guarantees for the 2028 host, basically no more than constructive suggestions. The Extraordinary Session had been attended by 83 of the then existing 95 members. All that now remained was the presumed willingness of LA and acceptance by the Session in Lima for LA to be the hosts of 2028.

In the wake of the Russian nightmare, the IOC and its wilful leader might rightly celebrate, as Bach did with French president Emmanuel Macron, who had attended the Extraordinary Session in Lausanne, pronouncing, 'We are ready to work with the IOC on this win-win-win approach.' Mayor Hidalgo was equally euphoric, 'Fully committed with the Paris team to putting all our creativity and my resolve into reaching an agreement for Paris to experience once again this Olympic adventure for which it has been longing for a hundred years.' Those previous occasions had been 1900 and 1924. From LA mayor Garcetti there was a touch of humour, 'In Olympic history there's only been 37 times in which there has been a tie for a gold medal. Maybe today is the 38th.' Bach's observation was pragmatic, 'Ensuring the stability of the Olympic Games for the next 11 years is something extraordinary, which is why this is a great day for these Olympic Games and for the Olympic Movement, and not least these two wonderful cities.'

With LA obligingly and predictably agreeing to be the later host, it was calculated that the city would benefit by several million dollars' increase in broadcast and sponsorship revenues, Garcetti forecasting, 'I can look people in the eye and say this is a much stronger deal financially.' US President Donald Trump had duly bandwaggoned in July, 'For the first time in a generation the Olympics are coming back to the United States. I want to congratulate our Olympic committee for developing a plan that will ensure LA demonstrates the best in American creativity, innovation and hospitality.'

When the minor army of officialdom embraced by the multiple organisations which constitute an Olympic Games had gathered in Lima, there was bare necessity for the election confirmation of the two known appointments; LA privately celebrating that by its voluntary decision in accepting 2028, its hosting would be funded by an additional $1.8bn in respect of the longer planning period, and in order for the IOC to increase participation and access to youth sports programmes in the preceding years. After all the months of Russian misery, Olympic morale was now once more riding optimistically, and it was a relaxed IOC president who at the opening of the Session in Lima could thank head of state Pedro Pablo Kuczynski 'for remaining steadfast in commitment to hosting this Session despite such floods earlier this year'. With a new sense of momentum, the Session would also take stock of implementation of other reforms under Agenda 2020, as Bach reflected, 'Showing a sceptical world that we are making the Olympic Movement stronger, living up to our values and responsibilities. We have reformed and we have changed.' Simultaneously, President Kuczynski was emphasising Peru's political goal to strengthen sport in the school system embracing eight million children.

While celebration might have been the mood of the moment, Bach had remained sanguine during his address to the Session, acknowledging that the Olympic arena existed, 'In a world of crises, mistrust and uncertainty, with a worrying trend towards isolationism on many levels. More than ever the world needs Olympic values, peace, respect and understanding … as we all know, the coming Winter Games in Pyeongchang will be taking place under difficult political circumstances. In all our conversations with organisation in Pyeongchang, we have never been put in doubt, we could always feel support for our objectives. Any Olympic Games must be beyond political intentions, not be a tool for political manoeuvring, but a stage for communal dialogue, a symbol of hope and peace. To discuss political scenarios for the Winter Games would send the wrong message: would undermine the efforts of those working towards a diplomatic solution, so that peace will prevail on the Korean peninsula.'

There are those who mock the IOC's concerted attempts to embrace its morality and function within extraterritorial affairs of political organisations, yet the acquisition of the former UN secretary-general Ban Ki-moon as new chairman of the Ethics Commission could not but raise the accountability and transparency of the IOC. Ban, the only candidate to replace outgoing chairman Youssoupha Ndiaye, enjoyed a landslide welcome with 74 of the 78 votes. The 73-year-old South Korean had been proposed by the Executive Board and his role would commence following conclusion of the Lima Session. Ban was aware as any of the IOC's pressing need to repair global image, following accusations of corruption across several channels: Nuzman's interrogation on vote-buying in Rio's election, alongside Diack's involvement as IAAF chief, and further accusations against IOC member Frankie Fredericks of Namibia for comparable improper financial procurement activity.

For the moment the IOC was riding, as it were, the funfair magic roundabout: their future commissioned to a couple of dynamic leaders of prospective Games, Tony Estanguet and Casey Wasserman, in whose care Olympic reputation would now be entrusted. Estanguet was an Olympic champion of no little substance: three canoeing gold medals in 2000, 2004 and 2012, five world and four European titles, and countless other medals. A man of unlimited energy who was brimming with confidence without being unduly immodest, 'I did not undergo any training to become president of the organising committee, but I was curious about everything I learned from Bernard Lapasset, our former head of World Rugby, from Jean-Claude Killy, Thomas Bach, Christophe Dubi, all those who have been involved in organisation before me. But after a while I wanted to function as I did when I was an athlete. Initially you feed off advice from coaches and athletes who have been there before you, then one day you have to go on your own, take the responsibility.' Estanguet's ambition is to create in this third Paris hosting an ambience in the city unlike anything known previously: embracing the unique scenic beauty of the French capital to draw the population more intimately into the drama of the world's greatest social festival.

Wasserman is a different breed. As a boy he attended the opening ceremony of the second LA Games, in 1984, with his grandfather, Hollywood mogul Lou Wasserman. The event profoundly affected a ten-year-old – nowadays chairman and chief executive of a global sports representation and marketing group. He was invited to chair LA's campaign by mayor Garcetti, and knows his city has an inbuilt advantage, 'The unique aspect for LA is that we don't have to build anything – including an Olympic Village.'

The name Wasserman is still referred to with reverence because of his grandfather's achievements, an effective creative influence in Hollywood and building one of the industry's most powerful studios. Yet his grandson has created a reputation of his own with the foundation of a sports agency now of acknowledged global influence, embracing superstars from a multitude of major sports, which is said to outshine renowned IMG of Mark McCormack. If anyone is entitled to administer a competent Games beyond expectation, it should be Wasserman.

10

PENINSULA FALSE DAWN

THOMAS BACH will readily tell you that the Olympics are 'all about the athletes'. Self-evidently as true as ever at Pyeongchang where unassuming, relatively unheralded Czech snow orchid Ester Ledecká soared to unique ski-snowboard double: a dual performance that stunned previous champions, moreover when using old skis formerly belonging to American champion Mikaela Shiffrin. Yet since Bach's competitive days 45 years ago, two radical aspects have altered: in many of the major spectator sports, whether individual or team, firstly they are now professional; secondly, if from among the top 15 podium-prominent nations, likely medal recipients will have had the benefit of substantial NOC and/or government-funded investment.

In Britain, many millions of pounds invested were triggered in the early 21st century by former prime minister John Major's Lottery-funding Olympic subsidy. This has a relevant bearing upon any athlete's attitude towards evident doping by rivals. In the 'good old days' – my time pre-1960 as a fringe would-be Olympic competitor – everyone competed for the honour, the exhilaration, with occasionally the glory: superstar minorities such as middle-distance gladiator Derek Ibbotson trousering clandestine cash (maybe twice a week, Dublin to Cologne, say, with £50 from each, equivalent of then two months' salary). Today, for the elite, the race *is* their salary: they cannot withdraw in dissent from a competition which they suspect may be bent. Or even have the evidence. Thus some of front-line sport, especially the Olympic Games, is doubly compromised: the clean and the guilty equally committed, the clean because they too have spent four years in devoted preparation. How might they demonstrably become involved in constructive exclusion of the cheats, if the administrative bureaucracy fails?

This conundrum had been apparent long before the tarnished succession of Games, from 2008 to 2014, and now hung heavily across prospects for Pyeongchang's Winter Games of 2018; never mind that Russia's corruption had been blitzed by 2016. There were many other cheats out there hitherto, and likely some again, summer or winter, roaming free. A dilemma was posed by Angela Ruggiero, ice hockey Olympic champion with 256 collective matches for USA, IOC member 2010–2018 and Executive Board member, when elected Athletes Commission chair in 2016. In her preface to the chapter preceding the Pyeongchang Games, for my *Official History of the IOC and Olympic Games, 1894–2018*, Ruggiero wrote:

'As new chair of the Commission, I see my role as ensuring that athletes' priorities shape every aspect of decision-making: not just those final months of fine tuning. It was an honour to be elected by commission colleagues. With Tony Estanguet as vice-chair, along with new members Yelena Isinbayeva, Ryu Seung-min, Britta Heidemann and Dániel Gyurta, we are better equipped than ever to play an integral role in meeting Olympic challenges.

'Most pressing is reform of the anti-doping system. I spent Rio's Games listening to global colleagues, many angry that clean Russians were excluded while convicted cheats were present; many angry that Russians were there at all. Anger is acceptable when incontrovertible flaws in the campaign against drugs have been exposed. Our commission is representative for athletes worldwide, our resources extensive: talent, expertise, ambition, reach and relevance. We must capitalise on that and channel that anger, so that when athletes arrive in Pyeongchang, and subsequently in Tokyo for the Summer Games, they will be certain of a level playing field. I will make it the mission of an efficient, professional Commission to place the rights and needs of clean athletes at the heart of anti-doping renewal.'

Sterling stuff. Ruggiero is a distinguished Olympian, enthusiastically elected to the commission and a worthy figurehead protecting prized interests. She deserved unqualified support. Yet absent from her forthright stance was a salient issue: positive proposals from clean athletes of practical steps to eliminate criminal athletes: such as, say, refusal to compete with those previously suspended for grave positive tests. If the commission is important, should it not negotiate with the IOC, and WADA, the means to disenfranchise unexcluded offenders who are poisoning public trust?

Behind the scenes, a satisfactory independent foolproof process of adjudication still had to be determined. If clean athletes desire state-of-the-art facilities, they need to collaborate, practically, on effective sanctions. The advent of cheating by the entourage surrounding an athlete had compounded the problem for IOC and WADA. The threads of evil had had several sources, individual and collective. The balance between Olympic ideology and wilful infamy had trodden a fine line for half a century: frustratingly, the honourable continue to vastly outnumber the cheats, yet too often are outwitted by them.

In the author's opinion, it behoves the IOC and the commission, in conjunction, to introduce in the Charter a clause authorising the commission to demand the exclusion from any Olympic event of any competitor convicted of a serious drug offence within the past four years since the previous Games. The would-be guilty then know the consequence. The athletes, who comprise the Games, need to be granted such absolute right to terminate the inclusion of known current cheats continuing uncensored by IFs. It should then be conditional upon every NOC to accept this right of athletes to be active in their own disciplinary process: such a Charter clause to be instrumental for any entry in that sport: with the legal proviso of right of appeal.

This author's view could be termed as 'hindsight irrelevance' if the optimism expressed elsewhere, by Witold Bańka, current president of WADA, proves justified: that testing is now foolproof. Time will be the judge of that: moreover, if international imposition of permanent suspension from continual practice following serious misconduct is legally acceptable in professions such as medicine, law, academia, banking etc, why not sport? Athletes should not be legally protected by their 'right to earn a living'.

Prior to the Rio Games, and again during the approach to South Korea's second Olympic hosting in 30 years, there was ceaseless flack fired at Thomas Bach by critics from every quarter – Russia's rival NOCs, individual athletes, media, some lawyers, even some IOC members – incensed that uniform collective exclusion had not been imposed on Russia's entire team; the allegation of his personal prejudice believed to be coloured by Bach's perceived friendly association with President Putin, in liaison with the acceptable importance of Russia within the Olympic arena as one of the 'big three'. Bach is frank about the quandary, legal and emotional, confronting the organisation of the most global social picnic, 'You can always argue on behalf of the IOC on either of the two fronts – collective discipline, by imposing suspension, or acceptance of the innocent. Of course we were embarrassed by what was revealed, especially by the second McLaren Report. We suffered security threats when calculating sanctions in the wake of the Samuel Schmid special commission. If we had decided on a blanket ban, we would have been accused of being biased, and we didn't want to be judged as taking revenge, yet neither did we wish to be viewed as being protective of the Russian NOC, though there was no evidence Russia's NOC had been active participants. We needed to address the legal evidence. Otherwise, the IOC could have been overruled by CAS.'

John Coates of Australia, vice-president and admittedly in harness alongside Bach since his 2013 election, is satisfied the adjudication was correct, 'Russian appeals were addressed by CAS, all parties had the opportunity to express opinions – WADA, IOC, Russia. The Athletes Commission was urged to impose a sense of responsibility on the new generation of athletes.' Well, yes, though was it not irrational for clean athletes to accept or consider it was exclusively other people's responsibility to penalise the cheats? Do not instances of libel prompt private litigation? Most athletes cannot afford that route.

The initial expulsion of an official Russian team from Pyeongchang had come in early December 2017: not the first such state exclusion, Germany and Japan similarly ousted following two world wars; South Africa for three decades on account of apartheid; Afghanistan from Sydney 2000 for prohibition of women; now multiple Russians, in bureaucratic confusion in 2016, 2018, 2020 and 2022, simply for being mammoth cheats. Appeals on all sides were inevitable, repetitive and expensive, the IOC's incriminating evidence emerging from 'investigative' reports, rather than prosecutorial, by McLaren and Schmid.

In 2016, the IOC/WADA originally banned Russia for four years as a nation and NOC; subsequently under CAS jurisdiction, while Russia's NOC was banned until December 2022, innocent competitors were accepted as non-representational 'Olympic Athlete from Russia' (OAR). This would equally madden the 'hygienically approved' Russians, themselves, their sceptical rivals, and all the spectators who still viewed the 'team' as 'those damned Russians': like attending your daughter's wedding to a three-times divorcee. And this alongside the doughty principle of a conscientious IOC president who riled more observers than he consoled: notwithstanding that CAS ruled the IOC's decisions 'were fair and not carried out in a discriminatory, arbitrary or unfair manner, that to create an invitation list of Russian athletes to compete as "Olympic Athletes from Russia" could not be described as a sanction, but rather as an eligibility decision'.

It was observed by sceptics that judgement of Russia's compliance in response to their disgrace would depend how they treated the three key whistleblowers for exposure of their villainy: competitors Yuliya Stepanova and her husband, and front-line coach Grigory Rodchenkov. The fact that the three of them had fled abroad for self-protection remained validation for those offended by any lenience towards Russia. In early 2018, 42 Russian individuals had appealed to CAS. Of these, 28 appeals were successful, but others had their sanctions upheld in accordance with the weight of evidence against them. The number of clean Russian athletes that would participate in Pyeongchang was 168, selected from an original pool of 500 under consideration. Opinion within Russia was divided on acceptance of reduced participation: a public poll revealed 86 per cent were against the indignity imposed upon the nation by competition as 'neutrals': many fans attending the Games would blatantly wear Russian colours, chanting their nation's name in defiance.

If Russia's potential involvement with Pyeongchang had been in turmoil for 18 months, the diplomatic relationship between North and South Korea was permanently so. It was an exceptional beam of light in one of the globe's darkest tunnels when, in his 2018 New Year Address, North Korea president Kim Jong-un suddenly and unexpectedly proposed talks in Seoul for consideration of participation in the Games. This was momentarily unfathomable: due to frigid relations between North and South, there had been concerns over security for the Winter Games, especially in the wake of tensions regarding the North's continuing missile and nuclear tests.

On 20 September 2017, South Korean president Moon Jae-in felt obliged publicly to promise security for the Games; the minister for youth affairs and sports in France,

Laura Flessel-Colovic, had warned of withdrawal if safety continued uncertain, this threat echoed by both Austria and Germany. In early December the US ambassador to the UN, Nikki Haley, had suggested on television that participation was under consideration. Whence on New Year's Day came Kim's proposal of unprecedented participation in the Games, eliciting the first such talks between North and South for more than two years. These were held on 9 January, with mutual participation acceptance, while eight days later it was further announced that North and South were agreed to field a unified Korean women's ice hockey team, the two entering together under a Korean Unification Flag during the Opening Ceremony. Such spectacular development met with some opposition in the South, critics suggesting this was a ploy by the government to encourage pro-North sentiment; that a unified hockey team would be of no account, that such a joint venture would tempt the Games to be termed the 'Pyongyang Olympics' (Pyongyang being the North's capital). Japan's foreign affairs minister Taro Kono warned the South to be wary of their neighbour's charm offensive. However, on 20 January a meeting between Kim Il-guk, the North's minister of sport and NOC leader, and Do Jong-hwan, the South's minister of culture and sport, confirmed the deal: that the two nations would march together under the unified flag for the first time since the uneasy truce that halted the Korean War in 1953. Thomas Bach was quick to fasten upon the opportunity to emphasise, 'It is the objective of the Olympics to build bridges, never to erect walls, this development hopefully opening the door to a brighter future on the Korean Peninsula and inviting the world to join the celebration.'

With the Olympic Movement threatened on several fronts, a harassed Bach could not have asked for a more energising and emotional injection for the third Games of his troublesome presidency: expanding an Olympic stage which flies the flag of harmony. With IOC approval, the North would be sending

22 athletes to compete in five disciplines across three sports – hockey, skating and alpine skiing – together with two dozen coaches and a bevvy of journalists. This sensational move would be highlighted by the unified women's hockey team, embracing 12 players from the North: President Kim exploiting the development with a boastful rhetoric aimed at Washington in response to US alarm at the North's advancing mass weapons capability. Despite this political aside, the South actively welcomed the potential for a mood veering away from the North's recent provocations, Bach reflecting, 'Such an agreement as this would have seemed impossible only a few weeks ago.' The North had also negotiated acceptance for a cheering squad of over 200 as part of the charm deal: support, in addition to the hockey team, for a figure skating pair, Ryom Tae-ok and Kim Ju-sik, plus two male short-track speed skaters, Jong Kwang-bom and Choe Un-song, and three competitors each in cross-country and alpine skiing.

The novelty of the North's initiative was more than a new year's gift. The rival nations had marched together at previous multi-sport competitions, most recently 11 years previously at the Asian Winter Games of 2007 in Changchun, China, but never previously assembled a joint team in competition – beyond twice, as one nation, at the World Table Tennis Championships of 1991 and FIFA's World Youth Championship the same year. Now the ice hockey IF would belatedly have to determine the numerical size of this joint team, the South privately intent on not reducing the numbers of their own squad. Their coach openly spoke of 'damage' to her team's integration, saying it was too late to be adding new players this close to the tournament: the South's team the only one operational in the country because of limited talent pool, and the current group having been preparing for this moment for the past three years. South Korea were ranked 22nd in the world, and on the rise, while the North were 25th and declining: the pair last meeting the previous April in division two of the women's world championship in which the South had comfortably triumphed 3-0. The coach's view was that being obliged to dispense with three or four players to provide access for the North's inclusion 'was simply asking too much'. Additionally, the combined team might create crowd hostility towards players from the North, news of the agreement immediately provoking complaints for lack of prior consultation.

Whatever the outcome of joint participation, the potential was widely viewed as revolutionary for the peninsula's future. Shamshad Akhtar, under secretary-general of the UN, and executive of the Economic and Social Commission for Asia and the Pacific, expressed her optimism in the organisation's Policy Society publication the same month, 'Sports fans worldwide eagerly await the Olympics, and this time there is cause for cautious optimism that sport diplomacy may lower tensions on the Korean peninsula. Leaders, diplomats and citizens, from the world over, will witness North and South Korean athletes walking side by side. There could be few better places than Pyeongchang, which means peace and prosperity goals integral to the mission of the UN and the 2030 Sustainable Development Agenda are visibly on view … in this spirit, the first Olympics in South Korea in 1988 served to foster relationships at a time of rapid geopolitical shifts. Those Games featured many participating nations, including the US and Soviet Union, establishing diplomatic relations through the thaw in relations, the Republic of Korea becoming a member of the UN in 1991 … the Olympics also heralded the economic transformation of the South, now known as "the Miracle on the Han River".

'For the decade after the Games, the economy grew at an average rate of 8.5 per cent per year, transforming the South from an aid recipient to a key aid donor … between 1960 and 1995, GDP increased more than 100-fold, reducing poverty of more than half of the population to less than five per cent … this miracle was linked with the key value of the Olympics and international collaboration via the UN.'

For Bach's address at the opening ceremony of the IOC's Session prior to Pyeongchang's eagerly awaited Games – its successful third bid – his acclamation for an opportunity to pour oil on the Korean peninsula's politically troubled waters, under the Olympic banner, was an advertiser's dream. The president proclaimed, 'North and South Korea will send a powerful message of peace to the world when they march together under one flag at our Opening Ceremony. The Olympic spirit has brought two sides together that for too long were divided by mistrust and animosity. The Olympic spirit has brought real hope for a brighter future for everyone in the peninsula. While the Olympics has opened the door for talks between two Koreas, it was important to see the process through to completion. This initiative gives all parties the chance to reflect on what the future could look like, if we were all guided by the Olympic spirit. Yet Korea's mutual journey does not end here, the political tensions will not disappear overnight. Sport itself cannot create peace, but the Olympic Games can open the way with its powerful symbols. For many, North Korea's participation in the Olympics where North and South had formed a unified team had seemed impossible. However, such worries have disappeared and become a reality.' Bach's unalloyed gesture was buoyed by the news that Kim Yong-nam, the North's ceremonial leader, was to make an unprecedented visit to attend the Games.

As the Games' outdoor ceremony commenced, South Korean president Moon Jae-in shook hands with Kim Yo-jong, sister of the North's leader and herself a prominent figure in the regime: the first time since the Korean War that a member of the ruling Kim dynasty had visited the South. However, a blip in diplomatic etiquette, there was less courtesy towards US vice-president Mike Pence, a civility cancelled by the North at the last minute. Pence was seated alongside Japanese Premier Shinzo Abe, witnessing the entry of the largest ever US winter team of 242. There was, too, a slight shift in perspective from

Bach, adjusting focus to the issue of clean athletes when warning competitors, 'You can only really enjoy your Olympic expectations if you respect the rules and are clean, only then will your memories be that of a worthy Olympian.'

Kim Yong-nam was there to celebrate the march of joint teams beneath the Unification flag of blue and white, jointly held aloft by Chung Su-hyon from the North and Park Jong-ah from the South, the flame then ignited by queenly figure skating champion from 2010 and runner-up in Sochi, Yuna Kim. Russia, clad in neutral white, their Olympic flag borne by a volunteer at the head of a team minus its 47 suspensions, roused applause only from their own supporters. Erin Hamlin, first US women's luge medal winner, carried their flag in a parade adjusted unavoidably over the last fortnight by director Song Seung-whan to accommodate the unexpected neighbourly guests. For a Games which had endured controversial economic preparations, the stage was a relatively small stadium of 35,000 which would hold no subsequent events and then be dismantled.

It is the spontaneous, extravagant touch of genius from youth that occasionally produces pinnacles of Olympic fame, and seldom had there been anything more spectacular than the emergence of 22-year-old Ester Ledecká: daughter of one of the Czech Republic's most popular singers and musical composers. Ledecká personified much that distinguishes the Olympic arena. Prominent as a snowboarder while ranked only 43rd on the Super-G World Cup skiing circuit, she now unleashed a performance that stunned previous ski champions such as title-defending Anna Veith of Austria and American Lindsey Vonn. Ledecká soared to an unexpected Super-G title and then, in snowboard's parallel giant slalom, her supposed preference, comfortably defeated Germans Selina Jörg and Ramona Hofmeister.

Ledecká was modest about her fame:

'It's hard to explain the difference between skiing and snowboarding, for me the two together are normal. Until this moment I'd considered I was a better snowboarder, so when I looked up at the television screen from the Super-G finishing pan, I was wondering what had just happened, thinking it was a mistake ... OK, they're going to change my time, I'll wait a bit and they'll adjust it. Still staring at the screen, nothing happened, everyone was shouting and I thought "this is weird", yet every time I stand at the start of either discipline I'm mentally going for gold, saying to myself "do your best and see what happens". Now it really did happen, yet I didn't expect this so soon on skis ... at the finish I met my mum, neither of us really understanding what had happened, asking her if I didn't miss any gates, thinking it was not such a good run that I'd made mistakes. Yes, snowboard helps my skiing mentally. I'd been dreaming since I was five about gold medals, but so many had said the double was impossible.'

Pyeongchang's ambitious winter venture was a low-key echo of Korea's innovative achievement at Seoul 30 years earlier: friendly, efficient, security prominent but light-handed, transport efficient, with apparent puzzlement among the local provincial population, unfamiliar with the outside world, at the sudden arrival of 100 foreign nations. A slightly guarded attitude was evident towards the small, noisy shoal of northern neighbours, alongside a veiled disdain for over-enthusiastic Russian spectators: they and their 'clean' competitors effectively 'quarantined' like ghosts at the banquet. Unlike Seoul 1988, the Games only marginally roused the country nationwide, the imposed restrictions on Russian eligibility promoting a mood of siege mentality.

The implausible project of the unified women's hockey team was a synchronisation nightmare for coach Sarah Murray, whose father Andy once coached Los Angeles Kings. Taking charge in a country without a league or formalised club structure, Murray had begun to install the squad's integration when suddenly confronted by the North's additional 12 players: a different language and an obligation to inject four of them into the team with mere weeks in which to have done so.

The consequence was predictable: in front of raucous support, 'Korea United' fell 6-1 to Sweden, their only other goal from Randi Griffin coming in a 4-1 loss to Japan. Born to an American father and Korean mother, Griffin had joined the South's senior squad a year earlier: the balance of play could be judged by goalkeeper Shin So-jung's saving of 44 shots to retain respectability. Asked if the hockey IF might attempt to keep the two Koreas together, president Renee Fasel reflected, 'That might be a good idea until 2022, to keep a joint team for Beijing, retain this unified experiment as a message of peace.' Despite voracious support, notably from the North's prominent contingent of women, the team was outplayed in all matches by a 20-1 aggregate: nonetheless heroines of the tournament attracting 15,000 fans to their matches. Lee Hee-beom, head of Pyeongchang's organising committee, said it was rewarding to experience the symbolic presence of a joint team as a demonstration of unity beyond politics.

The North's delegation had been divided into three categories – athletes, administrators and security members – social integration with Southern rivals rigorously monitored. Television coverage in the North was restricted, unwilling to expose the South's global reach, never mind that *Rodong Sinmun*, the North's state newspaper, proclaimed, 'South Korea is grateful to us for assisting with their Winter Games, which risked becoming the least popular in history because of the political situation.' Predictably, anti-doping tests were of mammoth proportion, 3,149 in and out of competition. There had been rumoured a possible IOC approval for lifting suspension of Russia's NOC in time for the Closing Ceremony, enabling the OAR team to re-appear under the national flag, but this prospect sank with disclosure of two new positive tests in curling mixed doubles and women's bobsleigh. Inescapable evidence emerged that under rigid testing surveillance, Sochi's elicit Russian medal haul was unrepeatable.

In the refined precision of alpine events, versatility can assist the route towards medals. Marcel Hirscher of Austria had been a world champion six times, Olympic fame eluding him, his only success a silver despite never finishing below fifth in two previous Games. Now, in the super combined of downhill and slalom, he finally proved his worth: the slalom leg being definitive, for Hirscher no surprise considering his record of 55 individual victories. The organisers were accused of jeopardising safety when allowing the women's slopestyle final to proceed, in conditions described by competitors as dangerous amid multiple crashes. Ski jumping and snowboarding events were all afflicted by fearsome weather yet controversially slopestyle continuation was approved by the IF: immediately doubtful when six of the first seven riders crashed in 30mph crosswinds. By the conclusion, there had been only nine clean runs out of 52. Aimee Fuller of Britain, after finishing 17th when crashing on her second run, described conditions as the worst she had ever encountered. Anna Gasser of Austria, a favourite finishing 15th, described the outcome as 'a lottery'.

Supreme in freestyle events for years had been Shaun White, American millionaire from his half-pipe gymnastics: otherwise known, for his red hair, as the 'Flying Tomato'. He now achieved, in the wake of his failure at Sochi, his third Olympic title, overwhelming heir-apparent Ayumu Hirano of Japan with an extravagance of tricks. Hirano briefly snatched the lead during a spectacular second run, but back soared White with the improbably named twists and turns, such as a '540 Stalefish', to retain the judges' verdict and his elite status – open to question in the light of ongoing allegations of sexual harassment within the rock band which White simultaneously managed.

Almost equivalent fame was now afforded to compatriot Chloe Kim, Korean-American, who became the youngest Olympic champion at 17 in the women's half-pipe. An uncomfortable question increasingly overhangs Olympic prestige: the impact of financial investment, whether for instance it is an acceptable return, on UK's £32m for Winter Games, for Lizzy Yarnold of Britain to successfully defend her skeleton title aged 29: sliding alone consuming £6.5m over four years. Yarnold had been playing catch-up after a break from the sport, and almost scratched following an ailing first run, but responded with a track record of 51.46 seconds in her fourth.

Vying with Ledecká as the most promising athlete of the Games, Norwegian Marit Bjørgen's accumulation of medals arrived with the regularity of a rush-hour bus service, opening her latest spectacular haul when taking silver as runner-up in skiathlon behind Charlotte Kalla of Sweden: Bjørgen's 11th Olympic medal passing her previously existing tie with Raisa Smetanina (USSR/Unified Team) and Stefania Belmondo (Italy). Next had arrived bronze for Bjørgen in the 10k, followed by gold in the cross-country 4x5k relay, this marking a tie on 13 medals with fellow Norwegian superstar Ole Einar Bjørndalen. Number 14 came in the cross-country team spirit with bronze – the ultimate achievement being, as a mother and at the age of 37, the 15th with gold over 30k, unparalleled for man or woman. The Games were notable for all-round Norwegian dominance, leaving Russia in the shade with their 39 medals – 14-14-11 – from a mere 109 competitors in 11 sports.

In no other sporting environment do the respective sexual identities of men and women, both athletic and interpretative, so visually engage in mutually sympathetic response as in ice dancing. Alongside other ice disciplines, this event offers cultural potential, both physical and abstract, far beyond any others, and seldom was this more evident than with the performance of Gabriella Papadakis and Guillaume Cizeron of France, who finished as runners-up. Theirs had been, in both short and free programmes, the ultimate in synchronised refinement, eliciting from a ballet critic the tribute, 'They are not even two humans but one single being moving on the ice, an action by him merging with a reaction by her.' Their performance, embracing a routine to Beethoven's 'Moonlight Sonata', was rapture itself, a window into another space. Yet such were the judging priorities that athleticism was ranked above ethereal interpretation: the leaps and turns by the accomplished Canadians Tessa Virtue and Scott Moir sufficient to reward them with the title following a duel of absorbing contrast, the author uninhibitedly wishing for triumph by the French world champions. Yet an unfortunate theoretical turning point for the French pair had come with a dress malfunction during their short programme, a faulty neck halter snapping to expose Gabriella's breast, necessitating spontaneous adjustment of their routine: impact on the judges' marking potentially decisive in one of the most poetic contests ever observed.

Harmony at the Closing Ceremony was partially clouded by the North's delegate being General Kim Yong-chol, alleged to have been involved in the sinking of the South's *Cheongnan* naval vessel. The concluding festival also departed from convention, there being no free-for-all conglomeration of competitors but proceeding country by country, with the event punctuated by the medal ceremony for the women's 30k cross-country, involving Marit Bjørgen's 15th medal. The Olympic anthem was joyously sung by ten-year-old Oh Yeon-joon, and once again a global Olympic audience was treated to a bare-chested Pita Taufatofua from Tonga. The US was represented by Ivanka Trump, her husband tweeting 'You cannot have a smarter representative' as she sat side-by-side with President Moon Jae-in and his wife Kim Jung-sook, a somewhat grim-faced General Kim Yong-chol in the row behind.

Thomas Bach duly passed the Olympic flag to Chen Jining, mayor of Beijing's hosting in 2022. The Russians moaned that their NOC status had not been returned in the wake of positive tests, preventing them from marching in conventional dress and carrying the national flag. Yet former ice hockey champion Igor Larionov remained realistic, 'Time needs to pass for the right to have our flag back, I think. Yet it's difficult for me to understand how any figure skater, hockey player or skier can win gold and stand on the podium without their flag.

That is sad.' Stanislav Pozdnyakov, Russia's delegation leader, admitted that the prospect of flying the national flag at the closing ceremony had meant more to the team than winning medals. He would have been unaware of the frustrated attempts by Russian computer hackers to disrupt the Olympics' internet and broadcast system and shut down ticket printing – thwarted by cyber security researchers injecting false flags to expose further Russian malevolence. Hitherto, Russian exponents had believed it was impossible to identify who was behind the shadowy world of cyberspace, their objective having been to indicate their falsified interference was sourced in North Korea or China, attempting to disrupt the Games in reprisal for Russian athletes' suspension.

There would be ongoing debate post-Pyeongchang, in the controversy surrounding Olympic expenditure and sustainability of venues: led for instance by Mintaro Oba, a former US diplomat involved on behalf of the South on North Korean policy. Quoted by *The Guardian*, he forecast, 'We will see a period of testing North Korea's intentions when the South outlines the strategy it wants to accomplish before any summit with Kim Jong-un, whether the North responds positively or attaches demands that Seoul cannot accept. The lull in tensions is unlikely to last far beyond the Olympics. Pyeongyang is likely to try to obtain concessions on economic sanctions in exchange for further dialogue or contacts such as reunions between families divided by the Korean War. How each side handles issues like this could give us a lot of insight into how flexible Seoul and Pyeongyang really are.' He and other experts agreed that once the South and the US resumed military exercises in the spring the North would express hostility, that tensions would rise again.

A further pessimism surrounded excess expenditure of £6bn having risen to £9.3bn. Andrew Zimbalist, professor at Smith College, US, and author of *The Economic Gamble Behind Hosting the Olympics*, forecast, 'Having the Games won't have changed the fact that outdoor winter sports are not traditionally popular in South Korea – the cost for maintaining the venues in Gangneung is unlikely to create a hot spot for foreign tourists, the IOC having warned that definitive legacy-use remained outstanding and suggesting they could become white elephants. Many winter sports rental shops had failed to prosper.'

Yet this pessimism was contradicted by subsequent analysis two years on at Manchester Metropolitan University by the Department of Economic Policy and Industrial Business under the title 'Supplementary Sustainable Legacy of 2018'. It recorded witnesses asserting that if forest restoration in the wake of the building of Pyeongchang's Alpine Centre would cost more than the building of the centre, then greater value would be added from expansion of Mount Gariwang for mountain tourism. A member of the Games organising committee claimed that despite environmental criticism, the venue was fully appraised for environmental impact and remained great value as an Olympic legacy. For local transportation infrastructure, more than twice the budget spent on the Olympics was spent on the development of high-speed trains and expressways that connected Gangwon Province to the capital Seoul. The aim of this network was not only to link the west and east of South Korea, but also to lower the psychological barrier surrounding Gangwon Province, which had taken the opportunity to promote its region as a logistic hub in north-east Asia, the state's next strategic goal.

The benefits of the Games corresponded with planning, suggesting that hosting a sports mega-event was an effective tool for promoting regional development. Gangwon had established itself as the mecca of winter sports in South Korea, in renown and in reality. Hosting a sports mega-event contributed to enhancement of the destination image in terms of tourism. Gangwon Province had previously lagged behind the balanced development of the Republic, with residents having a relatively low regional identity. The positive impact for local residents was an enhancement of their community sense, citizens who participated directly or indirectly with the Games could identify their pride in Gangwon Province's rise, it being clear the state had achieved the strategic goals they had originally planned.

The limitation of the study was that the proposed improvement in sustainability of such large events depended on the allegiance of both national and local government, the role of central government paramount in fulfilling national projects such as the Olympics. In the case of Pyeongchang, conflicts had existed between central and local government, because the bid was won under the initiative of the local government and then became a national project for central government. In terms of social legacy, hosting the Games had boosted the soft power of South Korea through North Korea's unexpected participation. Since the Olympics left a sustainable legacy in harmony with the economic, social and environmental pillars, this analysis of sustainability alongside previous Olympics was meaningful. Analysis of the entire project exposed the need for an independent agency to mediate between relative national authorities on any project of such dimension.

If Bach could feel satisfied with the reputation achieved by Asia's third Winter Games hosting – following Sapporo and Nagano – and the first of three consecutive Olympics in Asia, with Tokyo and Beijing on the horizon – he would have additional confidence that Agenda 2020 and academic analysis of Olympic objectives were financially in tune.

PYEONGCHANG 2018 MEDALS

Norway 39 (14-14-11)
Germany 31 (14-10-7)
Canada 29 (11-8-10)
United States 23 (9-8-6)
Netherlands 20 (8-6-6)
Sweden 14 (7-6-1)
South Korea 17 (5-8-4)
Switzerland 15 (5-6-4)
France 15 (5-4-6)
Austria 14 (5-3-6)
Japan 13 (4-5-4)
Italy 10 (3-2-5)
Olympic Athletes from Russia 17 (2-6-9)
Czech Republic 7 (2-2-3)
Belarus 3 (2-1-0)
China 9 (1-6-2)
Slovakia 3 (1-2-0)
Finland 6 (1-1-4)
Great Britain 5 (1-0-4)
Poland 2 (1-0-1)
Hungary 1 (1-0-0)
Ukraine 1 (1-0-0)
Australia 3 (0-2-1)
Slovenia 2 (0-1-1)
Belgium 1 (0-1-0)
New Zealand 2 (0-0-2)
Spain 1 (0-0-1)
Kazakhstan 1 (0-0-1)
Latvia 1 (0-0-1)
Liechtenstein 1 (0-0-1)

11

CONFRONTING COVID

FOR A president with ambitions to modernise the century-old foundation of the IOC, prospects for Tokyo 2020 a year hence could hardly have been more optimistic. There was every reason to expect the hub of Japanese imagination, ancient culture, inventive technology and industrial efficiency would deliver, in perception and deed, as exemplary a Games as 56 years earlier: then a burgeoning exhibition in the wake of humiliating World War Two defeat.

As a tyro visiting journalist in 1964, I had been transported by oriental efficiency: Bach in 2019 eagerly expected an injection of Olympic momentum during the 125th anniversary of the IOC's foundation, about to be celebrated with the opening of futuristic new headquarters in Lausanne. In his preface for the quarterly *Olympic Review* spring edition, he wrote:

'When we consider the tumultuous times that have accompanied the IOC since it was established, the endurance of the IOC and the Olympic Games stems from the fact that, from the very beginning, Coubertin saw sport, and its values of peace and friendship, as inherently linked. It is because of these timeless ethics that our mission, to make the world a better place through sport, continues to be relevant today.

'An important milestone will be the inauguration of Olympic House, the decision to consolidate all IOC offices here in Lausanne under one roof. More than simply another building, Olympic House is intended as a symbol and embodiment of our mission. The design of the building, which is inspired by the motion of an athlete, is intended to reflect fluidity and agility – important for any organisation – while the dove emblem visible from above is the universal symbol of peace, one of the values which define the Olympic Movement.

'Sustainability is another core element that we wanted to incorporate, which is why the building has been constructed according to the highest sustainability standards: electricity generated by the solar roof panels allowing the building to be self-sufficient in heating, ventilation, cooling and hot water. Transparency, too, is a key element of many of our Agenda 2020 reforms involving governance. This is reflected through the building's glass façades and open office spaces, intended to make the building welcoming and reflect our transparency.

'The design is by 3XN of Copenhagen in partnership with IttenBrechbuhl of Switzerland, contemporary in desire to shape the future with its glass façade creating openness and commitment to sustainability … a staircase symbolising the Olympic Rings to connect different floors, iconic without being ostentatious. Olympic House embodies five factors: symbolism, collaboration, flexibility, sustainability and integration with the historic Chateau, in combination with Louis Bourget Park landscape.'

Evolution of Lausanne administration, in continuation of the Agenda concept, advanced in June 2019, with Executive Board guidance on host city incentive, a crucial step to transform future host city elections: approval of changes projected a month earlier, creating an ongoing international dialogue to generate interest among cities, regions, countries, and especially NOCs, to attract both Olympic and Youth Games. Simultaneously to establish two Future Host Commissions, for Summer and Winter Games, exploring global interest and report back to the Executive Board: thereby to ensure an exclusive once-in-a-lifetime experience for the world's athletes, and to grant any IOC Session enhanced input by having non-

EB members forming part of these commissions. A role for the commissions would be to encourage prospective hosts for a more flexible view of innovative proposals, such projects not necessarily referring to a single city, and allowing more variable timing, adjusted to local context. IOC members would continue to be at the centre of the decision-making, granting Session approval.

An almost immediate host election was only three months away, for the Winter Games of 2026: the choice for which, with rampant withdrawals by four other hesitant contestants, had narrowed to a pair, Milan and Stockholm. The truth behind this decision, quite simply in the author's view, was that the IOC owed Sweden an overdue favour by 107 years: the time since the Stockholm Games of 1912 emblazoned modern Olympic virtues on a global audience in the wake of equivocal, exploratory festivals in Athens, Paris, St Louis and a chauvinistic event in London 1908.

It had been Sweden which had carved a gold medal as hosts, yet had never since been granted either a summer or winter award. Now, surely, was the moment for history, for the IOC, to recognise an enduring contribution to Olympic principles. And had not Italy, in the shape of Turin, been winter hosts as recently as 2006? It was more than evident that Stockholm, with its snow subsidiary host of Are, would be accommodating Agenda requirements of economy and sustainability, justifying Bach's intended adjustments. Of the 12 Winter Games staged within Europe since inaugural Chamonix in 1924, there had been three staged in France, two each in Austria, Italy, Norway and Switzerland, one in Germany, and none in Sweden. Yet in Winter Games medals ranking, Sweden lay fifth behind the USA, Soviet Union/Russia, the former GDR and Norway, Sweden boasting 20 per cent more medals than Italy. Now here the nation was bidding on the same near empty Scandinavian map as Rio back in 2009. I had no personal opposition to Milan, Italy always a strident source of Winter Olympics excellence, and providing prominent members of the IOC. It seemed simply not to be its turn: once more a moment for the IOC to heed their collective conscience. It was not to be.

For a while the Italians had fluctuated. A year earlier, there had been the likelihood of another bid by Turin, but within weeks that foundered and the Italian NOC (CONI) announced a project combining Milan and Cortina d'Ampezzo. Within a couple of months, Milan-Cortina had government backing, though without financial investment, this coming from the regions of Lombardy and Veneto, though by the spring of 2019 the government committed to financial aid: never mind that in July 2018 the IOC had confirmed a substantial funding contribution to any successful host city bid. When the vote came at the Lausanne Session in June 2019, Milan-Cortina enjoyed a majority of 13, 47-34, Sweden once more relegated to also-rans, while a satisfied Bach was able to claim, 'The new candidature process has demonstrated the success of Agenda 2020. We have lowered the cost and complexity of Games projects, which now serve the long-term development goals of host communities and have sustainability and legacy at their heart. This has led to a significantly reduced organisation budget and the use of 93 per cent existing or temporary competition venues. Milan-Cortina will feature iconic venues and beautiful settings, combining the attractions of a modern European metropolis with a classic alpine environment.' Was Sweden, with snow, less than classic?

Sustaining the IOC's advance on all fronts came the signing in June of the first joint TOP partnership agreement: Coca-Cola and the Mengniu Dairy company of China, a blend combining the non-alcoholic beverage and the dairy categories, gaining Mengniu a worldwide passport. The agreement was for a 12-year term through to 2032, including unprecedented investment in traditional and digital media, promoting Olympic values globally while extending Coca-Cola's association with the Olympic arena to a historic 104 years, the longest in the Games. Mengniu was the first Chinese consumer goods as a TOP partner, supporting ambitious growth plans as the leading dairy manufacturer worldwide by 2025. Bach reflected, 'This is another demonstration of the relevance of the Olympic Games – having our longest-standing partner Coca-Cola, iconic American brand, collaborating with a young Chinese company, illustrating the unifying power of the Olympics.'

At his 134th Session address, Bach stressed how maintenance of Olympic values in a disruptive world was essential:

'The ideals of de Coubertin have stood the test of time, now vital as we face an age of increasing crises, the significance of the Olympic Games as relevant now as ever. His idea of uniting the world through sport, so many years ago, is even more defining of our movement today. Now, as then, humanity is living in an era when the world is drifting apart, hardly a day without news of rising nationalism, mistrust or protectionism, witnessing more isolation, separation, confrontation and diminishing co-operation, thereby increasing the relevance of our Games.

'The enduring power of the Games is universality, and we are only able to achieve this by exhibiting universal respect. Fundamental within the IOC's resilience is distributing 90 per cent of our revenue to benefit athletes globally. This means $1.5bn is re-invested in sport: in the four years of an Olympiad, $5bn supporting athletes and sports organisations from every continent ... there is no one-size-fits-all solution. If de Coubertin were with us today, I think he would be pleased to find how still relevant is his Olympic dream. Knowing of his idealism, he would also have a message: keep striving, keep changing. The universality of the Olympic Games can only happen when everyone has mutual respect.'

Bach's first three Games in charge had been anything other than unmitigated satisfaction. Sochi, exceptional in context, had become a nightmare in retrospect, the consequences of which had thus compromised both Rio and then Pyeongchang. By the autumn of 2019, sport was gearing itself for the prospect of a welcome climax at Tokyo 2020. An ever-optimistic Bach expressed his expectation in the autumn edition of *Olympic Review*:

'A little under a year from now, all eyes will be on Japan as the world comes together in celebration of sport and peace and harmony at the Games of Tokyo 2020. I can truly say I've never seen an Olympic city as prepared as Tokyo is with one year to go. It will be the second time that the city hosts the Games, the first in 1964. Some of the venues used then will have another Olympic outing as they welcome athletes and spectators once more. These Games will be innovative in so many ways. Just as Tokyo 1964 transformed the Games technologically – live television images beamed around the world for the first time – Tokyo 2020 will also showcase the country's inventive prowess. Fleets of low-carbon-emission vehicles and automated driving solutions will be used to transport people: robots will assist with luggage at airports, give passengers directions, and recommend tourist attractions in Japanese, English, Chinese and Korean. The city's sustainability credentials will also be on show, embodied by the medals that have been made using precious metals extracted from discarded laptops, mobile phones and other electronic devices donated by the Japanese public.

'For the athletes, Tokyo 2020 will offer new opportunities. With a record 48.8 per cent female participation, these Games will be all but gender equal. Thirty-three sports will feature on the programme, five of them new: baseball/softball is returning, while karate, sport climbing, surfing and skateboarding make their debuts. Of the 339 medal events, 18 are new. Tokyo 2020 will be more youthful, more urban and more female than any Games previously. Interest in tickets has exceeded all expectation, 3.2 million being sold in the first access, while more than 200,000 people have applied to volunteer in one of the 80,000 positions required, so that they too may be part of the Olympic story. All the elements that comprise truly outstanding Olympic Games are in place. The athletes of all 206 NOCs, as well as the IOC Refugee Olympic Team, can look forward to an amazing experience.'

In mid-November emerged disciplinary detonation upon Russia by the Compliance Review Committee, WADA imposing a four-year ban across a complexity of sports in the wake of non-compliance. Agreement by WADA's executive would remove Russia from multiple major events, including the Olympic Games and many world championships across different sports. Russian refusal to see beyond the end of their own noses remained myopic: Umar Kremlev, head of Russia's boxing federation, scornful of the decision, insisting, 'Russia plays an important role in the development of global sport.' That was not, however, the way WADA considered things. 'The guilty should be punished in the toughest way possible,' the IOC stated in approval of the CRC.

The IOC condemned the manipulation of data acquired from RUSADA's Moscow laboratory, deeming it 'an attack on the credibility of sport', yet welcoming the opportunity for Russian athletes who were never found guilty of doping violations still to be granted access, despite the looming national ban. The CRC recommended Russia be stripped of hosting rights in any competition during a four-year period, with any hosting already awarded to be transferred to a different nation. With some sense of reality, the Russian Olympic Committee, any involvement in gross manipulation never alleged, called for total reinvention of the Russian Athletics Federation, several officials having been charged with obstructing investigations. ROC president Stanislav Pozdnyakov was requesting total overhaul of the federation's management, 'The indictment of its officials inflicts colossal reputational damage on our country as a whole.'

As 2020 was welcomed, and Switzerland summoned emotions for injecting momentum into Lausanne's hosting of the Youth Winter Games, none could have guessed the volcanic global health hazard that would erupt in three months' time, emanating from China and engulfing the globe.

When Swiss flag-bearer Thibe Deseyn entered Lausanne's Vaudoise Arena, the roar of an 8,000 crowd signalled another historic experience in the home of the IOC established by de Coubertin. The last time athletes had come to Switzerland to compete for Olympic medals was in 1948, St Moritz the Winter Games host. Seventy-two years on, Youth Olympians competing in sliding events would follow down the same track, the famed St Moritz Bob Run, though the heart of the Youth Games was now Lausanne: embracing sustainability while allowing maximum engagement of public and competitors.

A torch tour had travelled across 26 cantons to raise enthusiasm: now the Swiss team's youngest member, 14-year-old ice dancer Gina Zehnder, ignited the Olympic cauldron to trigger action, drawing 640,000 spectators to eight competition sites. When alpine skier Amélie Klopfenstein won the first gold medal in women's Super-G, she sparked a medal rush for the Swiss team. Skiing without fear, she added gold in the giant slalom, plus a bronze in combined to become a national heroine. 'I came here relaxed, didn't have any pressure, so it feels like a dream.' Other Swiss stars were twin brothers Thomas and Robin Brissard, competing in the new sport of ski mountaineering. Winning gold and silver in the individual event, they teamed with Deseyn and Caroline Ulrich to win mixed gold.

At the skating arena, Korean You Young stunned the audience with a winning total of 214 points, a 15-year-old who had already won four national titles, earning comparison with her idol, the 2010 Olympic champion Yuna Kim. Young was followed by another Korean, Seo Whi-min, soaring away with both women's 500m and 1,000m short track events. Women were widely prominent, with expectation for two years hence in Beijing. Kelly Sildaru of Estonia, already senior world champion, was exceptional in winning the slopestyle, extended in her victory by the challenge of China's Gu Ailing – fame awaiting in Beijing – to whose silver medal was added gold in half-pipe and big air on subsequent days.

Lausanne 2020 made history as the first bi-national Youth Games, Nordic events taking place at Les Tuffes in France, an Agenda 2020 manifestation. Alena Mokhova, Russian biathlete, claimed two golds, but home fans celebrated Mathieu Garcia and Gianne Richard winning the mixed relay. Mixed gender events being a Youth Games staple, outstanding was the curling victory when Norway won mixed team gold, half their team being Lillehammer-based, inspired by the event when staged at their home in 2016, and training for Lausanne ever since.

Buoyed by a vibrant Youth Games, Tokyo mood paused: news began to emerge of a rogue virus in a Chinese province. As yet there was no intercontinental mood of panic, certainly not in Europe. At an Executive Board meeting on 5 March, Bach reassured the Olympic Movement all was proceeding as normal towards the scheduled Games in August, announcing, 'I would like to encourage all athletes to continue their preparation for the Olympic Games with confidence and at full steam. We are confident that Japan will push through amidst the novel coronavirus disease outbreak. The Games will go ahead as scheduled and no Plan B is being considered.' The Executive Board vowed to keep athletes and NOCs up to date, having already established a joint task force with Japan's organising committee, Tokyo's metropolitan government and the World Health Organization, to discuss delivery of the Games. Tokyo's assessed measures to prevent spread of the virus during the Torch Relay restricted public access to ceremonies. The organising committee would also reduce its delegation to the torch-lighting ceremony in Greece, involving a cultural performance by 140 young Japanese high school students.

The Asia/Oceania qualifying boxing tournament was among the first of events to be impacted, moving from Wuhan in China – the plague's reported origin – to Amman, Jordan. The IOC established a task force to assess the full impact of the pandemic; by the end of February there were almost

80,000 cases in mainland China, even if as yet there was minimal impact in Japan where, with more than five months until the scheduled Opening Ceremony, both Japanese and IOC remained confident for a safe environment, as planned, by July. Yet by 11 March the WHO had declared Covid-19 to be a pandemic, the sporting landscape likewise changing by the day. 'We could see the progress being made in Japan, fighting the virus and the efficiency of measures being taken,' said Bach. 'On the other hand, the virus was spreading so rapidly, it increasingly became a question of whether the world could travel to Japan, and if Japan could afford to invite them.'

The escalation would unavoidably lead to Bach's confrontation with Premier Abe on 24 March. 'Human lives take precedence over everything, including staging the Games,' Bach said. 'The IOC wants to be part of the solution, our leading principle to safeguard the health of everyone involved, to contribute to containing the virus.' With dramatic increases in Covid-19 around the world and fresh outbreaks in different countries on different continents, the Executive Board realised the possible need to change the start date of the Games: the decision to postpone was not one the IOC could take by itself. The only unilateral decision in its power would be to cancel the Games outright, an outcome to be avoided at all cost, as it would crush the Olympic dreams of so many athletes. 'It was clear from the beginning that cancellation should not be something that the IOC would favour,' insisted Bach. With cancellation off the table, postponement could only be made with Tokyo agreement.

Within the space of a couple of weeks, the IOC's wilful façade of optimism – that a minutely prepared, financed and scheduled Games was indestructible – would crumple under the onslaught of nature: an innovative animal-originating infection, liberated whether or not inadvertently by Chinese laboratory research, had begun to overpower not just a sports festival but, at irresistible pace, entire countries on every continent. It was not consideration of athletes' health – an

191

essential issue – which finally provided the IOC with the inevitability of postponement of Tokyo 2020, but as the author understands from anonymous sources, additional pressure from key Olympic sponsors which subsidise the billion-dollar bill. Bach, all too aware of the potential infection cauldron of 10,000 athletes plus older officials gathered for three meals a day in the Olympic Village, and being widely criticised for continuing delayed action – speaking of a conclusion 'in four weeks' – was partially being stalled by Japan's oriental obsession, 'saving face'. Premier Shinzo Abe and Games leader Yoshirō Mori were praying that, during April, the pandemic might ease: a wholly unrealistic expectation with global deaths mounting by the day.

Anonymous springboard for postponement came, the author was advised, via an agent formerly working on behalf of two household-name sponsors. Alarmed that a Games shorn of many elite competitors would be downgraded, the sponsors discreetly demanded a halt to the 2020 venture. Bach, of course, could not point a gun at Japan's government, which was locked into emotional national expectation, the Torch Relay imminent and billions of dollars invested. The agent-adviser, from experience dating back to the presidency of Samaranch, was well aware the route to power and authority, even in sport, lies in money. The sponsors, discreetly, needed to be heeded. Meanwhile, Premier Abe, seeking political re-election, was agreeable to accept the lion's share of the postponement's additional costs, thought to approach $3m, but beyond that much was in doubt. Would the Olympic Village facilities survive? The major risk was an increased virus spike causing prohibition of travel, plus the threat to international federations already living beyond their means even without the stress of health-orientated rearrangements.

Also unknown was the attitude of authoritarian governments on foreign travel, and thereby reduction of foreign income. America's Anita DeFrantz, then the IOC vice-president, was cautious on how the IOC would handle

Emotional drive: Thomas Bach (front right), Olympic fencing foil team triumph in 1976 primed his energy to transform IOC administration four decades later.

Egyptian obstetrician, African swimming record-breaker, Rania Elwani reflects as 'failed' semi-finalist: 'If only media understood the immeasurable joy of participation.'

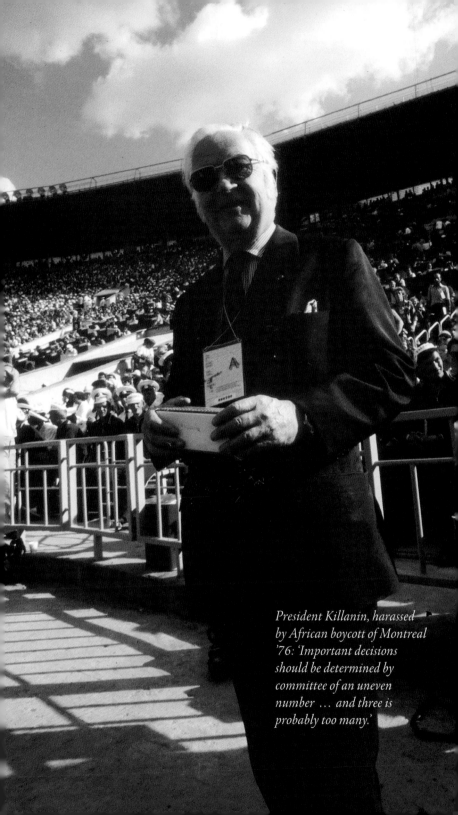

President Killanin, harassed by African boycott of Montreal '76: 'Important decisions should be determined by committee of an uneven number … and three is probably too many.'

President Samaranch congratulating five-Games champion Steve Redgrave (centre), having quelled Salt Lake '98 scandal through Constitution Commission 2000: a prompt for Bach's future Agenda.

Hand-in-glove misfit? Kuwait's powerbroker Sheikh Ahmad, head of both Asia's and world NOCs, may have clandestinely frustrated Thomas Bach's 2011 Munich bid for Winter Games '18.

Loser greets winner: Canadian Richard Pound (L) scuppered for IOC president in 2001 by adverse events, congratulates Thomas Bach's 2013 rout.

Charm, intellect, but no electorate: Richard Carrion, Puerto Rico banker, distant runner-up in presidential election, appointed by Bach as chair of promotional Olympic TV channel.

Jean-Claude Killy (FRA), triple ski champion of Grenoble '68, knew normal essentials as IOC co-ordinator for Sochi, unaware of deftly corrupted Games.

John Coates, Australian guru backing Thomas Bach's Agenda 2020 reformation, Monte Carlo 2014.

Not so friendly: Marius Vizer (left), president of both International Judo and SportAccord, encountered avalanche eclipse when recklessly advocating a World Games in rivalry to IOC.

Women were ski jumping for decades without jeopardising fertility, patronising Olympic males finally relenting: Germany's Carina Vogt soared to inaugural freedom in Sochi.

Francois Carrard, Swiss legal-eagle, director-general of IOC 1989–2003: 'Without Bach's innovations, the IOC might not have lasted another 20 years.'

Defending figures title of 2010, Korean Yuna Kim remained queen of style – but Russia's Adelina Sotnikova's jumps wowed 2014 judges. Carolina Kostner (ITA) (right) took bronze.

Still offering mutual goodwill post-hoc, Bach innocently and unwittingly engages President Putin at SportAccord Convention in 2015.

Alex Zhukov, Russia's Olympic chief, projects Vladimir Putin's veiled criminal Games ambition for Olympics at Sochi.

Bicentenario de la Independencia 1810
Centenario de la Revolución 1910

Master criminal detective: Canadian lawyer Richard McLaren itemised long extended Russian drug abuse.

Box of tricks: Grigori Rodchenkov, manipulator/whistle-blower of endemic Russian cheating, now exiled in USA.

Golden Try: captain Osea Kolinisau celebrates Fiji's unprecedented rugby sevens victory over Britain at Rio '16.

Mo Farah (GBR) emulates 1970s' Double-Double of Lasse Viren (FIN) in 5,000/10,000m, London and now Rio.

Tegla Loroupe of Kenya, marathon champion of Sydney 2000 and world record-holder, summoned in 2016 to head the inaugural Refugee Team.

Usain Bolt, Jamaican marvel, whose sprint sensations rescued World Athletics' tarnished reputation.

Michael Phelps, US phenomenon! 'I don't think I've ever swum in a clean race'.

Having swum to haul a sinking raft of refugees to safety, Yusra Mardini earns global acclaim as representative among the inaugural Refugee Team at Rio '16.

Andy Murray receives tennis gold from Richard Pound at Rio '16: did Roger Federer (SWI) generously go easy in front of a Wimbledon Final crowd four years earlier?

expansion of the pandemic, she anxious not to rock the boat, to protect the institution to which she had devoted her life since being an Olympic oarswoman and then village director at Los Angeles 1984. DeFrantz was alarmed by the extent to which many IFs were irresponsibly too dependent for survival on their share of Olympic revenue, likely to be much reduced within a postponed Games, 'The IOC is always willing to adjust, to adapt, and I admit we don't know what may emerge even next month. We have to be flexible, we are doing our best to ensure that athletes will still be able to compete, intent to preserve the Olympic ethic: that subtle blend of elitism and universality, all too aware that Covid-19 portends a future within which tomorrow would never be the former "normal", yet the Olympic Games are fundamentally about emotional integration.'

This crisis beyond imagination quadrupled the threat to a sporting empire which Bach had already been at full stretch attempting to hold together. Scheming its survival was now no longer a question of theoretical constitutional adjustment, but immediate stark reality. While the possibility of postponement had still hung in the balance, Bach released an interim advisory 'warning' – advocating global refinement of the sporting calendar to accommodate financial limitations inevitably imposed by health imponderables – advice not governed by panic but necessity, as relayed by agency Sport Intern, 'The Olympic Movement should look more closely into the proliferation of sports events, in order to streamline the calendar. It is clear that probably none of us will be able to sustain every single initiative or event that we were planning before this crisis, we'll need to look closely at the scope of some activities and make necessary adjustments. In this context the IOC is reviewing its own budget and priorities, shortly to be debated by the Executive Board. We may also have to look more closely into the proliferation of sports events, already discussed at previous Sessions. The financial pressure on all stakeholders, including NOCs, IFs and Organising

Committees may require tighter consolidation. As challenging as the circumstances may appear right now, if we draw lessons from the experience, we shall survive.'

Meanwhile, amid global anxiety, John Coates, Australia's head of the IOC's Co-ordination Commission for Tokyo, had negotiated a declaration by Australia's NOC, in conjunction with Canada, announcing that both nations would withdraw from the scheduled Games in July. Together with clandestine pressure from sponsors, the release of this news – breached through a media agency by the IOC's most senior member, Canada's former IOC vice-president Dick Pound – had effectively proved conclusive in Bach's protracted assessment of the crisis with Premier Abe. Postponement had become imperative.

A measured account of the multiple negotiations with all Games stakeholders, which had finally led to the postponement, was contained in the summer edition of *Olympic Review*, which had begun with Bach's preface:

'The decision to postpone the Games by a year is historic, never previously happening in 124 years, though the Games were cancelled on three occasions due to war. Yet despite the uncertainty dominating daily life and the resulting unprecedented decision, it has served to demonstrate the solidarity of the Olympic Movement. The decision could not have been made without the consensus of all parties: our counterparts in Japan, the Tokyo Metropolitan Government and the organising committee, including that of the Paralympic Games. We reached the most sensible decision in the circumstances. The health of those involved in the Games was our number one concern, aware that many athletes were worried about being able to train and qualify, while living in confinement. We reached out to them in a call to more than 200 athlete representatives. The announcement was welcomed by all 206 NOCs and by the Refugee Olympic Team, as well as by IFs and our broadcast and sponsor partners. This widespread consensus gives us confidence for the complex task of rearrangement a year from now. None of us know when the pandemic will end, normal life will resume, but we are encouraged to have the support of the entire Olympic Movement.'

With dramatic development of the pandemic, Bach called Games president Yoshirō Mori on 22 March, suggesting discussion including postponement. After consulting Premier Abe, Mori confirmed they were ready to debate different scenarios provided the IOC were committed not to cancel the Games, and further debate was scheduled for 24 March. By then, the WHO had announced further widespread infection and when Bach and Abe spoke, agreement on postponement quickly arrived. 'We could have decided on cancellation, on our own,' Bach admitted, 'but for postponement we needed full commitment with Japan, and this is what we achieved – the hope and assurance that the Olympic dream can still come true, even with delay. This is a huge jigsaw puzzle, and every piece will have to fit … this is why I really do not envy the members of the task force. I've seen proof of their professionalism, and the dedication of the organising committee, which had already made Tokyo the best prepared Olympic host city ever. I'm really confident that we can master this challenge. The Games have never been postponed before, we have no blueprint, but we are nevertheless confident that we can put a beautiful jigsaw puzzle together and have a wonderful Games.'

It was interesting, journalistically, for a lay observer to find amid an acute international crisis involving the lives of many hundreds of administrators, that the man in charge maintained a perspective of philosophical consideration alongside legal necessities. Reflecting on an ancient philosophy, 'May you live in interesting times', Thomas Bach had one moment observed:

'We must accept that in some circumstances the IOC itself becomes a target. We were not the only ones estimating criteria which were changing day by day, with governments everywhere doing the same. We had to respect not one government but

205 in an ever-changing scenario, the worst at the time in Japan, but the figures rising alarmingly worldwide. Then came the WHO declaration of "global pandemic", with forecast of imminent mutations from South Africa, and I remember an urgent summoning of the EB, a 12-hour debate, further calls to Tokyo, the safety of the Games on a knife edge, consideration of postponement, Japan acknowledging their readiness to agree on the one assurance that was no cancellation. I told them this was never in my mind. That possibility had to be addressed. I confirmed that the formality of cancellation could only come from the IOC, but that what was needed was collaboration on both sides, that with cancellation off the table postponement became the option, the collaboration with Premier Abe was one of trust, the key to Japan's reliability, the mutual sense that we must protect the athletes and live up to our mutual mission to preserve the concept of the Games.'

For the athletes, concerns about their health were a major factor from postponement; they would now be faced with re-scheduling training and adjusting to a new timetable. Among other challenges were re-scheduling all 339 separate events and ensuring that all 42 competition venues would still be available. Similarly, ensuring that the Olympic Village remained accessible, as the 5,000-apartment complex built for 2020 was planned to fulfil a long-term housing need following the Games. Fortunately, measures introduced as part of Agenda 2020 meant that the IOC had a closer working relationship with Tokyo than with previous organising committees, making the decision process more agile and flexible than ever before.

Christophe Dubi, IOC Olympic Games executive director, reflected, 'We were able to navigate through complicated discussions, because everyone was speaking with one voice. This alignment between all parties helps each of us make the right decision at the same time. The Olympic Movement has walked in unison through this crisis, and the support we got was remarkable. It was understood by everybody that this was the best solution in this context, and shows Olympic

Movement unity is strong. Postponement is never ideal, but at least we had all the conditions in place to deliver the best event possible.'

Bach and Abe believed that the Olympic Flame had a powerful role to play during the pandemic. 'We agreed the flame should stay in Japan, as a symbol of our commitment, a symbol of hope,' Bach said. 'We both envisaged that next year these Games could be a celebration of humanity, by having overcome this unprecedented crisis. The Olympic Flame can really become the light at the end of this dark tunnel which the whole world is experiencing at this moment.'

If Bach and Dubi were entitled to feel quietly triumphant, extended collaboration with Japanese counterparts having rescued a doomed Games with unprecedented postponement, a burning arrow was added to the social furnace in late April by hurdles champion from Montreal 1976, Frenchman Guy Drut: a lone voice bellowing for rationality among ambitious self-centred athletes and equally selfish IFs. The immediacy of Drut's challenge lay with the responsibility of Paris to host the Olympic Games of 2024. Belatedly, it might be said, Drut was ascending the platform which Bach had mounted six years earlier: the campaign for Olympic financial prudence. Drut's was a verbal assault, 'Contemporary Olympic administration has become obsolete, outdated, disconnected from reality. Current and future Games, while ideologically imperative in principle, cannot continue whatever the cost, forthcoming Games at Tokyo, Beijing, Paris, Milan and LA should establish revised criteria.' All very well, but a bit late you might say, Thomas Bach already being way down the road. President Samaranch, sponsor-wise, had erected the scaffolding of an ever-steeper sporting Mont Blanc, after which Jacques Rogge had marked time. Bach had recognised with Agenda 2020 that modernisation was essential, yet the lust for inclusion by multiple fringe sports envious of the Olympic pay cheque, made the IOC and the Games, in the opinion of many, too big for their own boots.

Agreement was immediate from Gerhard Heiberg, Norwegian mastermind of Lillehammer's Winter Games of 1994, 'I understand what Guy is saying, after '94 I believed it was possible to increase the numbers for Winter Games, but sensed the Summer Games were already too big. I feel for Guy – let us choose a fresh format, less big and complicated. It would be difficult with so many new sports knocking at the door, but I think, as did Jacques Rogge, we should keep the number to 28: the number of athletes for additional events as well as sports has continued to grow. The time has come to say enough is enough. I sense there are huge risks for 2021, I'm sure we need to do something to protect the future. The timing now is right – the Games cannot continue to grow.'

Drut's anxiety was met with a swift response from compatriot Tony Estanguet, multiple Olympic canoe champion and chair of Paris 2024. He asserted, 'From the start, our purpose has been to create the Games of a new era, making adjustments, taking into consideration effects of the Covid pandemic with Games that are responsible, sustainable, socially conscious, and open for everyone in the public to be involved. The current context and the unprecedented crisis we are experiencing mean we need to go even further in the directions we already chose.' A particular change by Paris is reduction in the athletes' village capacity from 17,000 to 14,000, regarding the level of investment required and the legacy for the area Seine-Saint-Denis. Paris' intention to illustrate its determination to deliver an innovative and responsible new model for Games organisation was already in line with changes applied to the postponement of Tokyo.

While officialdom battled to hold Tokyo 2020 on course for its curtain-raiser a year late, some prominent athletes were busy wrestling with long-standing emotional issues: racism, social integration, employment prejudice – four centuries old in USA and visibly lingering elsewhere, including Australia: emotionally sustained by recollections of subordination for Jesse Owens in the 1930s, Smith and Carlos at Mexico 1968, alongside contemporary civic protests such as Black Lives Matter. In 2020, demand mounted within the IOC's Athletes Commission for the abolition of Charter Rule 50, prohibiting demonstration on the Olympic podium. It was, some claimed, an inalienable human right for an athlete's freedom to utilise the sporting arena to challenge racial prejudice. The new chair of the Athletes Commission, five-time Olympic swimmer Kirsty Coventry from Zimbabwe – succeeding Ruggiero – pooled her members and happily found a majority in agreement with protest prohibition.

Prominent among protestors had been Gwen Berry, US champion hammer thrower, disciplined for a staged protest during the Pan-Am Games. A mood was mounting to oblige the IOC to modify Rule 50 in time for Tokyo's Games. Bach intended to hold firm on the ancient Greek ethic: truce observed during any Games, intent on peace and friendship, but protest on the podium insulting to other competitors in a contest where all are equal. To relax Rule 50 would be to open the Olympic Games to theatrical anarchy: what might have occurred, say, at Barcelona 1992, with Spanish medal winners who were Catalan Separatists? Rampant disruption among medal winners? Fortunately, the wisdom of Coventry's advice – survivor from President Mugabe's racist regime – sustained the precious neutral symbolism of Olympic fame. The context of the Olympic Village remains available to campaign for further racial integration in a circumspect formal gathering.

Coventry's intervention had been comprehensive, emphasising that the Athletes Commission intended, 'To take a lead in the conversation, having more than 60 global Athletes Commissions represented in our poll, with a conviction that the venues, the Olympic spirit and the uniqueness of the Games needed to be respected – that there was a time and place for athletes to make their voice heard, but this should not be on the field of play or during a medals ceremony. This reflected the influence of our athletes. We are delighted that the EB fully supported our proposals.'

The Executive Board's acceptance of the principle in the summer of 2020 was a reflection of the views of over 3,000 athletes representing all Olympic sports, with gender-equal representation: increasing opportunities for athletes' expression while preserving the podium, field of play and official ceremonies from any demonstration. Support for the Athletes Commission additionally came from FINA's president Husain Al-Musallam, commenting, 'The victory ceremony is a moment that commands respect and triumph for sporting achievement and should not be remembered by personal expression.' Criticism of the athletes' response by *USA Today* immediately prior to Tokyo's Opening Ceremony fell on stony ground, and during the Games there would be no more than a couple of trivial incidents, including Chinese track cyclists wearing a Chairman Mao on their jackets on the podium. The decathlon gold medal of American-Indian Jim Thorpe in 1912, of Afro-American Billy Mills at 10,000m in Mexico 1968, Bantu South African Josia Thugwane's marathon in Atlanta 1996 and Aborigine Cathy Freeman's 400m in 2000 are the best of all demonstrations for racial integration. The beauty of Rule 50 is precisely for the reason that it excludes protest.

Throughout 2020, daily life and world affairs shrank beneath an ever-darkening sky, disease and possible death reducing horizons and ambitions to minimal proportion. Simple family survival, if fortunate. Yet an historic innovation, paramount to Olympic future, was about to puncture the gloom. One of the key areas addressed by Agenda 2020 had been host city candidate procedure, integrating economic, social and environmental planning rather than trying to accommodate local context: less expensive, maximising efficiencies with stronger emphasis on legacy, reforms allowing more flexibility. The impact had been considerable, with a one-year non-committal dialogue introduced in consideration for the Winter Games of 2026, resulting in cost reductions of both the candidature and proposed operating budgets of respectively 80 and 20 per cent below the previous average for 2018 and 2022.

So effective had been the partnership prior to the election of Milan-Cortina, that a working party was established to consider extended implementation, leading by October 2019 to continuous dialogue by potential cities with the IOC through two permanent Future Host Commissions. The deadlines of past campaigns would no longer exist. 'We must continue to keep up with the pace of change,' reflected Bach. 'Flexibility is a necessity for effective governance and the Games' future. Maintaining the magic, the principle of universality and commitment to the athletes is the crux of everything we do. We had exponentially fewer and fewer candidates which was why we had to have change, to follow guidance from the business world and other sports events organisers, to avoid the situation where one bidding candidate is attacking the others. This was not the best procedure, either for the future of the Games, nor for the reputation of the IOC.'

Francesco Ricci Bitti, confidante of Bach, knew the sanity of the change, 'This revived the leadership of Samaranch's reforms, and increased the influence of the EB. The incidence of a Session once a year could not follow the necessary speed of effective business management now that sport had become more and more relevant, faster in its evolution. There is still a major concern about the interference of outside financial sources in the governance of sport, of private equity firms which we have seen involved in volleyball, creating dangerous risks, disrupting long-term confidence. Now the process will be simpler. The most effective executive in sport I've known was Philippe Chatrier in international tennis, ideal in the business sense in the guise of a CEO, and today I think this is what Thomas Bach has become.'

Dick Pound likewise reflected, 'Thomas is so well organised, concentrating on change, his style when fencing: attack, attack. Under city selection by the Session, this was beyond some members, when in two minds, that had partially been the problem with the Salt Lake vote, the wisdom too narrow, the effect beginning during Rogge's presidency. With Samaranch, he mostly knew beforehand which way the vote would go after guidance from what was then the Evaluation Commission.'

The advent of the new format, following closely on the heels of the double Paris-LA election, was that removal of 'competition' from the candidature process would be the decline in publicity for Olympic affairs between Games: yet it was the publicity and competition between rival cities that had become self-destructive.

Though easily recalled, the promise by the IOC for a better tomorrow was no hollow boast. In his opening speech to the virtual 136th Session video conference on 17 July, Thomas Bach roused conviction for belief in a symbolic project:

'Last year we celebrated Olympic Day with the opening of our Olympic House. This year, we highlight health: half a billion people around the globe were introduced to our Stay Strong, Stay Active, Stay Healthy campaign through the world's biggest digital Olympic workout. This success was the outcome of our measures to protect people's health and lives from the onslaught of the Coronavirus crisis. We started the campaign ahead of World Health Day to stress how important is sport for physical and mental health, especially in times of lockdown and social distancing. Yet the importance of sport goes beyond health, its social significance the glue binding communities, its economic significance creating jobs. Sport is an essential factor not only during this crisis but for the recovery. This is why we have repeatedly called upon governments to include sport in recovery programmes. Our message has been understood by many ... all this would not have been possible without the unified support of so many, the IFs, NOCs, the athletes, our Japanese friends, our TOP partners and rights-holding broadcasters, Organising Committees, the WHO, the UN and of course you the IOC members and our staff. The crisis is far from over. As I expressed in April, the situation requires solidarity, creativity, determination and flexibility. We will all need to make sacrifices.

'During the Session in January, I stressed the growing misuse of sport for political purposes as a serious challenge. This threat has grown, in some minds the ghosts of the past are rearing again, those of boycotts and discrimination for reasons of politics or nationality. All this 40 years after the fruitless boycott of Moscow 1980 by some countries, some refusing to learn from history that boycotts have no political effect whatever. We must strengthen efforts to convince governments of the irreplaceable value of the Olympic Games, the only event that brings the world peacefully together, the core of our movement since the time of de Coubertin who said, "We shall not have peace until the prejudices that now separate different races are outlived. What better means is there to bring the youth of all countries periodically together for amicable trials of strength and agility?" His words still true today.

'With our postponed Tokyo Games, we are walking the talk [a deliberate turn of phrase by Bach], athletes from 206 NOCs and a Refugee Team will be living this value of non-discrimination, uniquely achieved by Jesse Owens: at home suffering the painful reality of segregation, in the Olympic Village living as equal with all athletes. Through his achievements he taught Nazi Germany a resounding lesson, befriending his German rival Lutz Long in iconic moments of respect ... Olympic champion Muhammad Ali, who had the Olympic flag as one of just two flying at his funeral, recalled, "I have learned whatever time we spend on Earth should be devoted to helping others, creating justice and equality for all, not out of pity or shame, but out of love for all people with the knowledge that we belong not to many races, but to one – the human race." Those words mirror the philosophy of Olympic solidarity, of distribution of 90 per cent of our revenue to solidarity action – this lying at the heart of our Corona crisis management, reflected by our aid package of $150m to sustain the prospect of our postponed Games next year.'

There have been challenges in history simultaneously heroic and forlorn, such as Scott's expedition to the South Pole. Belief in the value of Tokyo's sustained Olympic festival was to prove so socially memorable. If Bach was campaigning tooth and nail, with countless partners, to uphold the coherence, communication and culture between continents through sport, there was a concluding lightning strike upon Russia in the third week of December, with an imposing final verdict from the Court of Arbitration for Sport (CAS), following a year's contemplation on WADA's proposed four-year worldwide ban. This was the pronouncement on 17 December:

'The Court of Arbitration for Sport has issued its decision in the arbitration procedure between WADA and the Russian Anti-Doping Agency (RUSADA), with 50 intervening parties including the IOC, the International Paralympic Committee and the International Ice Hockey Federation (IIHF). CAS unanimously determines RUSADA to be non-compliant with WADA in connection with its failure to produce delivery of authentic Laboratory Information Management System data, and underlying analytical data from former Moscow Laboratory to WADA. Consequently, the panel issues orders which come into effect today, December 17, for a period of two years, until December 16, 2022.

'The orders are reproduced in attachment to this media release, and include, *inter alia*, the possibility during the two-year period for any athlete or athlete support personnel from Russia to participate in or attend the Olympic and Paralympic Games (winter or summer) and any world championships organised or sanctioned by a WADA signatory, on condition that they are not subject to a suspension imposed by a competent authority; that the uniform worn does not contain the flag of the Russian Federation, and contains the words "neutral athlete"; that the Russian national anthem is not played or sung at any official event venue. For RUSADA to be reinstated as a compliant signatory, all consequences imposed for RUSADA's non-compliance must have been respected and observed in full through the two-year period with all monetary fines and contributions paid.'

The 186-page arbitral award, issued by the CAS Panel composed of co-arbitrators Judge Mark Williams (Australia), president; Professor Luigi Fumagalli (Italy); and Dr Hamid G. Gharavi (France/Iran), contains the following concluding remarks:

'This panel has imposed consequences to reflect the nature and seriousness of the non-compliance and to ensure that the integrity of sport against the scourge of doping is maintained. The consequences which this panel has decided to impose are not as extensive as those sought by WADA. This should not, however, be read as any validation of the conduct of RUSADA or the Russian authorities. In making its orders, the panel is limited by the powers granted under the applicable law. It has considered matters of proportionality and, in particular, the need to effect cultural change and encourage the next generation of Russian athletes to participate in clean international sport.'

WADA filed its request for arbitration on 9 January 2020. A hearing took place from 2 to 5 November 2020 in person and by video conference. Twenty years earlier, Samaranch had negotiated IOC survival, through re-assessments of administration, in the wake of the Salt Lake City scandal. Now Bach, regretfully, had been partly instrumental in unavoidable punitive intervention against one of the three most powerful Olympic nations. The pall hanging over 'clean' Russians' participation at the postponed Tokyo six months later would remain for a third consecutive Games.

12

BRISBANE 2032 COUP

AMBITIOUS, WILFUL? Certainly. Few were in doubt about the qualities that drove Thomas Bach as IOC president in his first eight years. Yet his virtues included a dutiful and sensitive streak. Circumstance in March 2021 should have seen him offering himself for second-term re-election for another four years, amid enthusiastic surroundings at the spiritual home of Olympia in Greece: instead, he was battling, at a virtual 137th Session in Lausanne, as secluded as a balloonist drifting above the global pandemic, intent on preserving a potentially crippled, postponed Tokyo Olympic Games. His support, in isolation, was nevertheless emphatic: 93 votes out of the 97 electronically gathered, in the wake of a leadership that had ridden consecutive crises, currently one from nature.

He was obliged to be fulsome in response, 'Thank you very much from the bottom of my heart for this overwhelming vote of confidence and trust. For me, this is even more special considering the many reforms and difficult decisions we have had to take. You know that this touches me deeply, makes me humble. When you elected me as your president in 2013 in Buenos Aires, I said that I wanted to lead according to my campaign motto "Unity in Diversity" and be president for all of you and for our stakeholders. This commitment is also true for my second and last term. My door, my ears and my heart remain open for every one of you, hoping I can count on your continued dedication, support and friendship during the next four years.'

There were those who said he was close to tears, and die-hard media critics were swift to condemn his alleged obsequious response to his colleagues. Is a man who is responsible for co-ordinating one of the numerically largest global cultural organisations – nearly 300 affiliated administrations – not permitted to be emotionally moved by such a wave of loyalty, even when many of those voters owe their position directly to him? His was a responsibility tormentingly compounded by a ferocious virus, the constantly changing development of which baffled the world's leading epidemiologists. For a re-elected Bach, this was no moment to decelerate.

The following day, the Executive Board was scheduled to present an extension of Agenda 2020 with '2020+5', Bach reminding them, 'We will keep changing, keep turning challenges into opportunities, keep being proactive.' Now was a moment for one of his lesser but relevant innovations: to extend the historic Olympic slogan *Citius, Altius, Fortius* (Faster, Higher, Stronger), with 'Together', emphasising an element of unity and solidarity, to be confirmed at the subsequent Session in four months' time in Tokyo. John Coates, IOC vice-president, had observed following the re-election, 'At no time have you ever given any indication of giving up your attempt to inspire us,' while Sebastian Coe – elected by Samaranch to the inaugural Athletes Commission alongside Bach back in 1981 – reflected, 'He's always carried an unflinching passion for the welfare of athletes.'

Behind all the complements was quietly smouldering a Bach-designed revolutionary transformation – Coates-assisted – of the IOC constitution, soon to be launched in July: hinted at by Bach's own reference to Milan-Cortina's budget for the 2026 Winter Games having been reduced by 80 per cent to $5m, a part of the 2020 Agenda extension agreed by the Executive Board and now being rubber-stamped by the Session; economy surgery. This was continuation of the strategy, Agenda 2020+5 (Bach's 2025 retirement date): 15 recommendations approved by the Session after a six-hour debate on proposals covering such topics as the global sports calendar, IOC relationship with esports, athlete representation, gender equality and human rights. Bach's new roadmap would promote a clearer Olympic profile in the wake of disruptive doping and corruption scandals: scrutinising administration, digitalisation, sustainability and financial resilience, the president asserting, 'We must be ready for these adjustments, to shape our future, our vision of how the new world will adjust. Agenda 2020+5 addresses these inevitable trends.' He stressed the necessity to exclude within esports any video games that promoted violence 'contrary to Olympic values'.

Evaluation of these conclusions was voiced by Bach in the spring edition of *Olympic Review*, 'The coronavirus crisis has changed our world fundamentally, never like it was before. Once we have overcome the health crisis, we will face extensive social, financial, economic and political consequences, as leaders of the Olympic Movement we must be prepared … From cost-saving simplification to scaled-back service levels, to creative digital engagement programmes, the postponed Tokyo Games have opened the door for new ways of thinking by future organising committees. This situation will need all our creativity, determination and flexibility, the need to make sacrifices and to compromise. The priorities for rescheduling the Tokyo Games were daunting: agreeing new dates in 2021; rescheduling the international sports calendar; re-securing all Olympic venues and the Village; re-confirming competition schedule, on 33 sports; embracing additional costs; appropriate simplification to reduce costs; maintaining the workforce and volunteers; developing measures to mitigate the virus to ensure security for all.'

Christophe Dubi, Olympic Games executive director, expanded Bach's concerns, 'It was almost like starting from scratch, absolute dedication, planning and execution, a series of crucial decisions requiring collaboration between IOC,

Japanese and Tokyo metropolitan governments, organising committee of Olympics and Paralympics, despite the relentless surge of the virus and new variants, accommodating all pieces in place 12 months later. The lesson was that the [Olympic] Movement is really strong, all hands were on deck with the best spirit and intent.' By May 2020, the IOC had announced a financial package up to $800m to cover increased costs, including $150m in loans to NOCs, to IFs to sustain activities and support athletes. Tokyo announced by July that it had secured all 43 competition venues plus the Olympic Village and the broadcast centres, the public sale of Village apartments delaying access to residents by a year. Bach would conclude prior to the eventual hosting, 'None of this could have been achieved without the solidarity demonstrated across the Olympic Movement. As we prepare to celebrate these Games, unlike any previous edition, they serve as a symbol of what we can achieve when we stand united.'

Further developments in April 2021 had seen support for the Athletes Commission from the EB, relating to 'athlete expression' at the Games involving Charter Rule 50 and protection of the neutrality of sport. The commission's proposals resulted from extensive consultation across 3,500 athletes from a majority of NOCs and all 41 Olympic sports, embracing gender-equal opinion and supported by the World Olympians Association. The recommendations included increased opportunity for expression during a Games, while preserving the podium, field of play and official ceremonies from protest or demonstration. Commission chair Kirsty Coventry stated, 'The objective was to hear athletes' thoughts on existing and new opportunities to express their views, during as well as outside the Games. We want to amplify the voices of athletes, find more ways to support our values, and the consultation was important as part of the ongoing dialogue with our community. We appreciate the EB's support.'

At the same time, the IOC announced a landmark move into virtual sports by launching the first Olympic Virtual

Series, embracing partnership with five IFs: baseball and softball, cycling, rowing, sailing and motor racing. The OVS would mobilise virtual sport, esports and gaming enthusiasts in order to reach new Olympic audiences, further embracing Agenda 2020+5 proposals.

Tensions mounted throughout spring and summer among all Games organisation as the virus irretrievably expanded. 'It is regrettable that the Games will be staged in a very limited manner in the face of the spread of infections,' conceded Seiko Hashimoto, president of Tokyo's organising committee, regretting the government decision by Olympic minister Tamayo Marukawa that events would take place behind closed doors: the decision to abandon hosting events with limited spectator access following consultation with IOC and the Paralympic Committee in conjunction with governments, immediately in the wake of a state of emergency being announced until August 2022. At that meeting, Bach and Paralympics chief Andrew Parsons emphasised they remained committed to delivering a secure Games, Bach stating, 'We have shown this responsibility since the day of postponement, and will sustain any measure which is necessary for a safe Olympics.' Christophe Dubi was equally positive on health security among Olympic personnel. 'We are keeping the Covid risk at an absolute minimum,' he reiterated, more than 80 per cent of Olympic Village residents arriving fully vaccinated and Dubi stressing that contact between participants and the public was strictly limited. Games operations director Pierre Ducrey claimed Olympic personnel 'are the most controlled population in the world'. Toshirō Mutō, Games CEO, was also optimistic, 'We have been able to deal with Covid measures at a level within expectations so far,' confirming that Olympic personnel were in no way linked to record daily increased Covid infections among the domestic population, which had just risen to a peak of 12,000 in one day. The Olympic Village 'guest' community was thought to be the most tested in the world, in keeping with 30,000 daily tests amid the

Tokyo population. Ryu Seung-min, South Korean Olympic champion and IOC member, testing positive on arrival at the international airport and immediately isolating, revealed he was 'wholly asymptomatic', having been vaccinated, and regarded Tokyo's protective Covid administration 'sufficient to protect us all'. This view was echoed by Tokyo's Yuriko Koike, claiming increased vaccination rates in the wake of earlier inadequate reaction, and that hospitalisation and deaths were optimistically declining.

Thomas Bach, reassured that the visiting Olympic community were satisfactorily self-protected and unthreatening to domestic citizens, welcomed the decision to maintain schedule, 'A whole generation of athletes would have forfeited their career had these Games been cancelled.' The IOC decreed that only fully vaccinated members would present medals, and would be required to wear disinfected gloves. Only one IOC member and one IF representative would be present at each sports event, while athletes would remain on their own podium module during presentation ceremonies, but Bach optimistically forecast, 'These Olympics will be historic for another reason, the most electronically followed Games ever, with the world watching Tokyo, watching Japan, and longing for Olympic competition. Expectation is becoming the highest ever.'

As athletes assembled in late July, many anxious about the extent of five years of preparation seriously disrupted over the past 15 months, the IOC president sought reassurance among members and participants at the 138th Session. In a city besieged by mass infection yet still short on vaccination, widespread public scepticism regarding continuation remained rampant. Part of Bach's address to the 138th Session attempted reconciliation with a negative public mood:

'We can only be together today because of the heroic efforts of doctors, nurses and the many healthcare workers and volunteers around the world, so let us pay tribute to those supporting those in need, caring for society. We remember those here in Japan and worldwide affected by the pandemic, and ask you to stand for a minute of silence in honour of those we have lost.

'Dear friends, what a journey this has been. When Japan set out ten years ago to bring the Olympic spirit back to Tokyo after the path-breaking Games of 1964, none of us could have imagined the unprecedented challenges we would face: the Great East earthquake, the coronavirus pandemic ... the first ever Games postponement. We could only overcome these challenges because throughout the past eight years we had a trustful partnership, could always rely on you, made us admire even more Japanese virtues of dedication and perseverance. For this you need partnership. I express sincere gratitude to so many – the government under the leadership of Suga Yoshihide and previously Abe Shinzo, additionally to Tokyo's metropolitan government led by Yuriko Koike, to the organising committee and its president Hashimoto Seiko, her predecessor Yoshirō Mori, all of you demonstrating dedication in challenging times.

'Pierre de Coubertin once said, "The Olympic Games are a pilgrimage to the past and an act of faith in the future," words with special meaning on the eve of these Games, when we are committing such an act of faith in the future. Just as Tokyo 1964 marked a new era for peaceful and dynamic Japan, Tokyo 2020 will give humanity faith in the future.

'The best athletes in the world look forward to fulfilling their dreams, they share the experience of perseverance with the people of Japan, the stage set to shine and inspire the world. Their achievements, their joy and tears create the magic of the Games. A time too for Japan to shine, sending a powerful message of peace to the world, of solidarity and resilience. Billions around the globe will appreciate these Games, admiring the Japanese for what they have achieved. The international community is longing for the unifying power of sport, expressed by G7 and G20 countries, by the United Nations. We are delighted to welcome tomorrow the director-general of the World Health Organization, Dr Ghebreyesus, addressing us with a keynote speech. The secretary-general of the United Nations, António Guterres, now summarises this great appreciation of Japan in his address.'

Bach's duty to attempt to hold the Olympic world united had never been more prominent than now, so acceptance by the Session of his extended motto could hardly have been more appropriate, 'Faster, Higher, Stronger... Together'. 'We need to focus on solidarity, the meaning of the word 'Together', we can only go faster, aim higher, become stronger if we stand together,' he said. The president's ethical objectives had always been evident, including gender equality, this now apparent with the elevation of Nicole Hoevertsz, former synchronised swimmer from Caribbean Aruba, succeeding Anita DeFrantz as IOC vice-president and maintaining Bach's drive for gender balance. The 57-year-old had been a member since 2006 and on the Executive Board for four years, having chaired the Olympic Athletes from Russia implementation group governing Russian participation at Pyeongchang 2018. Meanwhile, Ban Ki-moon, former UN secretary-general, was re-elected as chair of the Ethics Commission; Mark Adams, aide to Bach, asserting there was no impediment to members electing the man who might well be investigating them if they breached ethical rules.

The IOC also grasped the opportunity for recognition of a minority in the field of Olympic performance. Nobel Peace Prize winner Mohammad Yunus of Bangladesh was awarded the coveted Olympic Laurel. Regarded as the 'banker of the poor', Yunus had founded the Grameen Bank which pioneered the concept for micro credit and micro financing in impoverished Bangladesh. 'Being recognised, that we can contribute to the Olympic Movement, gives us all reason to be happy and excited, will lead to many celebrations,' Yunus exclaimed. He was also the founder of the Yunus Sports Hub, which provided competitive facilities, youth engagement and sustainable events in one of the world's most testing environments. Bangladesh had yet to win any Olympic medal, yet Yunus suggested his award signified his country was qualified for recognition: 'The person who this time is receiving the Olympic Laurel is not an Olympian in any sense, and hasn't taken part in any of these activities, but that did not disqualify me, it widens the whole concept,' delivering his initiatives, including the Young Leaders Programme, the Imagine Peace Youth Camp and inspirational programme Athlete 365 Business Accelerator.

While an Olympic Movement seriously fractured by the pandemic convincingly clung to its ethical principles, extending them to the disenfranchised poor of Bangladesh, now the Session was about to authorise – for many, reveal – the most fundamental constitutional change since Samaranch formalised TOP sponsorship in the 1980s, and also separated, biennially, Winter and Summer Games in 1994. With conciliatory Executive Board approval, Bach divested founder de Coubertin's original format – selection of host cities by unalloyed membership voting. Never was a single act more designed to stem the IOC's potential disintegration from absence of financially confident hosts. The story of Brisbane's widely rumoured incubation, as likely hosts for 2032, was dramatically leaked by Insidethegames, the comprehensive website launched 20 years earlier by Duncan Mackay, former athletics correspondent of *The Guardian*: the flow of ITG's information by now the equal of Sport Intern's encyclopaedic breadth under the late proprietor-editor Karl-Heinz Huba. On 23 February, Mackay disclosed that, under Bach's inventive strategy of creating Future Host Commissions, there was already a designated candidate for 2032. Mackay had written:

'Queensland's bid to host the 2032 Olympic and Paralympic Games could receive a potentially significant boost tomorrow when it will be recommended to the IOC Executive Board that the Australian state is installed as the preferred candidate, the story confirmed via a senior IOC official. The EB announced it had entered "targeted dialogue" with officials over Brisbane and Queensland staging the Games in 11 years' time. Technically, this does not mean Brisbane has been awarded the Games, but something would have to go spectacularly wrong from here. With Australian officials having already sent financial guarantees to the IOC, there seems little to prevent Brisbane being formally confirmed as 2032 host city as early as July shortly before Tokyo's postponed Games. Brisbane's bid was borne out of the Gold Coast's successful hosting of the 2018 Commonwealth Games.

'John Coates engineered a meeting between prime minister [Scott] Morrison and Bach at the G20 Summit in Osaka in 2019. Morrison reportedly convinced Bach on Brisbane's bid, saying Queensland had full government support. This represented remarkable progress in a feasibility study sponsored by city mayors across south-east Queensland, chaired by Coates, released in February 2019. The following month the IOC Executive Board announced the formation of a five-member working group [Future Host Commission-initiated] to re-design the bid process after a string of difficult campaigns which saw cities lose referendums and drop out. "We gave a kind of blank cheque to organise themselves," Bach said. "We want this to become transparent and not appearing as a *fait accompli* where nobody knows who is talking to whom. The Olympic Games are too big and too important that you can make an arrangement with a city without public discussion, without anybody knowing except a committee. This cannot work for an Olympic Games any longer."

'Ever since being elected, Bach has sought ways to make elections cheaper and more efficient, where a city's bid could be cut off at the knees after rejection of the Olympic brand by voters in local referendums. "This was not the best procedure, neither for the future of the Games nor for the IOC's reputation," Bach stated, aiming critical comments at consultants and lobbyists hired by candidates. Coates, long a strategic confederate of Bach's, had reflected in 2019 that "we [the IOC] cannot continue to be damaged as in the past";

though Bach would deny Coates's participation in negotiations with FHC members. Among those who addressed the FHC had been Cathy Freeman, legendary figurehead of Sydney 2000.

'The 2032 race was expected to feature bids from several countries, including Doha, Budapest and Rhine-Ruhr. The decision to enter exclusive negotiations with Brisbane came before any of them could launch a formal bid. It is fair to say they are all privately fuming at the unexpected turn of events, but have largely chosen to remain tight-lipped in fear of jeopardising any future bids. Brisbane has the IOC's new bidding system to thank for being given the unique opportunity to be awarded the Olympics four years before the traditional process would normally have reached its conclusion. It was developed in part by John Coates, and seeks to find a winning host more efficiently, while avoiding turning other campaigns into expensive losers.

'The Australian model, with 21 Olympic venues shared between Brisbane, the Gold Coast, the Sunshine Coast and south-east Queensland, is the kind of regional concept that Coates's working group had recommended in May 2019. "I know the good the Olympics do for sport," Morrison had told Bach. "This is also an opportunity for the Australian government to stimulate sports at all levels." These kind of messages are music to the ears of Bach, a devout believer in the power of Olympism. From that point, Brisbane's campaign was in the fast lane.'

An early intention in Queensland's project was for the main stadium to be Brisbane's famed cricket home, the Gabba. Coates, both architect alongside Bach of the reformed election system and then negotiator on behalf of Queensland, recalls, 'We had a number of alternative considerations, both for the ceremony and for athletics, and this was discussed by both local and national governments, the question of rebuilding. However, Queensland's government opposed discussion, saying we should simply go with upgrading. There was a testy weekend when we were all a bit worried, the national government politically unstable, but ultimately Brisbane and the national government wanted to share all appointments, considering it was best to have a balance.'

When the IOC's Executive Board announced Brisbane as its preferred candidate in March, the next step was Morrison's agreement to cover half the costs, with contributions from both state and local governments. Coates concurred, 'The diligence undertaken by the IOC's Future Host Commission far exceeded what we experienced with Sydney's candidacy for 2000. Since opening the dialogue phase in February, we had supplied the FHC with detailed responses which led to a joint Olympic infrastructure agency being established.' The city would utilise over 80 per cent of existing and temporary venues, while additional facilities would be delivered well in advance and irrespective of election for the Games. Bach's concept of the FHC had created in one bold gamble a platform of common sense which might well protect the IOC and future Games through another century, so that he was able to forecast, 'There is already a pool of interested parties who want to organise the Games for 2036 and even 2040 ... the future of the Games indeed looks bright.'

Prior to inevitable rubber-stamping of the bid by the Session in Tokyo, Bach was asked why Brisbane had been selected so early. The answer was unhesitating, 'It was about a sports-loving country backed by the public, and from all levels of government across the entire political spectrum, for a clear, sustainable and feasible Games wholly aligned with Agenda 2020 and 2020+5 – somehow irresistible. These Games will occur according to an existing development programme for the region, already in place. The concept was there in Queensland, and by 2032 the Olympics can benefit from being aligned with a long-term vision.' The outcome would realise the president's objective 'not to have losers' in elections, in which millions of dollars could be wasted on sinking bids: as in the Winter Games election of 2015 when Kraków, Lviv, Oslo and Stockholm had all collapsed. Asked also why nothing had yet emerged from the FHC for Winter Games in 2030, Bach was unfazed, 'They are in dialogue with interest parties, and once there is substance the Executive Board will be informed. We are still nine years ahead, so it's work in progress – not a question of urgency but of opportunity, and this is the objective of the new procedure.'

The Session was duly impressed, and convinced: approval by 72 out of 80 votes, only five negative, for a bid costing 80 per cent below the budgets of all election candidates for 2020, 2024 and 2028; and thereby the IOC had ensured a decade of security, celebrating Australians having achieved Olympic hosting for the third time in the wake of Melbourne 1956 and Sydney 2000. Conspicuous was the election of a city with the lowest population, two and a half million, in 80 years since that of Helsinki in 1952 with a population of one and a half million. In intervening years, there had been 11 cities elected with upwards of ten million – five with more than 20 million – and half a dozen with between four and six million.

Kristin Aasen, Norwegian chair of the FCH, had observed, 'We have the best possible project on the table before us. As the world continues to experience challenging times, we believe that we have the chance to seize a unique opportunity to secure the future of the Olympic Movement.' Queensland premier Annastacia Palaszczuk celebrated this unusual but reformative outcome, 'It's something our city and our state has always aspired to, but never thought possible. Under the Olympics "new norm", we have over 80 per cent of our venues, we have co-operation with all three levels of government, and agreements to do the infrastructure already needed for our city. The Games will accelerate our future by providing this infrastructure sooner than expected, focusing and fast-tracking investment of all governments. We want to show the world that mid-sized cities and regions can host a Games without financial distress or missed deadlines. The keys are long-term planning, bipartisan support, and making the most of the city's natural and acquired resources.'

13

EMOTIONS RELEASED

THERE HAS been no anti-climax in the history of international sports events such as Tokyo's postponed Olympics of 2021: the scheduled occasion of 2020 an extravagant concept by a respected nation suddenly overwhelmed by a second, now global, disaster in the wake of earthquake and tidal wave. When Emperor Hirohito had opened the door to 1964's festival, it signalled Japan's audacious entry as a re-engaged, post-World War Two technical and industrial democratic power: of bullet trains, colour television, strident economy, eager opportunism. By the second decades of the 21st century, the economy was stalling, the population ageing, the birth rate falling. The hope for 2020 had been that when grandson Emperor Naruhito welcomed the world once again, it might regenerate that flourish of optimism in a nation which had lost confidence, which needed an infusion of international appreciation, simultaneously entertaining the domestic population, a million guests, and an Olympic cavalcade equally in urgent need of a positive shot in the arm. The prospect now in 2021 was gripped by doubt, by outright opposition within home and foreign governments scared by the accelerating health hazard: in Tokyo, hospitality cramped by a state of emergency, visiting delegates feeling uninvited, the government shamed by vaccination rates of barely 30 per cent, theatrical deflation with non-existent crowds, never mind that regular attendances continued for domestic basketball.

Moreover, local dignitaries had been dented by repetitive embarrassments. Tsunekazu Takeda, elderly but forthright leader of Tokyo's bid back in 2013, had been obliged to resign in 2019 following revelations of million-dollar fees paid to a 'consulting firm' in Singapore; allegedly cash finding its way to IOC delegate Lamine Diack, said to have campaigned for Tokyo. In February 2021, Yoshirō Mori, president of Tokyo's Games, quit in the wake of insulting female committee assistants. A month later, Opening Ceremony creative director Hiroshi Sasaki resigned after advocating a sketch involving a deformed female comedian. With the Games about to begin, Keigo Oyamada, composer of the ceremony's music, resigned following disclosures of abuse of disabled children when he was a boy. The same week, Sasaki's deputy, Kentarō Kobayashi, was dismissed for having joked about the Holocaust. To cap the discourtesies, former Premier Abe decided not to attend the Opening Ceremony.

Yet despite the foreboding, derogatory across international media, and for all the pessimism in Japanese polling against continuing with a militia-esque celebration, we were about to experience a remarkable element of humanity's resilience. Fortified by Japanese willpower and IOC faith – Bach inoculation? – Tokyo's postponed Games created a spontaneous spirit that was truly infectious. How wrong could the entire world's population be about its instinctive will to survive, to live, to believe in a future? A belief which Thomas Bach had striven to convince the doubters could be fulfilled. And now it was: led by the anonymous who had worked selflessly to provide the facilities, and in turn by previously unknown athletes such as Flora Duffy in winning Bermuda, smallest of Olympic nations, its first ever gold, in triathlon.

Against the stark reality of a stadium largely devoid of ticket holders, attendance limited to officialdom and a minority of athletes, Tokyo's moment of truth had opened with a firework display and a single runner entering the stage where a representation of Mount Fuji arose in the middle with its cauldron awaiting the Olympic Flame. The Japanese sense how to harmonise cataclysm with triumph. A dance programme of solemn Japanese dignity was followed by a moment of silence in respect of departed Covid victims, and this by a first reference in an Opening Ceremony commemorating the Israeli massacre of Munich 1972, the field blackened except for the Mount Fuji replica, now bathed in blue. A cultural presentation followed, a sequence creating the Olympic Rings, then tap dancing succeeded by more fireworks. The parade of nations, normally lengthy but now much reduced in numbers, passed more swiftly, delegations condensed by phased-event schedule arrival of athletes. Delegations had two flag-bearers, male and female. With a release of paper doves came representation of the Games of 1964, and parade of the individual sports pictograms invented at that time together with those of the contemporary Games.

Arrival of the Olympic Torch was protracted, begun with three-time Olympic wrestling champion Saori Yoshida and judoka Dr Tadahiro Nomura. They were followed by baseball legends Shigeo Nagashima, 81-year-old icon Sadaharu Oh, and former Yomiuri Giants star Hideki Matsui. In respect of medical staff confronting the pandemic came Dr Hiuroki Ohashi and Junko Kitagawa, with wheelchair Paralympian Wakako Tsuchida. Finally bearing the flag towards Mount Fuji were six school students representing regions devastated by the Fukushima disaster; passing the torch to international tennis superstar Naomi Osaka, who ascended the emblematic volcano, on which the summit opened to reveal a spectacular bowl for symbiotic ignition.

Wording of the Olympic Oath was revised, a novel format created with a male and female athlete from the Japanese team accompanied by two coaches and two judges for a ritual promoting gender equality: in this instance Ryota Yamagata (track and field) with Kasumi Ishikawa (table tennis), judges Asumi Tsuzaki (water polo) and Masato Kato (surfing), and coaches Kōsei Inoue (judo) and Reika Utsugi (softball). In successive pairs, each would proclaim, 'We promise to take part in these Olympic Games, respecting and abiding by the rules and in the spirit of fair play, inclusion and equality. Together we stand in solidarity and commit ourselves to sport without doping, without cheating, without any form of discrimination. We do this for the honour of our teams, in respect for the fundamental principles of Olympism, and to make the world a better place through sport.' The Athletes Commission led by Kirsty Coventry had advocated the amendment, part of their recommendations for adjustment of Charter Rule 50, giving athletes wider opportunity to express emotions, other than on the podium.

If the initial impact of Games competition would be the unreality of empty stadia, emotionally negative for some performers conditioned to applause, Dick Pound justified the strange, shrouded stadium mood in postponement, 'Around the world, millions will be transported by television's dramas, irrespective of empty seats. Action is all.' *Asahi Shimbun*, rampant Games opposition newspaper, would continue protesting in vain.

For Bach, it had been an arduously fraught journey even to reach this ceremony, and now his opening words attempted to justify the cause:

'Today is a moment of hope, different from what we had imagined, but let us cherish the occasion, finally all here together, the athletes from 205 national Olympic committees and our Refugee Team, living under one roof together. This is the unifying power of sport, the message of solidarity, of peace and resilience. We can only be together because of our gracious Japanese hosts, to whom we would like to express all our appreciation. The organising committee and the Japanese authorities have done extraordinary work on behalf of the athletes, with our deepest gratitude.

'Ten years ago, you set out to bring the Olympic spirit back to Tokyo, so we thank the unsung heroes, doctors, nurses and all the Japanese people who contribute to contain the pandemic. Special thanks to the thousands of volunteers, who despite all the challenges welcomed us wholeheartedly. Thank you to all Japanese for making a Games possible. Their perseverance is also true for you, my fellow athletes, facing great challenges, living with uncertainty, not knowing when you could train again, whether you could see your coach tomorrow, whether your team-mates would be there for the next competition, indeed, if the competition would take place at all. You struggled, never gave up, and today you are making your dream come true. You inspired us, the IOC, and the entire Olympic community, to fight like you to make this moment possible.

'I express thanks to all national Olympic committees, the international federations, all our TOP partners and sponsors, and broadcasters for standing together with us, a true community.

'This community is with you tonight and throughout the Games. Billions will be glued to their screens, distantly sending you their enthusiasm. Our Olympic community learned we can address challenges of our times if we stand together in solidarity, which means much more than simply respect and non-discrimination – it means helping, sharing, caring, to make the Games happen, to enable athletes rich or poor and from all sports to enjoy the Games.

'This fuels our mission to make the world a better place through sport, and in which we welcome the Refugee Team. The talent and spirit of refugee athletes illustrates what enrichment our refugees offer society, fleeing because of violence, hunger or just because you were different. We welcome you with open arms to a peaceful home: all equal, respecting the same rules. The Olympic experience makes us humble, feeling we are a part of something bigger than ourselves, united in all our diversity. We are grateful to you the athletes, expressing commitment to our values: non-discrimination, sport free of doping, inclusion and equality under our new Olympic Oath. The pandemic forced us to be apart, separated, even from our loved ones, a dark space. Yet today, wherever in the world you may be, we are united in sharing it together, the Olympic Flame an illumination for all of us. Now I have the great honour of inviting His Majesty the Emperor to declare open the 32nd Games of the Olympiad, Tokyo 2020.'

In her separate address, Games president Seiko Hashimoto welcomed the moment as 'a vision for the future that embodies peace and respect, ready to show Japan's recovery from the 2011 disasters, the torch relay having symbolically begun at the Fukushima village training centre which served as an operational base during the calamities'. Sports director Mikako Kotani promised, 'We aim to ensure that, after the Games, each person will continue to practise diversity and inclusion awareness they have gained at Tokyo 2020, thereby rooting it in society as part of our legacy.' Emperor Naruhito's formal words solemnised the raising of the Olympic flag in three stages: first by a cadre of six athletes, one from each continent and the Refugee Team, then a group of eight Japanese workers saluting their role against the pandemic, and lastly a seven-member group of the Japanese Self-Defense Force.

Coincidental yet perhaps symbolic, within an Olympics simultaneously as spectacular as ever in performance but riding a precipice of immeasurable health anxieties, would be the psychological stress affecting two of the forecast stars. Here was evidence that fame, involving physical excess, and emotional comfort are not always ambient partners: Simone Biles, US gymnast phenomenon, and Naomi Osaka, Japanese-American tennis zealot, were both compelled provocatively to withdraw from eagerly expected triumph. Such were their traumas in Tokyo that, within months, a joint memorandum would be signed between the World Olympians Association and the International Federation of Sports Medicine, aiming at research and treatment surrounding the competitive tension of sustained extreme emotional pressure. Under global focus, Biles and Osaka had each become punctured personalities:

momentarily condemned for weakness, yet soon acknowledged for their burden of expectation, both private and public. Their respective emotional disabilities had become apparent with a combination of performance decline and competition withdrawal.

For Biles, the emotional eclipse represented dual stress: the physical sensation she encountered – colloquially, the 'twisties', total loss of orientation and balance during gyroscopic acrobatics – in the wake of earlier years of infamous sexual abuse by US team doctor Larry Nassar. He had been ultimately imprisoned on the evidence, over decades, of importunely soliciting the intimate trust of countless girls. A third instance of stress in Tokyo was worth noting: shortly before her start, US sprinter Sha'Carri Richardson surrendered her prospects on account of drug abuse, marijuana, to help her handle news of her mother's death. Maybe it was not coincidental that all these young competitors were non-white, perhaps compounding their subjective sense of inadequacy, all of them now confronting expectation of fame with concern for private equilibrium. Also instrumental will have been emotional confusion underlying postponement of the Games: athletes no different from the rest of the population in the sense of isolation, trauma and disrupted schedules, a third of Americans, for instance, consulting therapists during the pandemic.

What was exceptional in the case of Biles, and the past history of destabilised competitors, was that she openly informed the public that her malaise was mental health and not a strained muscle. She was, in one sense, aided by the parallel trauma of Osaka, who had put her mental health ahead of fame and convention when declining mandatory interviews during the French Open in May, struggling with the burden of public scrutiny and unrelenting media access.

Thomas Bach was swift to offer public sympathy for the pair, as Biles provocatively withdrew from gymnastics vault and uneven bars finals, the IOC president reflecting, 'Her handling of the situation has been commendable as she continues to cheer for her team colleagues – a quality that is the Olympic spirit at its best.' Biles admitted, 'You want to compete for yourself, but you're too alarmed about what everybody else is going to say, to think, on the internet.' Predicted to win six gold medals, the 24-year-old finalist withdrew from the team event, causing the IOC to remind athletes of the daily available Mentally Fit Healthline in more than 70 languages.

Regarded universally as the world's best, Biles was the only remaining survivor of abuse by Nassar, continuing to be a prominent critic of the governing body, with retrospective protest alongside many other women. 'They cannot brush all that under the carpet,' said Biles. Fellow competitors now uniformly came out in her support, USA Gymnastics stating, 'Simone will continue to be evaluated daily to determine whether or not to participate in next week's individual event finals. We wholeheartedly support her decision and applaud her bravery in prioritising her wellbeing. Her courage shows yet again why she is a role model for so many.'

Rather than totally abandoning the challenge, Biles found the will to return for the final women's individual event, the balance beam: a discipline not obliging tormenting twisting and in which she would eliminate from her routine her double-twist dismount. She reduced the difficulty of her dismount so much, to a double pike, that she could not recall performing similarly for a decade. Merely watching her Chinese rivals, Guan Chenchen and Tang Xijing, accomplish double-double dismounts had provoked her latent anguish: that technique involving a double twist and double back flip even having acquired a definition of 'the Biles'. Her bronze medal was a tribute to rationality and bravery.

For Osaka, gleefully indulged in the honour of igniting the Olympic Flame at the Opening Ceremony, her stress was marginally less acute. Having re-established equilibrium since the breakdown in Paris, she was back on court for the opening of the Tokyo tournament and her first competitive match in two months, with an easy straight-sets victory over Zheng Saisai in the first round, as expected of the world's highest-paid female sportswoman. At ease now with the media, she reflected, 'When I lit the flame I was so honoured, a role you dream about. Now I'm so happy to be here, happy to play.' There was, of course, an absence of supportive spectators. Continuing celebration, however, was short-lived: in the third round Osaka was eliminated in straight sets by former French Open finalist Markéta Vondroušová of the Czech Republic. The 42nd-ranked Vondroušová controlled the contest with a subtle series of drop-shot winners, Osaka conceding afterwards, 'The scale of everything is a bit tough because of the break that I had taken.'

While Biles and Osaka may have sparked ignorant criticism among sections of the media – accusations of lazy, gutless, unfit – the plight of the two superstars elicited sympathy among rivals, aware how marginal can be temperamental equilibrium. At the same time, overdue public recognition – across social media – was belatedly exposed to the variable limits of rational sanity with which many champions travel in pursuit of fame and finance. I sympathised, as a would-be Olympian whose international football career hinged – perhaps – on a single missed open goal 70 years ago.

What Tokyo's postponed Games contributed to history, unexpectedly, was less the instability of extreme achievement than the spontaneous release of emotional happiness: seized again and again, not in mostly empty stadia, but by remote, euphoric appreciative audiences identifying with athletes' own joy. It is no exaggeration to say that a sporting contest can be as fulfilling for the audience as a symphony or a pop concert. A hundred times, Tokyo 2020 personified the commitment of both support-denied competitors and a tortured, detached audience. It was disappointing though perhaps predictable that American media, so accustomed to being at the forefront of Olympic celebrations, was conspicuous for complaining about the lack of drama: or rather, American drama. The

Los Angeles Times in particular bemoaned the abnormality, a perceived decline in 'normal' US dominance. Indeed, some of Tokyo's most cherished moments came when minorities had their moment in the sun, such as Bermuda, their only previous medal, Clarence Hill's boxing bronze in 1976. Now 35-year-old Flora Duffy achieved a Wizard of Oz experience by winning the women's triathlon. Duffy's triumph made Bermuda, population 70,000, the smallest territory ever to win a gold medal at the Summer Games. 'It's bigger than me, and that's such a cool moment,' Duffy admitted. 'The climax of the run was the longest kilometre of my life. I think I can get used to being called Olympic champion for the rest of my time!' It was indeed a turn of fortune in the wake of anaemia suffered six years earlier which temporarily put her out of sport, having failed to finish at Beijing in 2008 before a determined return. Following the cycle and swim, Duffy opened an early lead in the run to hold off the challenge of Georgia Taylor-Brown of Britain and America's Katie Zaferes. Duffy had been fortunate to survive a puncture in the cycle section.

As spectacular as Duffy was unheralded Ahmed Hafnaoui of Tunisia, no one's forecast for the 400m freestyle at the pool. In lane eight, he was a rank outsider, aged 18, yet surprised those more experienced with his winning time of 3:43.26 ahead of Australia's Jack McLoughlin, and American Kieran Smith, the three separated by less than a second. Hafnaoui had only qualified for the final by 14 hundredths of a second, hence his outside lane, yet his winning final time was three seconds better than his pre-Tokyo best. 'I was in tears on the podium when I saw the flag of my country and heard the anthem,' Hafnaoui said. He had begun swimming aged six: three years earlier he had finished eighth in the Youth Olympics at Buenos Aires. McLoughlin conceded, 'I was a bit surprised, but this is the Olympics where anything can happen, Ahmed coming out and achieving a huge PB, that's all credit to him, just one of those stories.' Also in the pool, Australian Emma McKeon became only the second woman in Olympic history to win seven medals in a single Games: the first since Soviet Union gymnast Maria Gorokhovskaya did so in 1952. McKeon's tally included four golds – 50m freestyle, 100m freestyle, 4x100m freestyle, 4xmedley – and three bronzes in 200m freestyle relay, 100m butterfly, and 4x100m butterfly.

Tokyo was a scene of inaugural sports. If Hafnaoui was a comparatively unknown champion, so among the wider Olympic audience were Brazil's Ítalo Ferreira and the USA's Carissa Moore, both inaugural Olympic surfing champions. The scene at Tsurigasaki Beach was appropriately dramatic in wave formation, Ferreira breaking his board only one minute into his final against Japanese favourite Kanoa Igarashi, yet recovering subsequently to post the best two scores. Moore was anything but a surprise within her sport: five times a world champion, with prize money in excess of $2m, and for the first time ever wearing the colours of USA. Born and bred in Hawaii, her customary attire was the flag of the Pacific island: her title was a predictable honour, comfortably winning the final against South Africa's Bianca Buitendag.

Perhaps fortuitous, perhaps simply national pride, Japan dominated skateboarding's inclusion with five of the 12 medals, with three of the four available gold: these by Sakura Yosozumi for women's park, Yuto Horigome in men's street, and Momiji Nishiya in women's street. Yet the name that commanded global attention was the second-youngest competitor in Tokyo, Sky Brown, aged 13, from Great Britain, bronze winner in women's park behind Yosozumi and her compatriot Kokona Hiraki, the latter even younger than Brown. Born in Miyazaki but residentially American, Brown could be considered almost more Japanese than British, though having taken her father's nationality: irrespectively, she astonished a world audience with her mobility, flexibility and stunts, notwithstanding that only three months earlier she had fractured her skull in a fall.

If the largest electronic Olympic audience of all time was looking for new drama, Brown epitomised memories from these unusual Games. It was a pride shared with a more domestic Brit from Corby, Charlotte Worthington. In the BMX freestyle final, Worthington had ploughed her first attempt at a hitherto unrevealed 360-degree back-flip, never previously landed in competition by a woman. Should she reduce, play safe for silver or bronze, or risk all? In a drama inviting parallel comparison with Tokyo's exceptional hurdles world record by Karsten Warholm of Norway, Worthington went for the kill, nailing it for an unprecedented judge's score of 97.5: another split-second spectacle from Tokyo momentarily past belief.

An urgency existed among written media at Tokyo, whether American or Chinese, Australian, Korean or British: almost as though they themselves being athletes, dwelling on the exceptional, to convince readers and viewers that these Games were as special as ever, never mind the virus. Commentators had their reward with men's 400m hurdles, Warholm, the self-proclaimed Viking from Norway, crunching his own earlier world record so comprehensively, even when under intense challenge, in 45.94s, that instant historians labelled the deed 'the greatest race ever'. Maybe: some recall David Hemery of Britain lowering the then world record by a similar margin 53 years ago in Mexico. Certainly, the race was phenomenal.

Besides world and Olympic, North American and South American records, also falling were those of British Virgin Islands, Kyron McMaster, fourth; Turkey, Yasmani Copello, sixth; and Estonia, Rasmus Mägi, seventh. McMaster had run the 15th-fastest time in history. Alison dos Santos of Brazil, in third place with 46.72s, would have broken the world record only a couple of months earlier. Warholm's new record, 0.76s inside his summit only a month previously in Oslo, which had itself been a phenomenon in breaking the record of Kevin Young 29 years earlier at Barcelona. Every man in the race would struggle somehow to rationalise his contribution: Rai Benjamin of America had recorded 46.17s, that itself more than half a second inside Warholm's former world record, and had gained merely a silver medal. Dos Santos, also runner-up in the world championship two years earlier, exclaimed, 'We're in a different stratosphere, the record will continue to climb, we tore the old record to pieces. Warholm's amazing.' The new champion was as impressed as any. 'I ran for my life – we should all share the glory.' A measure of Warholm's achievement was that such pace would have won him the year's 400m title in Britain, without hurdles.

There was some controversy in subsequent discussion about the relevance of contemporary track shoes by Puma for Warholm and Nike for Benjamin, each containing authorised sole supplements allegedly contributing pressure-lift, yet direct measurement of these physical assets are almost impossible to assess, any more than the lift from a 'synthetic' track surface. Whatever the ranking of Warholm's triumph, his exceptional status was emulated within 24 hours, by a woman. Or rather, women. Yet a spectacular world record by American Sydney McLaughlin, of 51.46s, carving 0.44s off the previous time at the age of 21, provoked marginally less astonishment despite its margin: three of the four fastest women in history were in contention, including Dalilah Muhammad, world record-breaker with 52.16s two years earlier at Doha's World Championships, ahead of McLaughlin. Femke Bol, of the Netherlands, now took the bronze. Muhammad was defending her title but was overhauled in a last lunge by McLaughlin in the final 20 metres.

Forty-one years previously a moderate Scottish long jumper had belatedly switched to 100m, aged 24, for the Games in Moscow. With the USA's sprinters scuppered by boycott, Alan Wells, coached by his wife, had snatched the 100m title all but anonymously. When American Fred Kerley, co-favourite and on the day runner-up in the 100m in Tokyo, was asked afterwards what he knew about upstart Marcell Jacobs, the answer was 'nothing!' No Italian man had ever previously made the Olympic final. To have transferred from being a minor long jumper two years earlier, failing to make a mark in the European Championships, now to become Olympic sprint champion, was profoundly unusual. Only three months prior to Tokyo had Jacobs broken ten seconds for the first time, yet now his European record in victory of 9.80s was faster than that of legendary Usain Bolt when winning the event five years earlier in Rio. Jacobs was as stunned as any viewer, which in Tokyo was not too many, 'To win the title after Usain Bolt is unbelievable, but it's unthinkable to draw any comparison between us. My switch began three years ago when I moved to Rome and changed so much, including my nutrition, and having a mental coach, so this is a dream come true.' Born in Texas with an American father, Jacobs had moved to his mother's Italian homeland as an infant, yet there was little explanation for this extraordinary change in fortune: in his first race in Tokyo he had broken the Italian record with 9.94s, improving on that in the semi-finals with 9.84s.

Alison Felix, competing in her fifth Games, against the odds claimed bronze in the 400m and a night later was party to the 4x400m relay gold: the most decorated female in track and field with 11 medals, seven of them gold, only surpassed by legendary Finn Paavo Nurmi's 12. Felix also surpassed Carl Lewis's record for the most medals by an American. Her total embraced: gold – Beijing 2008, 4x400m; London 2012, 200m, 4x100m, 4x400m; Rio 2016, 4x100m, 4x400m; Tokyo 2020, 4x400m; Athens 2004, 200m silver; Beijing 2008, 200m silver, Rio 2016, 400m silver; Tokyo 2020, 400m bronze.

Sifan Hassan of the Netherlands became the first track and field athlete to win medals in three individual events since 1988, claiming the 5,000m and 10,000m titles, in addition to bronze between the two for 1,500m. Remarkably, she had qualified in the 1,500 semi-finals in the morning prior to winning the 5,000m; two races in under 12 hours. With a lap remaining in the 1,500m, Hassan fell, lost 30 metres on the leaders, yet retrieved her rhythm sufficiently to qualify. In the 10,000m, leaving the field for dead in 90-degree temperature and 80 per cent humidity, Hassan collapsed at the finish, needing resuscitation.

Elsewhere, notable Chinese successes were Ma Long, confirming his status as one of the all-time greats of table tennis, becoming the first man twice to complete the sport's grand slam: Olympic, world and World Cup titles in the same year, now at the age of 32, and increasing his Olympic gold medal tally to five with a double of singles and team titles, in spite of knee surgery in 2019. Another 'elderly', Lü Xiaojun, became the oldest man to win a weightlifting gold when taking the 81kg category, also setting new Olympic records with gold at London 2012 and silver at Rio 2016.

Equally unforgettable in age scale at these unique Olympics was an unknown girl of 12 years and 204 days, the personification of Olympic significance. Hend Zaza, dodging the bullets of Syria's apocalyptic civil war, defied fate even to be there in Tokyo, becoming the youngest in table tennis Olympic history. Her preparation had been no more than a handful of matches when evading her country's borders. Zaza lost in the first round, earning untold respect from an Austrian three times her age. She symbolised Thomas Bach's Olympic message: that socially we all belong, whether audience, family or participants, to an integration which extends beyond mere winning or losing.

In a comparatively 'clean' Games, David Howman, chair of the Athletics Integrity Unit, reconfirmed that only 20 athletes had been deemed ineligible for Tokyo, Nigeria the highest with ten, Ukraine and Belarus both with three, Kenya with two and one each from Ethiopia and Morocco. In the lead-up to Tokyo, more than 1,600 out-of-competition tests were conducted, Howman concluding, 'It is clear that the relevant national federations in conjunction with their anti-doping bodies have begun to take their testing responsibilities seriously.'

Lingering criticism in Japan of both Thomas Bach and John Coates, for respective visits to Hiroshima and Nagasaki, and city memorial sites for the atomic atrocities of World War Two, had resided: their intentions the most courteous of civic formality, in the face of domestic accusation of political exploitation in the face of domestic opposition to the Games. Bach had assured local opinion that his action was no more than 'a peace mission by the Olympic Movement and a beacon of hope for a better future'. He had accompanied an 82-year-old survivor of the bombing for a tour of Hiroshima's Peace Memorial Museum.

When Bach came to consider his address to the Olympic community and the watching world at the conclusion of the Games, he was no Greek philosopher, but a contemporary intellect who for 16 months had just led – tirelessly and morally – a mammoth rearguard action to protect, on behalf of fellow athletes, the world's foremost cultural festival in the face of a paralytic plague. With collaborative redoubtable Japanese administration, and emotionally committed athletes, he had succeeded. Bach did not now need to be Henry V at Agincourt: just to find simple words of thanks to thousands of ordinary folk who had accomplished ordinary tasks within near impossible demands. For the majority of athletes, that had been private, anonymous triumph; for medal winners, a life-lasting, anxiety-liberating reward; for administrators, a relief beyond expectation; for a billions-wide audience, an unpredicted cascade of shared emotions with athletes revealing what we as people can achieve in extremity. These were some of the president's gentle, unaffected, heartfelt words:

'Over the last 16 days, you amazed us with your sporting achievements, your excellence, joy and tears. You created the magic of these Olympic Games of Tokyo 2020. You were faster, you went higher, you were stronger, because we all stood together … in solidarity. You competed fiercely for glory, while living socially together under one roof in the Olympic Village, a powerful message for solidarity and peace. You inspired us with this unifying power of sport, the more remarkable given the many challenges you had to face within the pandemic. In these difficult times, you granted the world the most precious of gifts: hope.

'For the first time since the pandemic began, the world came together. Sport returned to centre stage. Billions of people around the globe were united by emotion, sharing your moments of inspiration. This gives us the hope, our faith in the future. The Games of Tokyo 2020 have been the Games of hope, solidarity and peace. You, the best athletes in the world, could only fulfil your Olympic dream because Japan prepared the stage on which to shine. You, the Japanese people, can be so proud of the dedication you bestowed upon the event. A special thanks goes to all the volunteers, the smiles in your eyes warming our hearts. Yes, these were unprecedented Games: it took us, the IOC, and our Japanese partners and friends, an equally unprecedented effort to make them happen, which is why I thank the Japanese authorities at all levels, in particular prime minister Yoshihide Suga and governor Yuriko Koike for their steadfast commitment. Thank you for staying with us on the side of the athletes, who were longing so deeply to embrace these Olympics.

'Our deepest gratitude goes to the organising committee. Nobody has ever organised a postponed Olympic Games before. Thank you to the Games president, my dear fellow Olympian, Hashimoto Seiko, to the dedicated people in the committee for your devoted partnership and enduring friendship. The same is true for the solidarity from everyone in the Olympic community, with our thanks to national Olympic committees, to the international federations, our TOP partners, the sponsors and rights-holding broadcasters for their truly outstanding show of support. We all did it ... like athletes, and for athletes. We did it together. And now I have to mark the end of this most challenging Olympic journey, declaring the Games of the 32nd Olympiad closed.'

In the wake of the Games, retiring prime minister Suga, attending a UN General Assembly for one of his final engagements, expressed satisfaction, 'That Tokyo's Games have been a symbol of global unity, held with the aim of building a peaceful and better world through sport, under the truce resolution adopted at this very venue of the General Assembly. While there were various views about staging the Games, we, as the host country, fulfilled our responsibilities and achieved what we set out to do. Many people were deeply moved by the outstanding performances of athletes, which gave hopes and dreams to many across the globe. The Games demonstrated the barrier-free mindset to the world, with aspirations for an inclusive society where all people, with or without disabilities, support each other to live in harmony. Above all, while humanity has been faced with immeasurable hardships, the Tokyo 2020 Games proved to be a symbol of global unity among people around the world.'

Off-stage, Dick Pound, at 79 a 43-year member who might well have preceded Bach as president but for the conflicting tide of events, reflected in conclusion, 'While there were those who were shrill with doubt and ready to quit, others persevered on a road that may have been windy: always moving forward in pursuit of an objective that was, after all, achieved. There is an element of the Olympic spirit from which we can learn at least two things: first, that nothing is impossible, and second, that the Movement we represent, when it works together, is stronger than we might have believed.'

TOKYO 2020 MEDALS

United States 113 (39-41-33)
China 88 (38-32-18)
Japan 58 (27-14-17)
Great Britain 65 (22-21-22)
ROC 71 (20-28-23)
Australia 46 (17-7-22)
Netherlands 36 (10-12-14)
France 33 (10-12-11)
Germany 37 (10-11-16)
Italy 40 (10-10-20)
Canada 24 (7-6-11)
Brazil 21 (7-6-8)
New Zealand 20 (7-6-7)

Cuba 15 (7-3-5)
Hungary 20 (6-7-7)
South Korea 20 (6-4-10)
Poland 14 (4-5-5)
Czech Republic 11 (4-4-3)
Kenya 10 (4-4-2)
Norway 8 (4-2-2)
Jamaica 9 (4-1-4)
Spain 17 (3-8-6)
Sweden 9 (3-6-0)
Switzerland 13 (3-4-6)
Denmark 11 (3-4-4)
Croatia 8 (3-3-2)
Iran 7 (3-2-2)
Serbia 9 (3-1-5)
Belgium 7 (3-1-3)
Bulgaria 6 (3-1-2)
Slovenia 5 (3-1-1)
Uzbekistan 5 (3-0-2)
Georgia 8 (2-5-1)
Chinese Taipei 12 (2-4-6)
Turkey 13 (2-2-9)
Greece 4 (2-1-1)
Uganda 4 (2-1-1)
Ecuador 3 (2-1-0)
Ireland 4 (2-0-2)
Israel 4 (2-0-2)
Qatar 3 (2-0-1)
Bahamas 2 (2-0-0)
Kosovo 2 (2-0-0)
Ukraine 19 (1-6-12)
Belarus 7 (1-3-3)
Romania 4 (1-3-0)
Venezuela 4 (1-3-0)
India 7 (1-2-4)
Hong Kong 6 (1-2-3)
Philippines 4 (1-2-1)
Slovakia 4 (1-2-1)
South Africa 3 (1-2-0)
Austria 7 (1-1-5)

Egypt 6 (1-1-4)
Indonesia 5 (1-1-3)
Ethiopia 4 (1-1-2)
Portugal 4 (1-1-2)
Tunisia 2 (1-1-0)
Estonia 2 (1-0-1)
Fiji 2 (1-0-1)
Latvia 2 (1-0-1)
Thailand 2 (1-0-1)
Bermuda 1 (1-0-0)
Morocco 1 (1-0-0)
Puerto Rico 1 (1-0-0)
Colombia 5 (0-4-1)
Azerbaijan 7 (0-3-4)
Dominican Republic 5 (0-3-2)
Armenia 4 (0-2-2)
Kyrgyzstan 3 (0-2-1)
Mongolia 4 (0-1-3)
Argentina 3 (0-1-2)
San Marino 3 (0-1-2)
Jordan 2 (0-1-1)
Malaysia 2 (0-1-1)
Nigeria 2 (0-1-1)
Bahrain 1 (0-1-0)
Saudi Arabia 1 (0-1-0)
Lithuania 1 (0-1-0)
North Macedonia 1 (0-1-0)
Namibia 1 (0-1-0)
Turkmenistan 1 (0-1-0)
Kazakhstan 8 (0-0-8)
Mexico 4 (0-0-4)
Finland 2 (0-0-2)
Botswana 1 (0-0-1)
Burkina Faso 1 (0-0-1)
Ivory Coast 1 (0-0-1)
Ghana 1 (0-0-1)
Grenada 1 (0-0-1)
Kuwait 1 (0-0-1)
Moldova 1 (0-0-1)
Syria 1 (0-0-1)

14

VALIEVA'S TRAUMA

THE SOCIAL benefits derived from sport extend far beyond improvement in health and the emotional fulfilment of competition. Never has the social 'medication' in sport been more evident than at Tokyo's postponed Olympic Games of 2020: amid the repression of the pandemic, a flood of emotions were released among and between competitors and audience, never mind spectators were, sadly, electronically distant. This laudable achievement was the most powerful justification for the concerted effort by both IOC and Japanese organising committee to persist with a widely criticised objective. Dick Pound's optimism would have stood ground six months later, at Beijing's Winter Games, but for Putin's hallucinogenic war in Ukraine: widely predicted during the Games by Western intelligence but denied by Putin until the day it began; he and China's Premier Xi Jinping having shaken hands on a joint 'non-intervention policy' regarding the affairs of sovereign states. Really? An instantly revealed scurrilous lie with Ukraine's invasion.

Awareness of Tokyo's social perspective had been evident in Bach's extended objective of his election manifesto, Agenda 2020+5: this released in mid-June prior to the Games, a contract for official hospitality provider as part of reforms. By this innovative contract, the US-based company On Location was to become exclusive service provider for Paris 2024, Milan-Cortina 2026 and Los Angeles 2028 in promotion of formal hospitality facilities, as recommended in Item 15 of the Agenda extension. The objective was to 'innovate revenue generation models, creating a centralised Olympic service for the benefit of all stakeholders – a global licensing programme and marketing alliance embracing the International Paralympic Committee'.

On Location would expand planning across packages including stadium tickets, travel, accommodation and in-venue entertainment, extending opportunities to families and friends of competitors, with a dedicated ticket inventory. Projected income from On Location was expected to add almost $1bn over the course of the three-Games contract made with Endeavour Group Holdings, a conglomerate which additionally had absorbed the prolific sports agency IMG. Bach commented, 'This is part of the Agenda objective to deliver additional solutions simplifying the complexity of hosting a Games. This contract will secure essential facilities for supporters across the world at these three Games, an illustration of good governance, supplementing NOCs and particularly their athletes.' Giovanni Malagò, organising president of Milan-Cortina, welcomed this 'important revenue stream'; likewise Los Angeles 2028 leader Casey Wasserman, considering the project 'a major priority'. Bach admitted, 'The governance of the Olympic Movement has experienced risks in the ticketing system and its regulations. This opens new opportunities for all NOCs to participate in the programme with the benefit of additional revenue.'

One financial advance was jostling with another: the IOC president was able to announce prior to Tokyo's belated opening that The Olympic Programme (TOP) was scheduled to raise an expected $3bn during the 2021–2024 quadrennium, thanks to an acceleration of enthusiastic growth, first initiated under Samaranch 36 years earlier in 1984. TOP had exceeded $1bn in revenue between 2013 and 2016, culminating at the Rio Games, and had been set to more than double this from 2017 to 2020 prior to the pandemic, but remained optimistic still to do so. The commercial power of the sports arena across broadcasting and sponsorship remained powerful even against the backdrop of the global financial crisis, as would be demonstrated by broadcasting during Tokyo's threatened festival. NBC Universal once more exposed the enduring appeal of a Games when leading all TV networks every night for 17 days of Tokyo broadcasting, with unprecedented streaming consumption: dominant across every broadcast platform, enjoying the knock-on effect in parallel broadcasts of news programmes both national and international. NBC's nightly primetime audience averaged in excess of 15.1 million, while the next audience figures were one-third of that for rivals such as CBS. The audience numbers might have been substantially down from those for Rio, London and Beijing, yet nonetheless remained justification for NBC's valued contract with IOC, inclusive through to Brisbane 2032.

In the wake of Tokyo's coverage, NBC was able to boast 'the largest media event ever: the most streamed Olympics, with six billion minutes across the digital and social platforms, airing over 7,000 hours of coverage with more than 120 billion minutes of content across all platforms'. In the UK, the BBC acquired a record-breaking 104 million online requests, way ahead of the figures from Rio 2016. In Tokyo, national audience figures for the Closing Ceremony at 47 per cent had been exceeded only by the 56 per cent recorded for the Opening Ceremony of its previous Summer Games in 1964. Christopher Caroll, director of digital engagement and marketing for the IOC, similarly recorded 'the most digitally engaged Games ever'; a delighted Bach welcoming the fact that 'almost 90 per cent of the Japanese population have tuned in to Tokyo 2020', a reflection of an enduring public appetite despite the pessimism that had infected polling forecasts prior to the Games.

Pete Bevacqua, chairman of NBC Sports, while acknowledging that the pandemic had altered almost every aspect of the Games, pronounced, 'Once again, we have seen the unparalleled power that the Games has on media and our culture. There is nothing more powerful in media than the 17 straight days of Olympics dominance.' Tokyo had broken digital records from those of Rio 2016, attracting more than 50 million viewers on the Olympic website and mobile application, the majority of viewers coming from the USA, India and the host nation Japan, with more than two billion video views for the OlympicSpirit hashtag on TikTok. Yiannis Exarchos, CEO of Olympic Broadcasting Services (OBS), reflected, 'With all these digital engagement tools, we needed to learn a lot to use technology to highlight and emphasise what has been going on yet cannot be physically seen ... delivering the means to connect athletes to their families, friends and fans.' OBS had realised the concept of the 'Virtual Fan Cheer' in which a five-second video could be recorded and sent via a mobile app, to be shown online and on stadium screens; Bach himself in awe of the facility when observing 'the number of videos having been sent is incredible at more than 250 million'.

Further encouraging financial news, post-Beijing in March 2022, came with prediction that the 28 IFs at Tokyo would be allocated a five per cent increased share of IOC revenue compared with Rio 2016. Yet would there be any revenue, indeed any Games at Paris 2024 if the ambassador from Hades extended Ukraine's hell on earth?

There was a different kind of hell in Beijing, on three counts. Firstly, China's opportunistic exploitation of the Covid pandemic to suffocate any contact between visiting spectators – forbidden – or competing athletes and the media. These were Games isolated beyond the previous restrictions in Tokyo: compulsory 24/7 masks, contrived quarantines, incessant swab tests. Secondly, China's propaganda assault at press conferences, suppression of Western questions on human rights, promotion of Premier Xi's uncorroborated claim of 300 million winter sports enthusiasts (though undoubtedly there will be countless future Chinese medal winners, these produced on artificial snow). Thirdly, and perhaps worst, 13 of the 17 days were dominated by the scandal and simultaneous harrowing episode surrounding the bureaucratic drug manipulation of sensational 15-year-old Russian figure skater Kamila Valieva; pitifully dragooned with degrading deceit by her coaching entourage, a retrospective verdict by WADA which may take months to unravel, amid continuing anarchic Russian drug recourse, suspicion on them also rampant in the biathlon arena. Anxious to sustain Olympic sports' largest national population and the second largest economy dedicated to biennial Olympic participation, Bach jeopardised approval of the Games with his hasty compliments on Beijing's authoritarianism. Critics aplenty overlook Bach's dedication in Agenda 2020 to multiple social principles starkly absent in a communistic expanding plutocracy.

The malevolent focus of Beijing's socially fractious but competitively often dramatic Games erupted on the first Monday. It had been Valieva's stunning performance that had won the unambiguous Russian Olympic Committee the team figure skating gold, becoming first female to land a quadruple jump at an Olympics, and not one but two, with a Salchow followed by a toe-loop; confusion following when the medal ceremony was postponed. Valieva was exposed for a belatedly divulged doping offence from 25 December. In the wake of seven years of institutional cheating by Russia across Olympic sport, this latest infringement was, throughout the Olympic community, the last straw. Was not Russia supposed to be on track for a drive towards integrity and compliance, not just with WADA, but normal sporting life? The allegation of a positive test was more complex on account of Valieva being a 'minor' aged 15, there being in some circumstances dispensation in penalties for a junior. The issue was further complicated by announcement of her positive test, by an accredited laboratory in Sweden, not being declared for more than a month.

Her case now had to be referred to the Court of Arbitration for Sport (CAS): the IOC, skating's IF and the International Testing Agency (ITA) all appealed for the suspension to be upheld: the positive test only announced on 8 February, the very day the team figure skating medals had been scheduled for presentation, but the RUSADA instantly lifted the suspension. The controversy now was whether Valieva, so supreme in the team event that an individual gold medal was now viewed as inevitable, would remain eligible. Would a child sensation be given the benefit of the doubt by a compassionate CAS jury on account of her age and the hovering implication that if the test was correct, the guilt for a child must lie with her entourage? The three-member jury consisted of Fabio Iudica of Italy, American Jeffrey Benz and Dr Bergant Rakocevic of Slovenia: provocatively, splitting opinion worldwide, their verdict was to uphold RUSADA's lifting of the suspension 'considering fundamental principles of fairness and irreparable harm for an athlete who did not test positive during the Games and is still subject to a disciplinary procedure'. CAS stated they considered 'preventing the athlete from competing at the Games would cause her irreparable harm'. The roundabout analysis was that should Valieva subsequently be confirmed to have had a positive test, she could then be disqualified in the individual event, if a medal winner, and the results adjusted: perverse in the extreme.

In the event, following a flawless performance in the short programme, disaster overtook Valieva in her free discipline, reduced to tears and a fourth place. Compounding this disaster for a girl whose fortune had gripped global audiences was the reception in failure she received from Eteri Tutberidze: coach to all three Russian entrants, including Anna Shcherbakova and Alexandra Trusova, who took gold and silver. Interpreted from the rink by Reuters agency, the renowned aggressive coach was unforgiving in her greeting. 'Why did you let it go? Explain to me, why? Why did you stop fighting?' Watching on television, Bach entered the public fray, sensitive to the emotional trauma suffered by a prodigy three days after being cleared to compete. Bach's comments now magnified the controversy, saying, 'I was disturbed, seeing how the pressure must have been, pressure beyond my imagination, how she tried to compose herself. You could see in her body language, this was an immense mental stress, this chilling atmosphere. I can only wish for Kamila that she has the support of her family and friends.' There was widespread testimony to the hard-line discipline for which Tutberidze was renowned, and the relative brevity of the careers of youngsters for whom she was responsible.

Instant response came from Russian authority to Bach's provocative sympathy, Putin's Kremlin spokesman Dmitry Peskov stating, 'We respect his opinion but do not necessarily agree … everyone knows that the harshness of a coach in high-level sport is a key for their athletes' victories.' Dmitry Chernyshenko, deputy prime minister, claimed that Bach 'has his own fictional narrative on the feelings of our athletes'. Here was a story of legally flawed bureaucracy betraying a child, a so-called 'protected person'; Valieva had received the reverse of protection, particularly in the light of a clause in CAS regulations that if a protected person can prove they are not responsible for ingestion of an illegal substance, then the penalty should be no more than a reprimand. The scandal provoked widespread calls for competitors aged under 16 being ineligible for the Olympics, since logic demands that anyone guilty of doping must be subject to the regulations imposed: in other words, if old enough for the Games, old enough to be subject to the regulations. No 15-year-old is going to be asking for heart medication.

Valieva's grief was a sinister reflection on a recent conversation I had had with the confident new head of WADA, Witold Bańka from Poland, who had succeeded Craig Reedie early in 2020. Bańka had served as European representative on WADA's executive since May 2017, a former track specialist at 400m, representing Poland internationally, junior and senior, from 2005 to 2012, with a World Championships bronze medal in 2007. Bańka's opinion in 2021 was one of optimistic confidence that the Olympic arena was finally in command over long-standing Russian malpractice, 'You never know who are the attempted cheats, the everydayness of the malaise, but we are now much stronger than in the past, when Russia, and others, were so often corrupt, and WADA was not in position to act legally. Now we are in a completely different place compared to the past, thanks to different organisation, with new tools, stronger compliance regulations in every country. Regarding Russia, CAS adjustments have confirmed our powers to sanction a country, and we must hope there will never be another Russia. Recently in 2020 our executive approved a new phase in our structure, and we've increased the presence of the Athletes Commission, giving them a more constructive role, so I think WADA is on the right course. My philosophy as a former athlete is that our role is never to be part of political attitudes. We have a new investigative unit, strategy for ten-year storage of samples going back three Games.'

When Bańka came initially to estimate the ongoing adjudication for Valieva, he was confident that all would be clarified, that any infringement would be punished; in line with the IOC's appeal that the suspension should have been upheld following an A sample in her test having been prohibited. Bańka's view is that for a minor involved in senior competition, the same rules must apply, 'I think our position is clear.' Yet there now had to be sincere doubts about the authenticity of RUSADA's alleged reorganisation, Bańka having emphasised, in his first meeting with Russia's new sports minister Oleg Matytsin, that the need for RUSADA to retain independence was crucial, and there should be no attempt of the Russian state or sporting authorities to interfere with any of its operations. In compliance, Russia had repaid $1.27m to WADA for costs incurred over prolonged investigation. 'Our common goal is to ensure the stability of the global anti-doping system and jointly to prevent any attempts to undermine it by individual countries,' Matytsin had said. 'The Russian Athletics Federation now adheres to clear principles of zero tolerance to doping in sport and implements in its policy a consistent approach to eradicate it.'

Bańka had stated to Polish newspaper *Rzeczpospolita*, 'In Russia, we have no longer to deal with an unprecedented system of doping support which once shocked the world of sports.' Was he now to be plunged back into WADA's past nightmare scenario?

Inevitably, accompanying Valieva's alleged guilt was the regular self-righteous protests of that example of American hypocrisy, Travis Tygart of USADA, who selectively chooses to overlook the past history of conspicuous American cheats such as Marion Jones and Justin Gatlin. As the ensuing war mushroomed in Ukraine, with appalling degradation of humanity becoming evident at the end of the first month, the IOC and the rest of the world sports authorities were unanimously in agreement for the suspension of Russia, together with sycophantic neighbours Belarus, both from hosting and participating in all international sporting events, together with the withdrawal by IOC of Putin's Olympic Order. The response to such global moral condemnation produced an extraordinary reaction from Chernyshenko, CEO of Sochi's defamed Olympic Games. At a Kremlin gathering of domestic sports authorities titled 'We are together – Sport', the deputy prime minister had the nerve to claim that the rest of the world 'have wiped their feet on the Olympic Charter with their condemnation'. As a die-hard colleague of the madman in charge, Chernyshenko asserted, 'When we see that international sport has become the most powerful means of political struggle, when all the principles and ideals on which we grew up are violated, all the rules of the Olympic Charter are ignored, and by those who did not write it, we see how the humanitarian mission of sports is being destroyed right before our eyes, and it is important that we stay together. Russia has a special role that will preserve these values, despite the fact that others have wiped their feet on them.' If and when charges and conviction for war crimes and genocide are ever achieved,

Chernyshenko must share the responsibility for Ukraine's iniquitous civilian bloodshed.

In the same blind face-saving conviction, more than 50 of Russia's national federations of individual sports planned to submit appeals to CAS against their inevitable rejection by IFs from global sport. One of my oldest, truest of Olympic friends, John Boulter, of 1960s vintage, phoned to say, 'What a mess the world is in.'

15

BURGEONING CHINESE SPORT

IF BEIJING'S Winter Games were to be lifted from exaggerated Covid lockdowns, it needed spectacular performance intervention on the acres of artificial snow established at monumental expense. This arrived in droves, the most extreme display from an apposite amalgam of the USA and China in the shape of Eileen Gu, otherwise Gu Ailing, born in California of a Chinese mother and American father, part raised by her then visiting grandmother Feng Guozhen, now 85, native of Nanjing and all-round sportswoman from Jiaotong University. An accomplished pianist, linguist and skier, Gu, a mere 18, had won two golds and a silver at Lausanne's Youth Games in 2020, two golds and a bronze at Aspen's winter X Games the following year, and was now aspiring for three Olympic golds against a controversial background of having gained Chinese citizenship in 2019.

Inflexible China's communism forbids dual citizenship. Does Gu retain her US passport: has she become, discreetly, a propaganda pawn for China's feigned social global expansion, while retaining her US residence? In celebratory press conferences, Gu was not quizzed on the respective relationships by China with Russia or the US, merely commending approvingly China's international integration. Amid the frenzy surrounding her sweep of two golds and a silver in big air, half-pipe and slopestyle, with provocative charm she declined to confirm if she retained her US passport.

Gu set the Games alight with her first event, the big air. In bright sunshine and under scrutiny of mass media, Gu lay in bronze position with one jump to go. Her attendant mother Yan Gu had offered advice to persist with a 1,440-degree spin which would have lifted her to silver position. Daughter had other ideas. She landed what is termed a 'left double 1620 with safety grab', the first time she had attempted this trick: it earned the points to vault her to gold, leaving French rival Tess Ledeux with silver. Gu reflected, 'I wanted to represent myself and the competitive spirit I take pride in.' Asked afterwards about her citizenship, she answered that 30 per cent of the year was spent in China, 'to use sport as a force for unity, to foster interconnection between countries and not a divisive force'. A wave of relentless attention followed Gu's silver in slopestyle and second gold in half-pipe, becoming the first freestyle skier to win three medals in a Winter Games. Adding political nuance to this dream performance was the presence in the audience of Peng Shuai, alongside Thomas Bach: the newsworthy Chinese tennis player enmeshed in social-political mystery, seemingly at ease within a cloud of speculation engulfing her sexual harassment by a senior politician. We did not know whether her presence in public view was by political arrangement (of supposed freedom) or private inclination.

If life was a dream for Gu, it was more a matter of relief for Lindsey Jacobellis whose sporting career had courted ridicule since the Turin Games of 2006 when she was 20. In youthful innocence, approaching the finish of the snowboard-cross final and seeming triumph, she risked the flourish which would remain vivid for the next 16 years. With 50 metres remaining and on the second-to-last jump, she had showboated, unnecessarily placed a hand on her board, floundered and crashed as Tanja Frieden of Switzerland glided by for gold. A silver medal never tasted worse and the error would live with Jacobellis through subsequent unrewarding Games at Vancouver, Sochi and Pyeongchang. As a girl she had been known as Lucky Lindsey, but that label evaporated: though

250

she progressed to six world titles, ten more in X Games and 30 in the World Cup, she had been unable to erase the Olympic memory of Turin. Finally, now at 36 the oldest snowboard champion in history, she realised her ambition, racing like a champion from start to finish and even including a saucy method-grab on one of her jumps for gesture. 'That gaffe had helped to keep me hungry, kept me fighting. Disaster doesn't define you if you are a winner,' she said.

The personnel of Winter Olympic competitions are influenced by the lottery of climate: there are few with the effective physique and temperament characteristic among African or Central and South Americans from European former colonies who are adept on snow or ice, though this disinclination is reducing. Black competitors are no longer such a rarity. American Erin Jackson became the first black woman to win a speed skating medal at the Olympics, her gold in the 500m sprint both a shock and a relief to have made this imprint within a former 'closed shop'. From Ocala in Florida, she joined fellow American Shani Davis as the only black athlete to win a long track Olympic medal thus far. She reflected, 'I hope this will do something for the sport, that more will see this and be encouraged.' Back home, her coach Renee Hildebrand observed, 'Maybe girls and boys unaware of roller skating or ice skating will see Erin and realise people our colour are out there, why not?'

With the time of 37.04s, this victory was America's first since that of Bonnie Blair in 1994 and involved a rare show of generosity from Brittany Bowe, Jackson's Ocala colleague. She had won the US trials but relinquished her place in favour of Jackson, though subsequently receiving third place selection prior to departure for Beijing and finishing 16th. Jackson had made her break towards prominence in 2016 when spending time in the Netherlands, throne of this particular art, then qualifying for Pyeongchang in 2018 and finishing 24th. This time Miho Takagi of Japan took silver, Angelina Golikova of Russia bronze. There was American black celebration elsewhere, redoubtable Elana Meyers Taylor extending her prolonged bobsleigh record with silver in a career, with bronze in the two-woman event, silver in the monorace, for a grand total of four gold, five silver and three bronze medals including World Championship races.

Bobsleigh has indeed become something of a speciality for black Americans ever since Vonetta Flowers wept during the national anthem in Salt Lake 2002, becoming the first athlete of colour to win any gold medal at a Winter Olympics. In 2022, seven of the eight members of America's World Cup bobsleigh team were black, as were four of the five in Beijing. One of them, Aja Evans from Chicago, who failed to make it for a medal, remained positive, 'This is a sport for everyone.'

Being an old-fashioned and less than expert pursuer of exercise on snow, I am no doubt one of many remaining baffled by the language involving much of snowboarding. I would be glad to know precisely how one sets about achieving a 'cab double cork 1260' – which they say involves three and a half rotations with two of them overhead. Anna Gasser, from Austria, now made history, becoming the first woman to land such a trick, and thereby the first back-to-back Olympic champion in women's snowboard big air. Zoi Sadowski-Synnott of New Zealand took silver, Kokomo Murase of Japan the bronze. At 30, one of the oldest riders, Gasser is regarded as a trendsetter, including – I am told – the triple cork. Sadowski-Synnott had earlier become New Zealand's first ever winter gold medal-winner when claiming slopestyle, a longer run of obstacles, rails and jumps.

In a sporting arena not short on personality, Chloe Kim of the US is anything but backward: one of those enviable characters who is out there as much for the fun as for ambition, yet her enthusiasm enabling her to be the first woman to win two snowboard half-pipe Olympic golds. In the sport's introspective language, she was the first in women's competition to attempt a 'cab 1260'. Five-time Olympian Queralt Castellet of Spain won silver, Sena Tomita of Japan the bronze. Kim's rivals were unanimous that she had raised women's half-pipe to a supreme level, that they were struggling to keep pace. Kim admitted, 'At Pyeongchang 2018 a "frontside 1080" wasn't that common, now it seems every girl can do it.' In Korea, Kim had become the youngest female to win Olympic gold on snow at the age of 17.

With the background of my father's theatrical career, I confess to a prejudice towards the musical symmetry and stage elegance of ice dancing, and not just on account of following the early emergence 40 years ago of magical Torvill and Dean. For the two most recent Olympic Games there has been an exhibition of such supreme harmony by a French couple, Gabriella Papadakis and Guillaume Cizeron. I would dare to place their lyrical synchronisation above that of the British pair who so mesmerisingly enchanted audiences at Sarajevo in 1984, and then again, though infamously denied by prejudiced judges from winning the title, at Lillehammer 1994.

The French pair, embraced in unison as though a single figure, had been robbed of gold in Pyeongchang by a dress malfunction, momentarily exposing Gabriella's breast and necessitating a rhythmic compromise. Now in Beijing they were, in my estimation, even more supreme. Gabriel Fauré, French composer, can be simultaneously alluring and grave, and the French entwined with his 'Elegy' to such a pitch that the audience was anaesthetised with admiration. Their victory in the free skate with 226.98 points over Victoria Sinitsina and Nikita Katsalapov of Russia was captivatingly comprehensive. They have been a unit for a decade, winning four world titles with such elegance that they are in a world of their own, so close to ballet that at times it is possible to forget that they are wearing skates. Since the Korean incident, they have lost only one competition, the European Championships of 2020, where they were defeated I know not how by the Russians.

If perfection can come in style, it can also be there with endurance. German speed skater Claudia Pechstein, days short of her 50th birthday, became the first woman to compete in eight Winter Olympics, serving as one of Germany's two flag-bearers in the Opening Ceremony. At 3,000m, she competed against 22-year-old Ahenaer Adake of China, Pechstein ranking last on a 20-strong field but witnessing her 20-year Olympic record finally lowered by Irene Schouten of the Netherlands. Pechstein admitted, 'I was not too fast today, but I could smile when I crossed the finishing line because I had achieved a private ambition.'

Competitive sport is not all joy, not least in the Olympics, and many experience the reverse, as we witnessed with the crumpled decline of America's formidable gymnast Simone Biles in the recent Tokyo Games: the girl who had everything reduced to an apologetic shadow of her unrivalled brilliance. A similar distress now overtook American Mikaela Shiffrin, who a decade earlier seemingly had waiting an Olympic career without parallel: Beijing became a trough so ordinary that few could believe they were watching the same woman: once a teenage phenomenon with talents which left rivals adrift. This was her third Games, expectation having magnified on each occasion: first at Sochi in 2014, then Pyeongchang, but either fortune, the climate or schedules defied her, limiting her to gold in Pyeongchang's giant slalom and silver in combined (downhill and slalom). She arrived in Beijing as one of the most heralded in the frame, scheduled for five events, admirers wondering how many she could win. By the conclusion, the question was more whether she would be able to finish a race, subject to the similar emotional pressures which had undermined Biles. Shiffrin's regular two best events were giant slalom and slalom: she completed neither. It had been a decade since she failed to finish consecutive slalom races; moreover, out of 229 World Championship, World Cup and Olympic races, she had previously failed to finish in a mere 14. What had happened?

Two years ago, her father Jeff had died suddenly in a home accident in Colorado. Shiffrin had not skied for the following nine months, shorn of motivation in 2021. Jeff, a medic and competitive skier, had been an emotional solace behind all the frictions that impinge on a touring competitive life. The impact on his daughter now seemed transparently evident. Shiffrin admitted in an interview, 'Everything I thought I knew about my own skiing, my slalom and racing mentality, makes me second guess the last 15 years.' In downhill, rarely her forté, she came 15th: in the combined, her last and prime event, she failed to finish. Shiffrin's extensive audience can but wish her recovery from such an uncharacteristic public and private ordeal, just as the watching world hoped for the unique Simone Biles.

Geopolitics is ever present in China–US emotional scales: domestic ecstasy on behalf of Gu, open hostility towards US-born Nathan Chen, men's figure skating champion with Chinese parents. Antipathy to Chen had arisen at Pyeongchang 2018, when he performed to the music of *Mao's Last Dancer*, attempting to identify with his genetic roots. He was seen as a defector, the music having featured in an Australian film that was banned in China. Chen aggravated the Chinese by agreeing that the issue of China's human rights record was an offence to humanity. Now he was seen in Beijing as a social outcast. Performing his free routine as the last competitor, his jumping was immaculate, leading in the short programme: his final points total of 332.60 was far beyond two Japanese, runner-up Yuma Kagiyama and bronze winner Shoma Uno. Both had complex routines, but each was undermined by error alongside a flawless Chen. Worse mistakes by their compatriot, Yuzuru Hanyu, in fourth place, denied him gold for his third Olympics in a row.

The most challenging of all disciplines, downhill, guarantees maximum attention: in Beijing focus was on Frenchman Johan Clarey, at 41 becoming by five years the oldest medal winner in alpine skiing, his World Cup career launched in 2003. With silver, he was obliged to yield to Beat Feuz of Switzerland, who echoed former icons such as Franz Klammer and Toni Sailer by adding Olympic gold in the same season as winning at Kitzbühel. The artificial snow presented, in severe weather on the Yanquing slopes, a demanding challenge, yet the physical power of Feuz matched the complex route designed by Bernhard Russi.

Comparable supremacy came from Ayumu Hirano of Japan with his display, for the first time in Olympic competition, of a 'triple cork' to command half-pipe gold and confirm his status as the current expert in his final run. Hirano was one of the first to achieve this trick, a geometric challenge thus far beyond all rivals: moreover, it was the opening manoeuvre on all three of his runs. Genting Snow Park course at northern Zhangjiakou was widely awaited on account of this being the final appearance of the event's enduring expert, American Shaun White. It was a formidable field, with four Japanese snowboarders in with a chance, plus Scotty James of Australia in addition to White, the three-time champion and still a serious talent. However, Hirano's 96-point ride on his final run assured him of gold ahead of James, and Jan Scherrer of Switzerland. At 35, White had still a commanding presence, though by now less of the media frenzy that had accompanied his exceptional career, having won his first X Games championship at 16 and already Olympic champion at 19 in Turin. Twice more in subsequent Games he had seized the title, though now he lay ninth in the world rankings at his fifth Olympics. I had long witnessed his eminence, but the podium eluded him: fourth after a fall on his final run. He was modest on reflection, 'I'm proud of the life I've led, what I've achieved in this sport, but these younger riders, they've been on my heels a long time, and to see them finally surpass me is, I think deep down, what I've always expected.'

Despite speculation on development of China's winter confidence, there was already growing evidence of prodigality, to be expected from a massive and ambitious range of would-be specialists. Su Yiming was one, demonstrating his scorn for gravity with triumph in the men's big air final at Shougang Industrial Park. There is longer experience in China than

In Brazil there is only THE sport: Neymar supplies THE answer, Rio '16 football final.

Moon-shot: double election agreed in 2017 for 2024–2028: (L to R) Tony Estanguet (IOC/FRA, Paris chair), Anne Hidalgo (mayor of Paris), Thomas Bach, Eric Garcetti (mayor of LA), Casey Wasserman (president, LA bid).

Peninsula expectation: Kim Il-guk, NOC president of North Korea (L), Thomas Bach and Do Jong-hwan, minister of sport, South Korea, celebrate unique joint Games in 2018.

Ester Ledecka (CZE) stuns rivals in two sports at Pyeongchang: here skiing's Super-G, and snowboard.

Kirsty Coventry (ZIM), Olympic silver for 400m medley in 2008, subsequently Athletes Commission chair, touted as 2025 presidential successor.

Fastest woman in world sport: Lizzy Yarnold (GBR) retains skeleton title, Pyeongchang '18.

Fatigue shrouds expressions of Japan's Prime Minister Shinzo Abe and Thomas Bach as they contemplate an exceptionally postponed Tokyo Games of 2020.

(L to R) Adrian Schrinner (lord mayor), Richard Colbeck (senator), John Coates (IOC member), James Tomkins (IOC member) and Annastacia Palaszczuk (Queensland prime minister) jubilant for Brisbane's historic host city election 11 years in advance.

Heroine's demise: supreme US gymnast Simone Biles surrenders to mental disorientation, 2020.

Tennis luminary Naomi Osaka ignites Tokyo's postponed flame.

Greatest race of all time? Norway's Karsten Warholm heads glittering world record 400 hurdles at Tokyo 2020.

Prize-money millionaire Carissa Moore (US) predictably triumphs in expanded Olympic programme.

Social equivocation: Thomas Bach and China's 'empire' builder Xi Jinping share earnest ambition at Beijing '22 but not mutual world politics.

Western political hostility greeted selection of Dinigeer Yilamujiang, Chinese Muslim (left), international medallist, as Beijing's joint final torch-lighting bearer with Jiawen Xhao.

Whether, controversially, Chinese or American, Eileen Gu is the Big Air freestyle sensation for Beijing's slender live audience and millions elsewhere.

Erin Jackson's 500m Beijing speed-skating gold for USA emphasises black women's Winter potential.

Fallen mask: scintillating Kamila Valieva, 15-year-old Russian, enchants the world (left) before drugs ignominy crushes a child and again condemns a nation.

Gabriella Papadakis and Guillaume Cizeron of France elevate ice dance to theatrical wonderment in Beijing, as they had four years earlier.

Snowboard recovery: iconic Lindsey Jacobellis (USA) dispels previous Olympic embarrassment of victory snafu with snowboard gold at Beijing.

sceptics were prepared to admit: Su had begun snowboarding at the age of four and had swiftly shown himself to be without fear when perched on the lip of a 60-metre slope: by the age of nine he had felt able to declare the ambition to become Olympic champion, and now China's first Olympic gold in snowboarding.

Pride of a different kind came to Max Parrot, Canadian snowboarder who had been diagnosed with Hodgkin's lymphoma in 2018. Yet he not only thwarted cancer but an array of experts to win slopestyle in the wake of his silver in 2018. Joy will have been profound: life expectation with this disease is no more than four or five years, but Parrot had not been intimidated, 'Holding out was tough, I even thought about quitting treatment. Months of hospital visits, no life, no sport, it was really hard.' Yet this three-time Olympian piled up the tricks to be the only racer with a score in the 90s. 'I've never previously done two triple cork jumps in a row, and everything was so clean,' he said. Adding to China's emergence, and predictable eventual dominance, was Yan Wengang when claiming bronze in the men's skeleton, the nation's first Olympic medal in any sliding sport; in behind dominant Germany's almost automatic gold and silver from Christopher Grotheer and Axel Jungk, domestic ambition seeing another Chinese, Yin Zheng, in fifth place. Wengang's bronze was only the second time a rider from outside Europe or North America had reached the skeleton podium.

And the achievements of Britain? This is not – within the competing bullseye of converging climate forces of the Atlantic, Scandinavia, Central Europe and Northern Africa – a nation equipped to excel in winter sport. We nonetheless try so hard, because it is in character to prove this island capable. In the 21st century, financially buoyed by Lottery funding, Britain has for some years spent many millions in pursuit of medals; for Beijing 2022, revealingly, in excess of £22m, and came home with merely a gold and silver from curling, which you can attempt anywhere indoors. Thrilling though both performances were, elsewhere – alpine, freestyle skiing, cross-country and snowboard – the investment was £9.5m, on skeleton (a previous forté) £6.4m. The price of curling medals was £5.3m; that for zero reward in bobsleigh, luge, figure, short-track and biathlon skating collectively, £0.9m. These are statistics which demand serious review ahead of the Milan-Cortina venture in 2026; even if allowance is made for Covid repression of training in our land without much snow or multiple ice rinks, the minor consolation being this was not taxpayer expenditure. There had been reasonable expectation for Dave Ryding, recent spectacular winner on Kitzbühel's formidable slalom, his only victory in 97 World Cup races. Beijing did not produce another. He admitted, 'We have to make it easier in the lower ranks to get on the snow more often.' Which raises the question whether Britain should bother spending £850,000 a year alone on alpine ambition.

Silver in men's curling was no disgrace. In Niklas Edin of Sweden, Britain were confronted by probably the world's most accomplished player, with three Olympic campaigns previously earning fourth place, bronze, and silver. The drive for gold found Edin in unbeatable form throughout the match, Bruce Mouat and his colleagues Grant Hardie, Bobby Lammie and Hammy McMillan, all in their 20s, barely in with a chance. Edin, a former tank commander, had defied physical stresses of the sport, including multiple operations, but was so supreme that Britain could still welcome the outcome as an achievement. You can hardly argue with an opponent who has five world titles. Not that Mouat should have felt inferior to Edin: nine years younger, he had won ten of their previous 22 meetings prior to the final, including the European Championship, but the Swede's dominance for his team proved conclusive.

In resounding compensation a day later, and closing the Games, Eve Muirhead and British colleagues Vicky Wright, Jen Dodds and Hailey Duff rose to the moment with a 10-3 destruction of Japan, so authoritative that their opponents quit without contending the tenth and final end. Muirhead had led a British Olympic team when she was 19, earning bronze at Sochi 2014, then embarrassed by a failing final shot and chance of a second bronze at Pyeongchang 2018. That error had haunted her, but now she banished the memory with possibly the best stone of the encounter in the seventh end of the final. The Brits had been rampant and concluded with Muirhead's stone that removed a critical Japanese advantage: an unbeatable lead of 8-2, ending a 20-year wait for an Olympic curling title. This was the joint highest winning margin in a final since the sport was re-introduced to the Games in 1998, and erased the women's memory of Covid obstruction in preparation, struggles in the qualifying competition and more anxiety prior to the semi-finals.

In recent Games, the skeleton had brought Britain some sunshine, but sliders success had run off track in China: Matt Weston and Marcus Wyatt finished 15th and 16th in the men's event, Laura Deas and Brogan Crowley 19th and 22nd in the women's. Britain had become also-rans, never mind bronze for Deas in Korea four years earlier. The problem, with forthright admission, was not so much the riders as the machines: a frustrating characteristic that Britain's sleds appeared to be the slowest to have made the long journey east with a funding expense of £4.5m. There would need to be investigation, through the English Institute of Sport, to failing modification of existing sleds: Deas conceded that performances were 'nowhere near what I expected or wanted during two years' preparation'. While a British slump required domestic assessment, here surely is instance, in an equipment-dominated sport, where there should be uniformity of the artefact upon which competitors are dependent.

Following Beijing's election in 2015, in the absence of any other available and acceptable host, there had been seven years of scepticism about the capability of a relatively unfamiliar winter sports nation, more especially about its social attitudes. The latter remain open to doubt in coming years: on the sporting front it should be acknowledged that

China has, and will continue to have, outstanding prospects for the promotion of skiing and skating for the world's largest national population. China is not short on self-promotion, but *China Daily* may be forgiven for acclaim which it granted Swiss designer Bernhard Russi, downhill Olympic champion of 1972, who created the Alpine skiing centre on Xiaohaituo Mountain, an alleged paradise for elite skiers. Russi himself is confident that the artificial snow quality will continue to be ideal for top-flight competition. 'The snow is absolutely perfect, could not be better,' he claimed as chairman of the International Ski Federation Alpine Committee. 'It's just like paradise, racers can do what they want.' Russi had designed nine out of the ten Olympic alpine courses for Winter Games since Calgary 1988.

Although crosswinds could make racing difficult, many experienced competitors had time to praise the course, despite widespread doubt over China's lack of experience to prepare alpine venues. Russi had spent seven years analysing the terrain in north-west Beijing suburbs so as to deliver not merely an ideal surface but a visual thrill for viewers. Kjetil Jansrud, renowned Norwegian Olympic champion, had been impressed, 'From the athletes' perspective, having built such a fantastic venue, with opportunity to continue here for many years, it's something great. When we travel around, it's usually on the old hills with history. If alpine skiing is going to survive and have its place in Asia, this is a venue that really speaks for the future.' The 73-year-old Russi reflected, 'In order to have a perfect course for alpine, you need man-made snow for the quality, compact snow to meet the power which these racers are able to impose.'

While the world may not be persuaded about Chinese social principles, we should be confident about their committed interest towards skiers, not least their own.

BEIJING MEDAL WINNERS
Norway 37 (16-8-13)
Germany 27 (12-10-5)
China 15 (9-4-2)
United States 25 (8-10-7)
Sweden 18 (8-5-5)
Netherlands 17 (8-5-4)
Austria 18 (7-7-4)
Switzerland 14 (7-2-5)
Olympic Athletes from Russia 32 (6-12-14)
France 14 (5-7-2)
Canada 26 (4-8-14)
Japan 18 (3-6-9)
Italy 17 (2-7-8)
South Korea 9 (2-5-2)
Slovenia 7 (2-3-2)
Finland 8 (2-2-4)
New Zealand 3 (2-1-0)
Australia 4 (1-2-1)
Great Britain 2 (1-1-0)
Hungary 3 (1-0-2)
Belgium 2 (1-0-1)
Czech Republic 2 (1-0-1)
Slovakia 2 (1-0-1)
Belarus 2 (0-2-0)
Spain 1 (0-1-0)
Ukraine 1 (0-1-0)
Estonia 1 (0-0-1)
Latvia 1 (0-0-1)
Poland 1 (0-0-1)

16

DEFINING WOMEN'S SPORT?

IN CIRCUMSTANCES as alarming as looming Nazi aggrandisement of 1938, or the Soviet/Cuba ticking clock of early 1964, the Olympic Games of 2024 in Paris were not, in 2022, currently the foremost planned tourist engagement, even if athletes would be engrossed in single-minded preparation. In conversation with Thomas Bach in 2019, prior to Tokyo's postponement, he had relished the prospect for Paris 11 years into his presidency, 'The Games will be in full accord with our Agenda 2020, sustained and inclusive, gender equal, more youthful, more urban, with preferred new sports, the beginning of a new era.'

Will the delivery by Tony Estanguet, multiple former Olympic champion, be all for which we hope? The 'Aladdin' of Paris predicts, 'Since his election, Thomas Bach has been deeply committed to promoting a new Games model, rooted in the present era and in line both with athletes' and the general public's aspirations, especially those of youth. As a fellow Olympic champion, Thomas loves challenges: he undertook a consultation with us to re-think every part of the Games, the ambition to be more sustainable, inclusive and open. This work led to the establishment of Agenda 2020, those recommendations forming the framework from the start of the bid process by Paris for 2024.

'We fully embraced these ambitions: Paris will be a spectacular celebration that takes sport into unexpected places in the heart of the city. These will also be interactive Games, with the first mass participation events embracing the public, and more sustainable Games thanks to the maximum use of existing infrastructures and an extensive reduction of our carbon footprint. Our Games will be open to people like never before, while symbolically marking the return of the Games to the French capital a century since we last were hosts. To mark the event, we will raise the biggest flag ever, from the Eiffel Tower, a flag as big as a football field, some 5,000 square metres. We are fortunate to have the world's most prominent flagstaff. Our Opening Ceremony will allow hundreds of thousands of spectators to gather along the River Seine, while our Games will minimise the environmental impact, embracing iconic landmarks such as beach volleyball at a temporary arena in the shadow of the Eiffel, finding a balance between Olympic tradition and creative innovation.

Paris, and the Mayor must urgently revise crowd control in the wake of the disgraceful shambles at the European Champions League 2022 final. And Paris aims to reduce the Olympic carbon footprint by 50 per cent. Sport has to be spectacular but also sustainable.

'Around 170 boats carrying delegations are expected to travel six kilometres along the Seine, providing an alternative "runway for athletes" … Sport should not be kept within stadiums, it should be in the streets and in schools everywhere, every day. We all know recommendations from the World Health Organisation that we should do sport for half-an-hour a day as an adult, or an hour if you are a kid. Sixty-one per cent of adults in France do not do this, and 80 per cent of youth is not moving enough. We need to use Paris 2024 to develop sport, everywhere, every day and for everyone. And Paris aims to reduce the Olympic carbon footprint by 50 per cent. Sport has to be spectacular but also sustainable.'

If Paris will showcase Bach's long-imagined legacy, so too will Los Angeles four years later. Ever since that exploratory entrepreneur Casey Wasserman engaged in sporting ventures, the concept of a third Californian Olympics has been motivational. As Wasserman predicts, 'These days we are at an inflection point in sports, in culture and live events, as fans have more choice than ever before. Sport has always been something that uniquely brings people together across communities around the world. The Olympic Games represent the pinnacle of global sport, and our powerful platform to be used for positive impact, both on fans and athletes.

'There is no question, however, that sports organisation, just like business, must be flexible and adapt to changing market trends, to evolving consumer habits. Over the last decade, under Thomas Bach's leadership, the Olympic Movement has worked to advance the Games to engage the next generation of fans, and to increase its long-term global relevancy. The Los Angeles 2028 Olympic and Paralympic Games will be a spark to maintain that forward movement: our goal to bring fresh energy to the Games, and no place can do that better than Los Angeles. With the backdrop of such a creative, dynamic and diverse city, the LA Games can set a new standard for what the Olympics can achieve when moving forward.'

Bach, entitled to bask in the satisfaction of a joint election for 2024 and 2028 with that decision in 2017, expects to enjoy his US visit three years into retirement, 'LA will continue the imaginative trends we witnessed back in 1984, a continuation of their digital expertise, bringing the momentum of California's lifestyle. After the tribulations we experienced in Rio three years into my presidency, I had supposed that from there on the task would become easier, that I could relax: yet what followed were the multiple risks of Pyeongchang and its security hazards, the pandemic embracing both Tokyo and Beijing. Paris and LA should provide re-establishment of the social power of the Olympics, which commands attention of half the world's population.'

An aspect of LA may well be the arrival on the programme of esports, though Bach concedes this development has risks, 'The worst we could do is to ignore this issue, risks can be converted into opportunity, yet the IOC must realise esports could lead a younger generation increasingly to turn away from traditional sport and Olympic values. At present there is not a clear line to see the way into the Olympic Programme, there cannot be killer games contrary to our values, which must come first. We have to examine new evolving disciplines and techniques, telling egames that we are ready to discuss fair competition alongside mental health, to create perceptions which make the public curious.'

If social integration, in many guises, is one of the objectives of the Olympic Movement, increasingly evident is not simply that of gender equality, achieved at Beijing 2022, but regulations regarding transgender participation, sexual abuse – especially of teenagers – and acceptable sexual orientation of female dress code, as in beach volleyball. Torment of the supposedly weaker sex has multiple manifestation: sometimes unintentionally self-provoked. Both the IOC and the international federations are aware of the hazards as they strive to achieve participation uniformity: many fashion-conscious teenagers shun competitive sport in Britain because of hostile body-shaming, even by nationally appointed coaches.

It is disconcerting for the IOC, for IFs, not least for some athletes themselves and their rivals, to be genuinely confused, either anatomically or by endocrine definition, over what is their truthful acceptable sex for sporting competition. Before and even after formal testing began belatedly to be introduced post-World War Two – embarrassing genitalia inspection imposed on females – there were intermittent controversial allegations way before LGBT became a public issue: notably whether eastern European women, especially from the totalitarian GDR and the Soviet Union, were ineligible through drug enhancement as opposed to endocrine abnormality. Jarmila Kratochvílová of Czechoslovakia – as it was then – has held the 800m world record for 20 years, in company with other suspect middle-distance record holders Marita Koch (GDR) and Florence Griffith Joyner (USA), others also haunted by allegation being Christine Ohuruogu (GBR) and, for identified natural testosterone excess Caster Semenya (South Africa), she wretchedly and persistently persecuted by well-intended 'fairness' guidelines of World Athletics.

The dual transgender and endocrinology qualification debates for 'fairness' are all but insoluble. As Richard Budgett, IOC medical and science director, stated in 2021, 'It depends which you are minded by, the view of "inclusive" as the priority, or absolute fairness to the nth degree. The IOC is now reviewing data that would create a new framework, enabling each IF to develop specific participation guidelines, as there is no "one-size-fits-all" [e.g. safety in women's rugby]. But as you measure those levels, you can start to prioritise "inclusion" more than "safety".'

However, the moderation of the IOC – receding from its stance of 2015 and a 'presumption of performance advantage' and 'differences in sex development' such as Semenya's – is challenged by both the international and European federations of sports medicine. Their argument is that the IOC, its revision to be implemented post-Beijing 2022, now focuses on human rights rather than scientific, biological and medical elements, and is therefore 'unfair on [conventional] females'. The IOC counter, however, is that they are protecting fundamental rights of all 'regular' female athletes but do not exclude medical differences. Yet there is no single correct answer, in the eyes of Budgett, 'Competitor-advantage needs to be assessed for each sport. Good-performance evidence needs to be specific for each sport.' An impasse?

The public debate on acceptance in the Olympic arena of LGBTQ identities is one to be sensitively confronted: debated during participation at Beijing by Gus Kenworthy of Britain, who described China's attitude to the gay community as appalling for anyone insufficiently mentally and physically prepared. Kenworthy, born of an English mother and American father, settled in Colorado when he was two but reverted to British nationality after two Olympics and five X Games medals. He believes it is the duty of sports bodies to set the tone, 'It should not be up to the athlete, they have to use their talents, officialdom is responsible for social acceptance, so boycotting an event is not the answer.' Competing at Sochi in 2014, Kenworthy had not declared his disposition in Russia, a nation overtly criminalising the gay community.

At the heart of the debate in 2021 stood Laurel Hubbard, a New Zealand contender in the women's weightlifting snatch category at Tokyo, having been male into her 30s. Budgett had supported Hubbard's cause while sidestepping the issue of fairness, and Hubbard's qualification eligibility by testosterone measurement, never mind that Hubbard was eliminated in the first round; having been junior boys' champion but abandoning the sport in her 20s as her sex identity oscillated, transitioning in 2012. Her sense of achievement amid Tokyo adversity was evident yet leaves her, and the IF, in a quandary. With conspicuous cases of male–female transition in swimming, the instability, emotionally and physically, of sex identity threatens the entire arena of 'normal' women's sport, acknowledged by World Athletics chief Sebastian Coe, who stated: 'Maintaining integrity of female sport is essential. Transgender women must be allowed to compete, with regulation of testosterone levels. For athletes (with sexual variation) CAS is agreed on conditions being 'reasonable and proportional'. At the IOC's 139th Session, Thomas Bach agreed that 'no one size fits all', that the essence is "fair competition". World Athletics places fairness above inclusion. It is possible that transgender athletes should have separate competition, but we are not ready for this at the moment.'

One dilemma in female sport is: how should they appear visually? Should they dress for competition, comfortable convenience, even if that exposes and emphasises intimate erotic elements of their frame, as say in beach volleyball? This debate was also sharply evident at Tokyo 2020, where the USA's title-winning performance against Australia often momentarily seemed more like shots from TV's *Love Island*.

Female sporting accomplishment can be a double jeopardy, especially in events needing limited attire such as gymnastics, swimming, athletics and sand-friction-infected beach volleyball. Dame Jessica Ennis-Hill, world and Olympic heptathlon champion, has related the embarrassment of mini-shorts and the threat of 'malfunction', as happened to French ice dancing pairs favourites with Gabriella Papadakis at Pyeongchang 2018. In the fashion-conscious everyday world of female stereotype which dominates both private and TV-punctuated public life, Britain's low female level of teenage sports club membership is compounded by fear of being body-shamed by kit exposure. More comfortable to show off in the bar.

Equally harassing for females is sexual intimidation or abuse, especially of innocent, unsuspecting teenagers, and predominantly in events requiring limited clothing apparel – athletics, gymnastics, figure skating and swimming – when in close proximity with personal coaches. In the past four years there have been continental criminal court charges prominent in Canada, South Africa, the USA, France, Greece and Afghanistan, the latter in women's football. Most notable was the 175-year conviction of US gymnastics senior coach Larry Nassar, primarily confronted by global icon Simone Biles, temperamentally tormented into self-suspension at Tokyo 2020. It is perhaps significant that in the newly involved style-judged sports such as skateboard, dress is not designed by competition necessity so much as freelance flamboyance and personality cult. There is a discernible drift in audience appeal towards theatricality of judge-dependent sports, in which the 20th-placed can be as fascinating as the winner, whereas in finite exact measurement, 15th place never mind 30th, can be swiftly forgotten.

Of the flood of imponderables which the Olympic Movement, more specifically the IOC, must confront, the least contemplated is that of membership of the IOC. If it can be reasoned that of the two prime responsibilities of IOC members – determining host cities and the programme content – the first has been removed, and that decisions on marketing, finance and ethics are assigned to individual commissions, why should an intendedly democratic organisation which is arithmetically and continentally short of being genuinely democratic when self-elected, continue to need more than 100 members, many of whom are no more than convenient placements under the patronage of the president?

There is unspoken acknowledgement that Thomas Bach is by no means uncomfortable in administration of a global body in which his word is the predominantly controlling force. Yet now, to reduce the membership would be inviting turkeys to vote for Christmas, even if a fifth of them are known barely ever to have spoken at the Annual Session. The function of the IOC, with its vast subsidiary staff administering multiple functions in Lausanne, like any effective industry, has become increasingly dependent on close-knit professional expertise.

The governance of the Olympic Movement is far removed today from the ancient gentlemanly concept of Baron Pierre de Coubertin. For 126 years, the Olympic Games, under the IOC flag, have been a bastion of civilised conduct. In an era of many selfish ambitions – financial, political, cultural – how long can our emblem of honour, dignity and equality survive?

The BOA is wilfully optimistic. On the tenth anniversary of 2012, a plan was being quietly assessed to bid again for hosting in 2040. May my great grand-children enjoy that occasion as I have done in 1948 and a decade ago in regenerated East London.

INDEX

INDEX

271